NATIONAL
GEOGRAPHIC
KiDS

# YES! NO? MAYBE SO...

Julie Beer and Paige Towler

NATIONAL GEOGRAPHIC
WASHINGTON, D.C.

# CONTENTS

## CHAPTER 1

### Do Fish Notice They're Wet? Questions About Animals .......8

## CHAPTER 2

### How Deep a Hole Could You Dig? Questions About Earth ........ 34

## CHAPTER 3

### Who Invented Money? Questions About History ....... 60

## CHAPTER 4

### What Does Space Smell Like? Questions About Space & Physics ...................... 86

# CHAPTER 5

## Do Robots Have Emotions? Questions About Technology . . . 112

# CHAPTER 6

## Why Do We Dream? Questions About Being Human . . . . . . . . . . . . . . . . . . . . . . . . . 138

# CHAPTER 7

## How Were Sports Invented? Questions About Art, Food & Culture . . . . . . . . . . . . . . . . . 164

# CHAPTER 8

## Is Area 51 Real? Questions About All Things Weird and Wild . . . . . . . . . . . . . . . . 190

# WHAT IS THIS BOOK?

DO YOU HAVE A BURNING QUESTION YOU JUST NEED TO KNOW THE ANSWER TO? QUESTIONS LIKE...

WHAT WOULD HAPPEN IF YOU JUMPED INTO A BLACK HOLE?

WHY CAN'T I TICKLE MYSELF?

NO!

AND WHAT'S THE DEAL WITH ALL THOSE DANGEROUS ANIMALS IN AUSTRALIA?

# YES!

## THEN YOU'VE COME TO THE RIGHT PLACE, BECAUSE WE HAVE *(ALMOST)* ALL THE ANSWERS!

Get ready to discover the science behind all your wacky wonderings, from questions related to animals (Why do zebras have stripes? And do animals ever get bored?) to space (Is there life in space? When will humans live on the moon?) to the human body (Why don't people grow wings? And what's going on inside our brains?), and much more. Find the answers to all the questions you've been dying to ask ... and ones you might not have ever considered (Why do sloths travel so far to poop? What does space smell like?). Plus, read mind-boggling interviews with experts in the field, including a paleontologist who digs up dinosaurs and a scientist who taught brain cells how to play a computer game. Scour cool facts on real-life superpowers, terrific technology, mythical monsters, and more. And prepare to learn which wild questions no one knows the answer to (yet!). So, what are you waiting for? Your answers are (quite literally!) at your fingertips!

# CHAPTER 1

# DO FISH NOTICE THEY'RE WET?

## QUESTIONS ABOUT ANIMALS

They say curiosity killed the cat ... but what about humans who are curious about cats? Or whales? Or even dinosaurs? Get ready to find all the answers to your burning questions about wildly amazing animals. Like, what was the very first animal on Earth? Why do sloths move *soooo* slowly? And speaking of chill, do animals ever get bored? Think you know which animal sleeps the most? Take a guess now, and read on to find out.

# How do ANIMALS know WHERE TO GO?

Imagine you're about to set out on a long journey. What's the first thing you do? For most people, the answer is probably to plug the destination address into a GPS. But migrating animals don't quite have that luxury. Yet each year, millions of animals migrate long distances to find food, meet mates, give birth, seek shelter, and more. How do they know where to go?

DURING COLD WINTERS, SOME WORMS MIGRATE DEEPER INTO THE EARTH TO STAY WARM.

## PASS IT ON

Consider all the information that has been passed on to you from teachers and guardians. Things aren't so different for some animals! OK, they don't exactly go to animal school, but many do learn migration routes from older animals. In one study, scientists found that young arctic sheep and caribou learned where to migrate by following or communicating with adults in the herd. In fact, they found that some sheep and caribou that had recently been reintroduced to the area didn't migrate at all until they found more experienced animals to show them the way. Thanks, Teach!

## NATURAL NAVIGATORS

Some animals find their way by paying close attention to the world around them. Imagine that you were trying to give someone directions, but you weren't allowed to use street names or road signs. Instead, you might describe certain buildings or landmarks. Animals can do this as well! Many animals navigate by remembering mountains, rivers, trees, and more along the route. Neuroscientists studying animal brains discovered that some animals even create maps of the land, sort of like a paper map, except these maps, called mental maps, only exist in the animals' minds.

Animals can rely on other features of their environment as well, such as the sun and stars. Many types of birds can find their way north

using bright stars, like the North Star or a star named Betelgeuse. Other birds, like starlings, use the sun's path to figure out which direction they are facing.

But what about places where there are no trees or stars, like in the ocean? Some ocean animals, such as dolphins, follow landmarks along the ocean floor. Others, including gray whales, tend to find their way by traveling along coastlines. And some ocean animals navigate by paying attention to the ocean currents, and either swimming along with them or against them. *Whee!*

## SPECIAL SKILLS

Over time, some animals have also developed special abilities that help them migrate. Believe it or not, scientists think that many animals can smell where they are going. For example, experts believe that wildebeests can migrate to grassy pastures by following the scent of rain. And it's not just mammals—salmon use their sense of smell to find the regions where they lay their eggs.

Some animals have another super sense available to them. Turtles, whales, bees, and many birds can sense the charged energy around planet Earth, known as the magnetic field. Though scientists aren't sure exactly how, these animals can use the magnetic field to figure out where they are and then chart a path to their destination.

EACH DAY, GOLDEN JELLYFISH ON THE ISLAND COUNTRY OF PALAU MIGRATE ACROSS A LAKE BY FOLLOWING THE SUN'S PATH IN THE SKY.

## Why can't HUMANS get around this way?

They can! It may not seem like it in today's age of technology, but humans have been using the environment to navigate for thousands of years. In fact, for most of human history, people have relied on the sun and stars, local landmarks, and knowledge passed down over generations. Many sailors also became familiar with ocean currents and used these to travel where they wanted to go.

Over time, people began to create tools that made navigating even easier, such as maps, compasses, and GPS systems. Today, because it is easy to rely on these tools, many people no longer use the environment to get around. But that doesn't mean we can't do it! In fact, some scientists think that humans might even be able to sense magnetic fields, just like certain animals can. The ability to navigate may be ancient, but there's still much to learn.

## Why do BIRDS FLY SOUTH for winter?

*Brrr*—have you ever wanted to escape winter's cold and head somewhere nice and toasty? You're not alone! Many birds migrate to warmer territories for the winter season. Part of this is to stay warm, but there's another reason: to find food. As temperatures drop, so do insect populations. To keep feasting, hungry birds often fly to areas where bugs are still buzzing.

# ANIMAL SNOOZEFEST

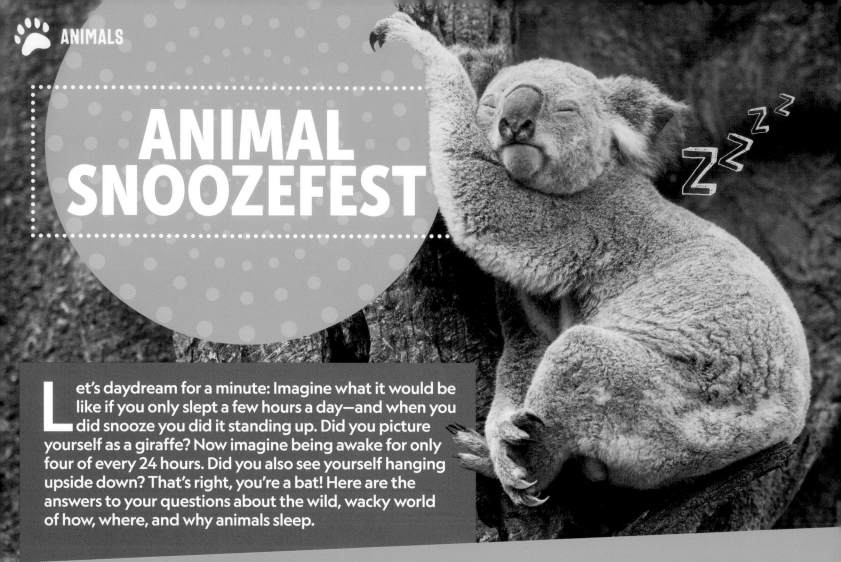

L et's daydream for a minute: Imagine what it would be like if you only slept a few hours a day—and when you did snooze you did it standing up. Did you picture yourself as a giraffe? Now imagine being awake for only four of every 24 hours. Did you also see yourself hanging upside down? That's right, you're a bat! Here are the answers to your questions about the wild, wacky world of how, where, and why animals sleep.

## HOW MUCH SLEEP DO ANIMALS NEED?

It depends! Grown-up humans typically need seven to nine hours of sleep at night—and kids need even more because they're still growing. But animals are all over the map with their snooze time. Let's start with giraffes. They might be the tallest animals on Earth, but they need less sleep than most. They catch quick naps throughout the day that add up to about two hours. They do most of their resting while standing, although they will occasionally lie down and put their heads on their rumps.

Brown bats, on the other hand, are major snoozers. They look busy fluttering around the sky at dusk, hunting and filling up on insects. They are efficient, too: Bats can eat 1,000 insects in one hour! But for the 20 hours a day that they aren't eating, they're resting—upside down in their roosts, including caves, trees, and rocks.

## DO ALL ANIMALS CLOSE THEIR EYES WHEN THEY SLEEP?

Nope! Snakes don't have true eyelids, so they can't close their eyes. But that doesn't mean they don't sleep. Snakes don't rely much on their vision—they often sense prey through vibration caused by movement. They really only notice things when they move. Most fish don't have eyelids either. Land animals often rely on eyelids to keep their eyes moist. That's not an issue if you live in the water.

## ARE THERE ANY ANIMALS THAT NEVER SLEEP?

Almost all animals need some sort of sleep, but there are a few that are capable of staying awake for a very long time—and they have a special trick to pull it off.

A dolphin, for example: One-half of a dolphin's brain is able to fall into a deep sleep while the other half is wide awake, swimming and on the lookout for predators. Talk about multitasking! This means that 24 hours a day a dolphin is alert and aware of what's going on around it.

Some birds use a similar tactic for long-distance flights. Frigate birds fly for months over the ocean—a tricky commute if you don't have anywhere to take a break. To make the flight, half of this bird's brain shuts down and goes to sleep for short bursts at a time, while the other half focuses on gliding on air currents. No need for autopilot!

## WHY DON'T HORSES FALL OVER WHEN THEY SLEEP?

Horses rest while they're standing up. They look like they're off in dreamland, but they're actually not in what's called "REM" sleep—the stage of deeper sleep, which for humans, is when we dream. (Horses do get short amounts of REM sleep by lying down, but they keep it to just an hour or two because they are more vulnerable to predators when they aren't standing up.) In order to doze while standing, horses have special tendons and ligaments that lock while they're standing, letting them relax into a slumber without the worry of falling over.

## HOW COME BATS DON'T FALL WHEN THEY SLEEP UPSIDE DOWN?

Bats are built for hanging around. In fact, it takes less effort for them to hang by their feet than to let go. That's because they have special tendons in their feet that stay locked in the hanging position without any effort at all. When they wake up and want to bug out, they contract a muscle to let go of their perch, then drop and fly away.

## HOW DO SHARKS SLEEP IF THEY NEVER STOP SWIMMING?

Some shark species—like nurse and tiger sharks—can stop swimming and snooze whenever they want. That's because they breathe by "inhaling" water into their mouths and over their gills. Other sharks—like great whites and whale sharks—rely on swimming with their mouths open to push water through their gills. If they stop swimming, they don't get oxygen from the water and will die. And other sharks use a combination of these methods to get their oxygen.

So how do those sharks that can't stop moving ever get any sleep? It's possible they don't! Scientists think that some sharks simply rest, instead of really sleeping. However, recently researchers observed a great white shark drifting in a shallow current of water with its mouth open and in an almost trance-like state, leaving open the possibility that the sharks do sleep, but in the right conditions where water is still flowing through their gills.

13

# Can DOGS TELL TIME?

**It's 6 p.m. and your pooch is prancing around her dinner bowl ... does she know what time it is? Yes and no.**

IT'S BEEN ESTIMATED THAT A DOG'S SENSE OF SMELL IS AT LEAST 10,000 TIMES MORE POWERFUL THAN A HUMAN'S.

Dogs don't keep track of time the way humans do, with minutes and hours. So, if you plopped your pup in front of a clock, he would have no idea what those numbers meant. But while you probably won't ever catch Fido wearing a watch, dogs do have their own ways of tracking the passing of time. For one thing, dogs can tell the general time of day—such as morning, afternoon, evening, and night—based on how light or dark it is outside. Dogs also have something humans don't: a super sense of smell. Scientists think canine companions can track the passing of time by noticing how scents change or fade. For example, let's say you usually head out for school in the morning and return in the late afternoon. When you leave, your scent starts to fade. Over the course of the day, the scent continues to get weaker. If you come home around the same time most days, your dog knows that when the scent reaches a certain weakness, that's around the time that you should be walking in the door. Of course, to you, it's just 3:30!

## SPEAKING OF SUPER SNIFFERS ...

Now we know that dogs don't just tell time—they smell time. And their noses can smell a lot of other things that human noses can't. Dogs can sometimes even smell when their owners have a disease, like certain kinds of cancer. For example, one woman from upstate New York, U.S.A., only found out that she had skin cancer after her pup repeatedly sniffed a spot on her nose. The spot disappeared, but the pooch kept sniffing the same area, leading the woman to get her nose checked by a doctor. It turned out to be cancer, and her dog's smart schnoz saved her life.

## Can animals RECOGNIZE THEMSELVES in a mirror?

Mirror, mirror on the wall, who's the smartest of them all? Being able to recognize yourself in a mirror means you understand how you physically appear. Researchers have given mirror tests to many different animal species and only a few have passed. And the ones that did might surprise you.

When most animals see a mirror, they either flat out ignore it, or they treat their reflections as strangers that need to be examined or attacked. Parakeets interact with mirrors like they've met new friends, but they don't realize their new BFFs are, well, themselves.

One researcher found that orangutans, at first, treated their reflections as other beings, but in time they started examining their reflections, checking out parts of their bodies. When dots were painted on the orangutans' faces and they looked in the mirror, they realized the dots were on their own faces. Chimps had a similar response. Scientists have debated if other animals have this same self-awareness, and so far, the short list of animals that have proven they do includes dolphins, elephants, and magpies. But recently, the cleaner wrasse, a type of tropical reef fish, got some attention for the way it interacted with mirrors. In a study, the fish approached their reflections upside down, and swam quickly toward them and then stopped. When researchers put a brown gel on their throats and the fish saw themselves in the mirror, they tried to rub the gel off onto other surfaces. When they didn't have a mirror, they didn't try to rub it off. Researchers think these fish—and other animals overlooked in the past—may be more aware of themselves than we knew.

# Why do SOME animals GO EXTINCT?

You've heard of *Tyrannosaurus rex*. But you've never seen one—except maybe its fossil. This is because *T. rex* is one of the many kinds of animals that have gone extinct over the years. A species that is extinct is one that has completely died out. This can happen for several reasons, including evolution, mass extinction events, and human interference.

SCIENTISTS THINK THAT WOOLLY MAMMOTHS WENT EXTINCT SOME 3,500 YEARS AGO, WHEN IT BECAME TOO RAINY, CAUSING THE PLANTS THEY FED ON TO DIE OUT.

NOT ALL SPECIES OF DINOSAUR WENT EXTINCT. SOME SURVIVED, EVOLVING OVER TIME INTO THE BIRDS YOU SEE TODAY.

## BIG CHANGES

As species of organisms exist, generation after generation, they change over time. This process, called evolution, leads to the rise of many new kinds of animals. But it can also lead to extinction. This is because as animals evolve, some become better suited to their environments. They may develop body parts or characteristics that make it easier to hunt or live in their homes. This may also make it harder for other animals to survive. For example, if one species of animal becomes very good at eating up a food source, another animal that also depends on that source may not have enough to eat and can eventually go extinct.

## BIG EVENTS

Extinction caused by evolution tends to happen very slowly. Other times, animals can go extinct more quickly, because of something known as a mass extinction event. During an extinction event, either disease, a natural disaster, or an impact by a space object—such as an asteroid—causes so much sickness or destruction, certain species of animals cannot survive. One of the most famous extinction events happened about 66 million years ago, at the end of the Cretaceous period. Scientists believe that an enormous asteroid struck Earth, driving up plumes of debris, dust, and gas that led to the deaths of

AN EXTINCT ANCESTOR OF WHALES KNOWN AS *AMBULOCETUS* WAS ABLE TO WALK ON LAND.

about 75 percent of the organisms on Earth—including the dinosaurs. But this wasn't the largest extinction event on Earth! That record goes to the Permian–Triassic extinction, which occurred around 250 million years ago. After a series of enormous volcanic explosions heated up Earth's atmosphere and ocean, more than 90 percent of all life on Earth—including many reptiles, plants, and ocean animals—went extinct.

## HUMAN INTERFERENCE

So, if extinction tends to happen over time or after extinction events, why are there so many animals in danger of becoming extinct today? Unfortunately, this is because of human interference—the actions of people. Extinction can happen when people destroy animal habitats or hunt a species until there are no more left. In the 17th century, for example, people hunted and ate so many dodo birds that the entire species went extinct.

Over the past several centuries, human pollution has led to climate change. Earth's increased temperatures create conditions in which some plants and animals cannot survive. Because of this, plants and animals have become endangered. Many conservationists are fighting against climate change and to save species.

ROUNDUP

## BACK FROM THE DEAD

Sometimes scientists make mistakes—after all, they're only human! Here are some animals that were rediscovered after they were declared extinct.

>> Fernandina giant tortoise: This species of tortoise was thought to have gone extinct back in 1906. But in 2019, researchers discovered a female member of the species that was more than 100 years old!

>> Coelacanth: In 1938, a fisherman in South Africa stumbled upon the discovery of, well, many lifetimes—a type of giant fish thought to have died out with the dinosaurs.

>> Chacoan peccary: In the 1930s, researchers found the fossilized remains of a piglike creature that they assumed was long gone. Imagine the surprise of the scientists who, some 40 years later, encountered the living animal!

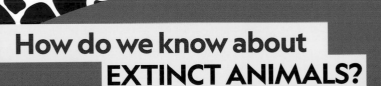

## How do we know about EXTINCT ANIMALS?

The truth is that we don't always know! When it comes to modern animals, conservationists have a lot of different ways to keep track of them. Scientists use tools such as camera traps, drones, and GPS collars to monitor wild animals. They can also search for clues such as droppings and tracks. But it can be very tricky to spot animals in the wild. In fact, there are still many species we have yet to discover! This means that there may also be many species that have gone extinct that we never knew about in the first place.

The same is true for extinct animals from long ago. Today, scientists know about many of these animals thanks to the traces, known as fossils, that they have left behind. Experts have discovered hundreds of thousands of extinct species from the fossil record in the past few centuries alone. Imagine how many more are yet to be found.

# Why does AUSTRALIA have so many DANGEROUS ANIMALS?

Saltwater crocodiles. Box jellyfish. Taipan snakes. Funnel-web spiders. It's easy to see how Australia got its reputation as a hot spot for dangerous animals. But is Australia really more dangerous than any other place? Yes ... and no.

PLATYPUSES ARE ONE OF ONLY TWO MAMMALS TO LAY EGGS.

A SYDNEY FUNNEL-WEB SPIDER'S FANGS ARE CAPABLE OF BITING THROUGH A FINGERNAIL OR LEATHER SHOE!

## WELCOME TO THE NEIGHBORHOOD

First, let's take a closer look at Australia's famous residents. At the top of the list is perhaps the most unique one: the platypus. The animal's venomous glands deliver toxins through a spur on its back legs, making the male platypus one of the most venomous mammals on Earth. Scientists think the platypus, with its ducklike snout, webbed feet, and beaverlike tail, is one of the earliest modern mammals.

Sydney funnel-web spiders are perhaps Australia's most dangerous spiders—capable of causing death in as little as 15 minutes. Since an antivenom was developed in the 1980s, there haven't been any deaths reported as a result of a bite. With a body about two inches (5 cm) long, the spiders get their name from their funnel-shaped web, which they use as a burrow or to trap prey.

Australia's dangerous animals aren't all on land. Some of the most notorious live in the waters offshore, including great white sharks, box jellyfish, blue-ringed octopuses, and saltwater crocodiles. (The crocs are a double threat— they live on land and in the water, including wetlands, tidal basins, and even far out in the sea.) Blue-ringed octopuses are the size of a golf ball but are capable of killing a human in one bite. (Luckily, they only attack in self-defense.) Box jellyfish are considered one of the most venomous creatures on Earth, stunning or killing prey that get tangled

IN AUSTRALIA, CROCODILES ARE CALLED SALTIES.

in their tentacles. These creatures don't exclusively live in Australia, but they certainly contribute to the country's "dangerous" reputation.

## PERILOUS PREHISTORIC PAST

Australia is not only a country, it is an island—and it happens to be the smallest of Earth's seven continents. It's also the most isolated continent. About 180 million years ago, Australia, Africa, South America, Arabia, India, Madagascar, and Antarctica were all one giant landmass, called Gondwana, that slowly started to break apart. Australia broke off from Antarctica 30 million years ago and has been slowly drifting toward Asia ever since, in what is called continental drift.

But let's go back to that giant landmass of Gondwana. It is believed to have had a population of venomous snakes living on it that were separated when the land broke apart. Almost all of the snakes on newly formed Australia evolved from that group of venomous snakes, called elapids, which deliver their venom through hollow fangs. While other continents evolved with a more balanced mix of venomous and nonvenomous snake species, Australia kept the venom line strong. Today, it's home to some of the most venomous snakes in the world, including the inland taipan snake. It contains enough venom in one strike to kill 250,000 mice. Fortunately, this snake is shy, lives in remote parts of the outback, and rarely crosses paths with humans.

## ON THE RECORD

So, is Australia's reputation earned? If you're just looking at the number of species capable of killing, yep. But many places around the globe have dangerous creatures. In fact, Brazil and Mexico have more venomous snakes than Australia. And even though they're labeled "deadly," many of Australia's most notorious animals are hardly ever seen. But if you do find yourself on the wrong side of a fang or stinger, researchers have created antivenom medicine to prevent serious harm.

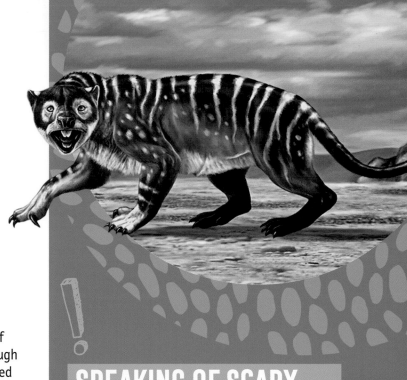

## SPEAKING OF SCARY...

You wouldn't want to encounter the prehistoric animals that once roamed Australia. If you lived in Australia more than 45,000 years ago, the marsupial lion would be one of your biggest concerns. It was bigger than a modern-day leopard. The female carried her young in her pouch, like koalas do. Also like koalas, marsupial lions climbed trees. But that's where the similarities with cute, shy koalas end. Marsupial lions had huge teeth designed to slice flesh, and they bit with almost as much force as modern-day African lions. And if that wasn't enough, they also had specialized thumb claws that ripped into prey like a can opener.

## What is the MOST DANGEROUS animal in Australia?

It's not a snake. It's not an octopus. And it's not a jellyfish. The animal most likely to send you to the hospital in Australia is one that is much, much smaller. Scientists recently looked at statistics of Australians who went to the hospital because of venomous stings and bites over a 12-year period and found that more people sought help for bee, hornet, and wasp stings than any other creature. Almost a third of people who sought medical attention because of bites and stings had these venomous arthropods to thank.

# What was the FIRST ANIMAL?

Hundreds of millions of years ago, Earth's first animal appeared. It was a species that would change the face of the planet forever. It was a majestic ... blob-shaped animal. The truth is that scientists don't know for sure which animal was Earth's first. However, they have some guesses—and yes, all of them are blob-like!

## EARLY ANIMALS

What exactly is an animal? Sure, you know one when you see one, but what makes an animal scientifically different from, say, a plant? Animals and plants are both living organisms made up of tiny building blocks called cells. To survive, animals must eat other organisms (such as plants, other animals, and more). Plants, on the other hand, create their own food. There are also other organisms on Earth that are neither plant nor animal, including tiny microbes that are each made of only one cell. These organisms existed on Earth long before animals did. Scientists think that over time some of these single-celled organisms evolved into clusters of separate cells that worked together, eventually becoming animals.

To figure out which animal first appeared on the planet, some scientists have turned to the fossil record to determine which fossils are the oldest. Among them is that of *Dickinsonia*, an oval-shaped marine animal that lived around 600 million years ago. However, other scientists disagree, claiming that sponge-like animals were the first animals in existence. In fact, some scientists think that they may have discovered ancient sponge-like fossils nearly 900 million years old!

*DICKINSONIA* COULD RANGE FROM A FEW INCHES TO SEVERAL FEET!

## Why aren't scientists sure WHICH ANIMAL came first?

It may seem like it should be an easy question to answer—can't we just go with the oldest fossil? However, the answer is a bit more complicated. With soft-bodied animals such as sponges, it can be difficult for scientists to determine what is a fossil and what is not. Because sponge fossils look so similar to nonfossil rocks, experts often have to examine the supposed fossil's chemical makeup—but that can be very tricky and not always accurate.

To answer this question, some scientists think it's better to avoid examining fossils altogether. After all, it's possible that the earliest animals didn't leave any fossilized traces. Instead, some scientists are attempting to unravel the mystery by studying and comparing genetic information—or the building blocks that make up living things—from different groups of animals. By looking at this information, researchers think they can trace the chain of evolution back through history. So where does it lead? These experts believe the planet's first animal was not *Dickinsonia* or a sponge, but a comb jelly—a kind of translucent (and oval-shaped) sea creature.

## Do scientists know what the FIRST LAND animal was?

Maybe! The record for oldest known land animal goes to a millipede-like insect that lived some 425 million years ago. However, as with marine life, there may be older fossils that scientists have yet to discover. And, of course, there may be older animals that never left behind fossils at all. Even so, this discovery means that we know that insects have been scuttling around the planet for at least 425 million years.

## Were animals the FIRST LIFE on Earth?

Nope! Scientists believe that the first life on the planet consisted of simple microscopic organisms, called microbes. In fact, experts have discovered fossils of microbes related to bacteria, known as cyanobacteria, that are about four billion years old. These cyanobacteria could likely get their energy from the sun—and may be the ancestors of all living things!

## Which CAME FIRST, the chicken or the egg?

Ah, an impossible question—or is it? Actually, scientists are pretty sure they know the answer to this one, and it's the egg. Chickens likely first appeared around 10,500 years ago in Asia. The oldest known eggs, on the other hand, are fossilized dinosaur eggs nearly 200 million years old—and fish may have been laying eggs for billions of years.

But what if the question is slightly different? Eggs definitely came before chickens, but what about chicken eggs in particular? In that case, some scientists think that the chicken itself must have been first. This is because the shells of chicken eggs require a special protein to form—one found only in chickens. Because of this, chicken eggs could only be laid after a chicken had evolved.

# Do ANIMALS ever get BORED?

"Oh, another day of catnip and catnaps? *Yawn—* how boring!"

**AT ONE SANCTUARY, BATS USE PAINT BRUSHES ATTACHED TO THE ENDS OF FRUIT PIECES TO "MAKE" MASTERPIECES.**

Yes, it's true—companion animals like cats, dogs, pet rodents, and even pigs can get bored, just like humans. Studies show that pets can get bored when they have lots of energy but not enough to do. For example, pet rodents that lived in homes with "fun" additions like water pools, tunnels, and chew toys showed less boredom than those without.

Just like humans, animals that do get bored often try to seek out excitement—and not always in ways that please their owners! Bored dogs or cats may chew on things and shred furniture, or act out in other ways.

**SCIENTISTS THINK THAT FEELING BORED OCCASIONALLY CAN INCREASE CREATIVITY.**

## Wait, what *IS* boredom?

You probably know what boredom feels like—but what is it, exactly? Boredom is a reaction to repetitive brain patterns. When activity in the brain is too predictable, it can cause the brain to release fewer chemicals that make people—and other animals—feel happy. Scientists think that boredom may be an evolutionary tool that helped develop curiosity, especially in young animals and people. Feelings of boredom may have inspired these animals to try new things, or even strike out on their own. However, it can also lead to feelings of restlessness and sadness.

## So, how do you **PREVENT** boredom in pets?

There are many safe and healthy ways to keep pets entertained. Like people, pets enjoy socializing and exercise. Taking a pooch for an extra run or even spending some quality cuddle time can keep it interested and happy. Some pets, especially dogs, enjoy having a job to do, such as working as sled dogs, police dogs, and more.

Some experts have also developed special puzzles and toys for pets. In the same way a 1,000-piece puzzle might keep you busy (or not—maybe you're a whiz at them!), puzzles challenge pets to sniff out treats and stay engaged.

## What about **WILD** animals?

Animals in the wild are often too focused on survival to get bored! They are constantly figuring out where their next meal is coming from. However, wild animals in captivity, such as those at zoos or wildlife refuges, can feel bored if they do not have enough to do.

To help keep animals engaged, behaviorists have developed different kinds of animal enrichment activities. These include puzzles, activities, and even specially designed parts of the animals' surroundings that keep their minds active. Some enrichments focus on providing fun social activities for an animal, while others encourage an animal to move and spend energy or even hide if it is feeling overwhelmed.

### ROUNDUP
## ANIMAL BOREDOM BUSTERS

Check out some of the enrichment activities experts have designed to help wild animals feel interested and at ease in captivity.

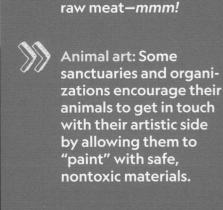

>> Training sessions: Using obstacle courses, interactive puzzles, and other forms of training, experts help animals stay active and alert.

>> Toys: From chew toys to hammocks to giant balls, toys provide delight for all kinds of wild animals.

>> Snacks: Food-based puzzles encourage wild animals to work for their meals, just like they would in the wild. One example? Meat "ice pops" for big cats, made of frozen chunks of raw meat—*mmm!*

>> Animal art: Some sanctuaries and organizations encourage their animals to get in touch with their artistic side by allowing them to "paint" with safe, nontoxic materials.

# HOW HAS NATURE INSPIRED INVENTORS?

**N**ature has been evolving and improving on itself for hundreds of millions of years. So when scientists try to figure out a way to solve a problem or make something better, instead of re-creating the wheel, they sometimes look at the ways nature deals with it and, well, copy it. This is called biomimicry. As it turns out, nature has inspired some pretty cool inventions!

## AN IDEA THAT STUCK

It all started with a dog walk. In 1948, Swiss engineer George de Mestral was out in the woods with his dog and discovered his clothes and his pup's fur were covered in burrs. The prickles were fairly easy to remove, and he could even stick them back on, which got him to wondering how exactly they attached themselves to fiber and fur. So, he pulled out a microscope and was surprised to find that the burrs were covered with tiny hooks, which were very good at grabbing on to fur and fabric. This concept was eventually applied to make the fabric fastener we all know as Velcro.

## LEARNING FROM THE PROS

In 1505, Leonardo da Vinci designed a flapping device called an ornithopter that mimicked the flying motions of birds' wings. But alas, he never built it or took it to the skies. In the late 19th century, engineer Otto Lilienthal was intent on building an aircraft and published the book *Birdflight as the Basis of Aviation*. The Wright brothers were the first to find success in flight in 1903, after figuring out proper wing angles by studying vultures glide in circles.

## ANCIENT TOUGH STUFF

It's hard to know what the very first nature-inspired product was, but one of the oldest for sure is silk. Humans have been spinning silk into material for 6,000 years. Silkworms produce silk threads to make their cocoons. The silk comes from tiny holes in their jaws. One cocoon is made up of about 1,000 yards (900 m) of silk. But silkworms aren't the only ones that spin a material that is of interest to us. Spider-web silk—specifically, Darwin's bark spider silk—is the toughest biological material. This spider, found only on the island of Madagascar, spins webs across rivers as wide as 80 feet (24 m)—that's the length of two school buses! Its silk is as strong as steel, but it is also stretchy, which means it can absorb energy without breaking. This makes it even tougher than Kevlar, the material used to make bulletproof vests. That's why scientists are studying spider silk to create new materials for medicine and engineering.

## LEAF IT BE

It's hard to imagine a time when people didn't have umbrellas. Nearly 2,000 years ago, a Chinese man, Lu Ban, and his wife are said to have invented that handy tool that keeps us dry on a rainy day. They weren't inspired by an animal, but a plant: Children were using large lotus leaves to stay dry on a rainy day. Lu Ban used silk to replicate the flexibility of the leaves to create what is believed to be the first umbrella.

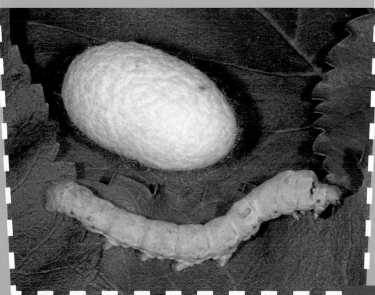

# Why do SLOTHS travel so far TO POOP?

**For animals that have a reputation of not moving around much, sloths go the distance when it comes to going potty.**

Generally speaking, sloths take their time with every-thing. They hang around in the tropical forests of Central and South America high up in the tree canopy and travel less than half the length of an American football field in a day. Most of this movement involves climbing along branches for food. Luckily, everything they need to eat is all around them—mostly leaves, along with flower buds and fruit. They break apart their food by smacking it between their leathery lips—very slowly, of course—then they move their meals into their mouths. They chew for a while, and eventually, they swallow. After all that, they begin the slow process of digesting. The leaves are low in calories and don't have a lot of nutrition, so a sloth takes its time processing the food so it doesn't waste any energy. This means a sloth only has to poop about once a week. And that's when a sloth suddenly has somewhere it needs to be.

## A LONG JOURNEY

For a sloth, going poop is a long process that takes a lot of effort. It is the one time of the week that sloths leave the tree canopy and head to the forest floor. This is a risky trip because while sloths are relatively safe from predators in the trees, danger awaits below. As you can imagine, sloths aren't good at making a quick escape. And jaguars, a top predator of sloths, are quick to pounce. In fact, more than half of all sloth deaths occur when traveling up and down their trees to go potty.

Even beyond the danger, going number two is a lot of work for sloths. Sloths are very polite poopers. They dig a hole at the bottom a tree, go poop, and then cover it up. All that activity burns 8 percent of their daily calories. That's a lot of energy for these tree dwellers.

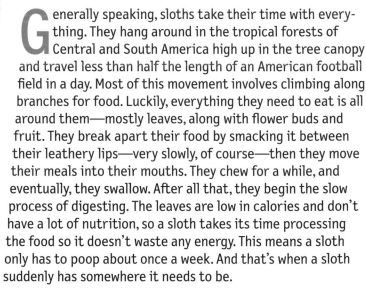

A SLOTH'S FUR IS HOME TO LOTS OF INSECTS. SCIENTISTS ONCE COUNTED 980 BEETLES ON ONE SLOTH.

## THE INSIDE SCOOP

So what's the benefit of these weekly epic journeys to poop, when sloths could hypothetically just poop from the treetops? Scientists who have spent time pondering this question have several ideas. Theory one: The poop fertilizes the trees that the sloths call home. The trees help the sloths, and the sloths help the trees. Theory two: Potty time gives sloths a chance to communicate with other sloths. Sloths live mostly solo lives, and this is a time when they might be near other sloths—or leave scent messages behind in their pee and poo. And theory three: Sloth poop provides a perfect place for moths to lay their eggs. Once these eggs become adult moths, they fly up into the canopy and nestle in sloths' fur. These moths provide nutrients in the sloths' fur that allow algae to grow on it. Then the sloths eat their fur algae, which contains important nutrients for the sloths. What goes around comes around!

## IT'S EASY BEING GREEN

This tasty algae has another benefit—it's green. And a lot of algae on a sloth's fur makes a sloth look greenish. What else is green? Leaves. As a result, algae affords camouflage in the tree canopy, helping protect sloths from predators like harpy eagles, which use their powerful talons to snatch sloths from branches. It's possible that sloths have their long poop journeys to thank for an otherwise comfortable life in the slow lane.

## Are sloths EVER speedy?

Yes—just not on land. Believe it or not, sloths can swim! They occasionally drop from their trees into a river below and go for dips. And they're surprisingly good swimmers, thanks to their strong arms, which they, of course, gain from hanging from branches all day.

SLOTHS MOVE THREE TIMES FASTER IN THE WATER THAN THEY DO ON LAND. THEY CAN SWIM 43 FEET (13 M) PER MINUTE, COMPARED TO THEIR TOP SPEED OF 13 FEET (4 M) PER MINUTE IN THE TREES.

# Do FISH notice THEY'RE WET?

## Fish are wet all the time. The question is: Do they notice it?

THERE ARE SOME TYPES OF FISH THAT CAN USE THEIR FINS TO "WALK" ON LAND OR THE OCEAN FLOOR.

SOME FISH COMMUNICATE WITH EACH OTHER THROUGH THEIR PEE.

So, do fish feel like they're wet all the time? Not quite. Experts may never know for sure, because they can't exactly ask a fish what it is feeling, but they can make a good guess based on how sense and perception—the ability to use your senses to understand something—work.

The truth is, the feeling of "wetness" is an illusion that your brain creates. All animals are made up of tiny units, called cells. Some of these cells are known as receptors: Their job is to respond to things in the outside world, such as temperature or touch. In humans, there are no receptors that can sense wetness! Instead, the receptors respond to other feelings, such as temperature, the amount of force something has, and texture. The receptors then send messages to your brain, which translates the messages into the feeling of "wet."

Is a fish's brain constantly telling the fish that it is wet? Probably not! For humans, the feeling of wetness occurs when we are touching something that sends unusual, or not normal, signals to our brains. But for a fish, living in water is normal. Just like we don't feel "dry" all the time, a fish doesn't feel wet. In fact, a fish's body is perfectly adapted to its watery home.

## How do fish LIVE in water?

A human being wouldn't be able to live in water for their entire life. But for fish, water is home. Fish are uniquely suited to their watery environment in many ways, starting with their shape. A fish's body is streamlined, meaning that it can move easily through water without being slowed down. The fish's flat, paddle-like fins and tail help it turn and stop quickly. In addition to this, fish have a special organ known as a swim bladder. The swim bladder helps the fish maintain buoyancy: It can easily stay where it wants to be in the water without floating upward or sinking downward.

A fish's body also lets it breathe in the water. Like humans, fish need oxygen to survive. Humans, however, have lungs to collect oxygen from the air, while fish have gills that let them take in oxygen from the water.

ROUNDUP

## WATER WORLD

Thanks to their adaptations, fish are right at home in the ocean. But what about marine animals that can't breathe in the water? Check out some of these adaptations that let mammals and birds thrive in the sea.

 **Blubber:** From seals to walruses to penguins, many marine animals have a special layer of fat that keeps them warm in cold waters.

 **Air stash:** Many marine mammals, like seals and whales, can store more oxygen in their muscles than humans. This lets them stay underwater much longer.

 **Waterproofing:** Some birds have organs called glands that secrete a waxy substance. The birds use their bills to spread this substance over their feathers, and water rolls right off the waxy surface.

## Why can't fish BREATHE on land?

If a fish breathes oxygen, why can't it breathe on land? And, for that matter, why can't humans breathe in the water? The answer lies in our organs. They're built for the environments we are meant to live in. For humans, even though our lungs can pull oxygen from the air, they aren't able to do the same thing in water. Similarly, a fish's gills stop working once it is on land. A fish's gills can only remain open while in the water. On land, they collapse, blocking a fish's access to oxygen.

# Why do ZEBRAS have STRIPES?

Few creatures stand out quite like zebras. But does their fashion have function? The jury is out!

PLAINS ZEBRAS BARK LIKE DOGS.

No one can deny that zebras have a unique look. Their bold black-and-white coats stand out against the backdrop of the African savanna where they live. And they're the only members of the genus *Equus*, which also includes horses and donkeys, to have stripes. Besides making a fabulous fashion statement, do zebra stripes serve a purpose? The debate is ongoing. Researchers have been trying to solve this mystery for more than a century.

## STRIPES ARE COOL

Scientists have proposed many theories as to why zebras have stripes. Other animals, like tigers, evolved to have stripes to help them camouflage. Do stripes help zebras camouflage to keep them safe from their number one nemesis, lions? Considering they mostly hang out on plains, not in the woods where stripes could help them blend in, camouflage likely isn't the reason.

Other scientists considered that perhaps their distinctive coats help them regulate their temperature. It gets hot—really hot—on the African plains, and being able to keep cool is key to survival. Here's the idea: The black part of a zebra's coat absorbs heat in the morning when it's cooler, and the white stripes reflect light when it gets hot, helping the zebra cool down during those blazing hot afternoons. The scientists even found that the hairs on the black parts of a zebra's coat stood up during early morning and noon. These hairs trapped heat in the morning and helped sweat evaporate once it warmed up, cooling the zebra down.

## NO-FLY ZONE

But there's one more theory that's all the buzz among scientists debating this subject. Zebra stripes might also keep flies away. Here's the scoop: In 2019, scientists gathered horses and put zebra-striped blankets on some, while letting the others graze as they were. When flies tried to land on a horse covered in stripes, they couldn't slow down the way they could on a horse without stripes. The flies either veered away or simply bounced off the "striped" horses. It seems the striped coats scrambled the flies' vision.

Sure, flies can be annoying, but why would zebras evolve this way specifically to keep flies away? Ultimately, zebra stripes probably have more than one function—not just deterring flies. But in Africa, biting flies carry diseases that can kill zebras. So the answer is rather black and white: Keeping flies away can mean life or death.

EACH INDIVIDUAL ZEBRA'S STRIPES ARE UNIQUE— LIKE FINGERPRINTS.

## Are zebras white with BLACK STRIPES, or black with WHITE STRIPES?

Here's a simple answer: black with white stripes. Their white stripes are actually fur that lacks melanin, the pigment that gives fur its color. Underneath their stripey fur, zebra skin is all black.

## What about TIGERS?

Even though zebras and tigers both have stripes, the purpose of these stripes seems to be quite different. Zebras spend most of their days together in a herd grazing in wide open spaces. On the other hand, tigers live alone in forests, grasslands, and mangrove swamps, hunkered down and waiting to ambush their next meal. Their orange-and-black stripes are the perfect camouflage for keeping a low profile before they're ready to pounce.

Here's another way tigers are different from zebras: While zebras have solid black skin, a tiger's skin is striped, just like its fur! The colored hair follicles in its skin are visible. If you were to shave a tiger, it would still be covered in stripes. (And in case you were wondering ... a giraffe's skin is tan—no spots.)

# AN INTERVIEW WITH DR. NIZAR IBRAHIM

**P**aleontologist and National Geographic Explorer Nizar Ibrahim spends his time researching, studying, and finding prehistoric animals. One of his biggest discoveries was unearthing new remains of the largest predatory dinosaur—*Spinosaurus*. It was longer than a school bus, and it had a head like a crocodile and tall spines on its back that looked like a sail. It was bigger than *Tyrannosaurus rex*. Before Ibrahim's discovery, only a few fossilized bones of *Spinosaurus* had been found—about 100 years ago. But those bones were destroyed by bombing during World War II. Ibrahim went searching for *Spinosaurus* remains in North Africa's Sahara, where there was once an ancient river system. And after lots of detective work, he found them.

**paleontologist**

## Q: HOW DO YOU KNOW WHERE TO START LOOKING FOR DINOSAUR FOSSILS?

A: Typically, we look at geological maps to find places where rocks of the right age are exposed at the surface. When I go to the Sahara, for example, I often look for Cretaceous-age rocks—the ones I am most interested in are about 100 million years old. I then spend a lot of time walking around the desert, looking for little bits of bone sticking out from the surrounding rock. That's kind of the ideal scenario, because it means there is a chance that the majority of a skeleton might still be underground, where it is protected from the elements. Sometimes other scientists—often geologists—or local people also tell us about places where they found bones.

## WHEN YOU FIND BONES, HOW DO YOU KNOW THEY CAME FROM DINOSAURS?

It's a bit of scientific detective work. We compare the bones we found to those of other animals. Dinosaurs share a certain number of anatomical features that allow us to confidently assign many skeletons to this group. When we analyzed the bones of our *Spinosaurus*, we compared them to the bones of many other dinosaurs. The similarities we saw to drawings and photographs of *Spinosaurus* bones were striking. Unfortunately, the only other associated skeleton of *Spinosaurus* had been destroyed in World War II, but the detailed drawings and publications of these fossils allowed us to refer our skeleton to this animal. One obvious feature: No other dinosaur has spines this tall. This is a unique feature seen in our skeleton and the "lost" skeleton of *Spinosaurus*. We now have several bones in our skeleton we can match to bones of the first *Spinosaurus* skeleton.

## HOW DO YOU KNOW HOW TO PUT THE BONES TOGETHER?

We can often see how bones fit together just by looking at the fossils. Some, for example, have a ball-and-socket configuration that shows us how one bone fits with the next. We also look at the skeletons of living animals to better understand how those of extinct animals worked. And sometimes, when we get lucky, a skeleton is actually preserved in "articulation." This means that the bones are still connected to each other, more or less the same way they were when the animal was alive. These finds also help us reconstruct less well-preserved finds.

## WHAT'S YOUR FAVORITE DINOSAUR?

That's a tough question. Typically, my favorite dinosaur is the one I just happen to be working on, because I spend a lot of time thinking about it and trying to solve its mysteries. Of course, *Spinosaurus* has a special place in my heart because the skeleton we are working on is the only one of its kind in the world, and also because *Spinosaurus* is such a weird creature: It's the first largely aquatic dinosaur known. I really like some of the long-necked dinosaurs—especially *Giraffatitan*, from Tanzania. I also have a soft spot for a preda-tory dinosaur with big horns—*Carnotaurus*, the "flesh-eating bull"—and, yes, *Tyrannosaurus rex* is also one of my favorites. Wow. I better stop, because this list is getting a little too long!

*Spinosaurus*

# CHAPTER 2

# HOW DEEP A HOLE COULD YOU DIG?

## QUESTIONS ABOUT EARTH

Earth is our home, so naturally we have a lot of questions about its past, present, and future. Like, how old is Earth—and how did people ever figure that out? How'd the oceans get so salty? And why can't we drink from them? How many people have lived on Earth since the beginning of time? (Hint: it's a really, *really* big number.) You know what else is big? Mount Everest. How did that happen? It's no mystery—there's a scientific answer waiting for you to uncover it. Ready to explore? Let's go!

# Is there ANYWHERE on Earth that HUMANS HAVEN'T BEEN?

Humans have been exploring Earth for tens of thousands of years. We've been to the very top of the highest mountain and traveled 6.8 miles (11 km) down into the deep sea. But, believe it or not, there are still places that remain untouched by humans.

## WAY UP HIGH

Gangkhar Puensum is the highest unclimbed peak in the world. Located in Bhutan, the mountain is not only remote and challenging to climb—it's off limits to climb by order of the government. The peak is considered sacred and home to holy spirits. No one is known to have ever set foot on the nearly 25,000-foot (7,620-m) peak, which is the 40th tallest in the world.

## HIDDEN LANDS

Some places are just now being discovered because they have recently been uncovered. Even though 80 percent of Greenland is covered in a single ice sheet, it is considered thoroughly explored. But melting glaciers are revealing never before seen or mapped islands. What once looked like mountains peeking out of the ice have now been revealed as a string of islands, leading mapmakers to go back to the drawing board to resurvey the area.

A SINKHOLE IN CHINA THAT'S 63 STORIES DEEP HAS A PRIMITIVE FOREST AT THE BOTTOM OF IT THAT MIGHT CONTAIN PREVIOUSLY UNKNOWN SPECIES OF SMALL ANIMALS.

# THE FINAL FRONTIER

The most undiscovered place on Earth isn't on land—it's the sea. Humans have been sailing the ocean's surface for thousands of years, but we've only been exploring its depths for a few decades. Thanks to new technology, such as deep-sea submarines and sonar, we are figuring out more about what lies beneath.

Even so, more than 80 percent of the ocean hasn't been mapped, explored, or seen by people. We have mapped more of the moon and Mars than we have the ocean floor. Why? For starters, the ocean is big. It covers 71 percent of Earth's surface and makes up 97 percent of the world's water. And it's also very deep. If you dropped Mount Everest into the deepest part of the ocean— the Mariana Trench in the Pacific Ocean—its peak would be a mile (1.6 km) below the surface. That depth creates an extremely hostile environment for exploration, with inky darkness and intense atmospheric pressure. In fact, it's easier to communicate with astronauts in space than with explorers on the bottom of the ocean floor. That's because scientists are still figuring out how to make electronics work well deep underwater.

Humans have done *some* exploring, though. In 1960, a Swiss oceanographer and a U.S. Navy lieutenant traveled in a bathyscaphe—a type of submersible—to the Mariana Trench, nearly seven miles (11 km) beneath the ocean's surface. That was the only time a vessel reached these depths until 2012, when inventor and filmmaker James Cameron became the first person to travel solo into this abyss.

James Cameron's submersible, *DEEPSEA CHALLENGER,* reaches the bottom of the Mariana Trench.

# THE LAST CONTINENT

Antarctica was the last continent discovered. People long suspected there was a continent at the southern end of the planet, but it wasn't formally spotted until 1820. The next "first" was getting to the South Pole—the southernmost point on Earth—which was achieved by Norwegian explorer Roald Amundsen in 1911. Today, a few thousand people live in the Antarctic to conduct research in the summer, but only a few dozen stay through the winter. While much of Antarctica has been seen by air, much less has been explored by foot due to its extreme terrain and environment.

Remote-operated drones help us explore extreme places, like Antarctica.

## What's in all those UNEXPLORED parts of the ocean?

We won't know until we go there. But scientists estimate there are between a few hundred thousand to a few million species still undiscovered. In 2022 alone, more than 30 new species were found on the ocean floor— and they're wildly weird! Scientists found feather stars that use their feathery arms to catch food, a translucent sea cucumber, and a bright yellow sea cucumber that earned the nickname gummy squirrel because it looks like a squirrel-shaped gummy.

the gummy squirrel

## MYTHS BUSTED

# THERE'S GOLD AT THE END OF RAINBOWS, RIGHT?

You've probably heard the legend that there's a treasure waiting to be found at the end of each rainbow. Unfortunately, there's no truth to this myth. Even if there were leprechauns to hide their gold (there aren't), you still wouldn't be able to find it. That's because there isn't an end to a rainbow!

That's right—rainbows may look like arches, but they are actually circles. When looking at a rainbow, you only see half the circle; the other half is below the horizon, or the line where Earth and sky seem to meet.

On top of that, rainbows don't really exist in one place. They are made of light, and they appear when there is a lot of moisture in the air—after it rains or when water sprays from a sprinkler or hose, for example. When sunlight hits the moisture at just the right angle, it causes the light to scatter into a rainbow.

THE FIRST MENTIONS OF LEPRECHAUNS DESCRIBE THEM AS WEARING RED—NOT GREEN! THE FAMOUS GREEN OUTFITS LIKELY APPEARED LATER THANKS TO THE COLOR'S POPULARITY THROUGH-OUT IRELAND.

## SO WHERE DID THE POT OF GOLD MYTH COME FROM?

Legends about tiny fairy spirits called *luchorpán* started appearing in Ireland by the eighth century. Over the centuries, people began to tell more and more tales about these secretive and mischievous creatures. According to folklore, leprechauns usually worked as cobblers, or people who fixed shoes. This eventually may have given them the name leprechaun, taken from the Irish term for shoemaker, *leath brogan*. And it also gave them their gold! Tales depicted leprechauns as storing their coins in large pots. However, possibly because they were distrustful of humans—or maybe just because they wanted to play tricks!—leprechauns were said to stash these pots at the end of rainbows.

Of course (as you now know!), no one would have ever been able to find this gold, given that there is no end to a rainbow. That's why, according to the legends, the only way to nab a pot of gold was to catch a leprechaun. Then, he might grant you three wishes, or hand over his treasure haul.

## IF SUNLIGHT CAUSES RAINBOWS, WHY ISN'T IT ALWAYS COLORFUL?

We often don't think of sunlight as having a color, because the light that shines down from the sun is white. However, this white light is made up of all the colors that exist. When the white sunlight hits moisture, it scatters into the different colors it is made of. This creates a rainbow. Until then, the light appears pretty colorless.

## WHY DON'T RAINBOWS HAVE EVERY COLOR?

Red, orange, yellow, green, blue, indigo, and violet—these colors make up a rainbow. Notice any missing? Even though white light is made up of every color, you'll never see brown in a rainbow. This is because some colors can only be created by mixing others, and not all colors have a chance to mix in a rainbow.

When light scatters, it splits into every color that humans can see, known as the visible light spectrum, as well as some colors that humans *can't* see. But because of the way the colors of the visible light spectrum split, some of the colors never touch other ones. For example, to make brown, the green and red lights would have to mix together. However, because they are not next to each other, this doesn't happen, so there is no brown light in the rainbow.

## ROUNDUP MORE MYTHOLOGICAL RAINBOWS

People have long thought that rainbows are pretty amazing; in fact, many cultures incorporated rainbows into their myths, folklore, and mythology. Read on to discover more amazing tales of rainbows.

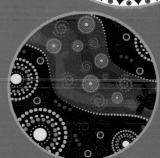

>> Putting the "bow" in "rainbow": In Sanskrit and Hindi, the word for "rainbow," *Indradhanush*, translates to "bow of Indra." This comes from Hindu mythology, in which Indra, the god of rain and lightning, uses the rainbow as his bow to shoot lightning bolts.

>> Shimmering serpent: In some Aboriginal Australian myths, the rainbow is part of a serpent that emerged from the sea to help create the world.

>> Rainbow bridge: In Norse mythology, a rainbow bridge called Bifrost connects the world of the gods to the world of humankind.

>> Respect the rainbow: In some cultures around the world, from the Lakota in the United States to the Kaiwá in Brazil, it is considered bad luck to point at a rainbow.

# Why is the OCEAN SALTY?

If you've ever gotten a mouthful of seawater *(blech!)* you know it's not good to drink—it's chock-full of salt! If you're wondering how all that salt got in there (after all, it doesn't rain salt water), stay tuned.

MARINE IGUANAS HAVE A UNIQUE WAY OF GETTING RID OF EXTRA SALT: THEY SNEEZE IT OUT!

Experts think that the ocean first formed about 3.8 billion years ago, likely from heavy rains that fell for centuries at a time. Back then, the ocean probably wasn't very salty at all. But over long periods of time—think millions or billions of years—that changed.

Over many years, rains and rivers can wear down mountains, rocks, and soil. These things are all made of minerals, many of which are salty. As water breaks down these things, it washes away the minerals. Where do the minerals go? Into rivers and streams—and eventually, into the ocean. That may not seem like quite enough salt to make the entire ocean salty, but over a very long time, enough salt collected to form the salty seas we know today.

## SETTLING SALT

Since minerals keep flowing from the earth to the sea, it stands to reason that the ocean will only get saltier and saltier. However, a lot of the salt in the ocean settles on the ocean floor, becoming what is known as sediment. This sediment does not add to the saltiness of the ocean. In fact, according to experts, the ocean seems to have reached a balance between salt that ends up in the sea and salt that settles as sediment.

THE DEAD SEA IS SO SALTY THAT FISH AND PLANTS CAN'T LIVE IN IT—HENCE THE NAME!

KNOWN AS THE DEAD SEA, A LAKE ON THE BORDER OF JORDAN AND ISRAEL CAN BE UP TO NINE TIMES AS SALTY AS THE OCEAN.

## A SALTY SITUATION

Even though the parts of the ocean are all connected, some parts of it are saltier than others. This can occur for several reasons. In some places where there is more rainfall, the ocean tends to be less salty. This can also happen in areas where freshwater ice melts, such as in the Arctic. In other areas, where it is warmer and water evaporates faster, the oceans can be saltier.

## Why aren't RIVERS salty?

Even though rivers and streams carry salty minerals to the sea, they themselves aren't salty. Not only is the water in them constantly running, it is also being fed by freshwater rains and mountain snows. Even so, it's not a good idea to drink from rivers and streams. They may not be full of salt, but they could harbor bacteria or pollution.

## How do animals SURVIVE in all that salt?

A human certainly couldn't live in the ocean permanently. Aside from not being able to breathe in water, all that salt would make them sick! But many animals do it with no problem. Over time, ocean animals developed special adaptations that allow them to thrive in briny conditions. Many ocean animals—from fish to dolphins—have special internal organs or body structures that help them get rid of some of the salt they take in. Then, they release the salt as urine.

## How much salt water can you DRINK?

Not very much at all! Of course, if you accidentally swallow some salt water while swimming, not much will happen—aside from it tasting unpleasant. But purposely gulping down salt water would make a human ill. For reference, experts recommend that humans get less than 2,300 milligrams of sodium each day—about the amount in one teaspoon of salt. By contrast, one glass of ocean water has almost two teaspoons of salt in it—nearly twice the amount of salt a person should have in an entire day.

When a human drinks or eats too much salt, it enters into their bloodstream. Like some other animals, humans have special organs, called kidneys, that can filter out waste and other things, like extra salt. However, kidneys need water (fresh water!) to function. This means that drinking or eating too much salt quickly leads to dehydration. Better to stick to fresh water!

# Why is MOUNT EVEREST SO BIG?

**Mount Everest is the highest mountain on Earth. Its peak rests 29,035 feet (8,850 m) above sea level—that's only slightly lower than the altitude airplanes fly at! But it wasn't always this tall.**

## WHEN CONTINENTS COLLIDE

Once upon a time, the gray spotted rocks at the top of Mount Everest were on the ocean floor. It's grown more than five miles (8 km) in the past 30 million years. Now that's a serious growth spurt! Let's go back in time a bit—around 200 million years ago, which happens to be the same time the Jurassic dinosaurs were beginning to emerge. That's when the supercontinent called Pangaea split into pieces. The Indian continent eventually broke free of Pangaea and went on a slow ride over the next 150 million years until it smacked into another continent—what we now know as Eurasia. Some mountain ranges—like the Sierra Nevada in California and Nevada and the Tetons in Wyoming, all in the U.S.—formed when stress between and inside tectonic plates caused cracking in Earth's surface, which moved rocks up and down. But the Indian continent and Eurasian

continent are made of roughly the same rock density, so when they collided, they crumpled the land. Eventually, this gave rise to the Himalaya, a mountain range that stretches 1,500 miles (2,400 km). In the entire world, there are only 14 peaks higher than 26,247 feet (8,000 meters) above sea level. Ten of those peaks stand in the Himalaya.

## GROWING UP

Mount Everest and the rest of the Himalaya grow by about half an inch (1.3 cm) each year because the continental collision that started millions of years ago is still (slowly) happening. But this probably won't go on forever. Scientists think the Eurasian plate is now stretching out, not rising up, so this growth will probably stop.

> THE BREATHABLE OXYGEN AT THE SUMMIT OF MOUNT EVEREST IS A THIRD WHAT IT IS AT SEA LEVEL.

## How much TALLER is Mount Everest than other mountains?

Mount Everest has a comfortable lead in the highest mountain in the world contest. K2, the second highest mountain, is located in the Karakoram mountain range of Pakistan, about 900 miles (1,448 km) northwest of Everest. It is 28,251 feet (8,610 m) tall, so about 1,000 feet (305 m) shorter. Despite its (slightly) shorter stature, K2 is considered a far more difficult mountain to access and climb. Everest is the more popular destination for mountaineers. Edmund Hillary and Tenzing Norgay reached the summit of Everest on May 29, 1953. Since then, more than 4,000 people have done the same, whereas only a few hundred people have climbed K2.

MAUNA KEA, LOCATED IN HAWAII, U.S.A., IS THE TALLEST MOUNTAIN ON EARTH—BUT TWO-THIRDS OF IT IS UNDERWATER.

## Is Everest the BIGGEST mountain... in the universe?

Not even close! Olympus Mons, a volcano on Mars, is the largest mountain in our solar system. It covers about the same amount of land as the U.S. state of Arizona! It is 15.5 miles (25 km) high—three times taller than Mount Everest. Olympus Mons was able to get so big because, unlike on Earth, Mars doesn't have plate tectonics that move a volcano away from its hot spot. The volcano stays in the same place and just keeps growing bigger.

## Are there mountains that are SHRINKING?

Yes! The Himalaya may be getting taller every year, but that's not the case for every mountain range. In fact, all mountains experience something called erosion—the process by which rock is worn away over time. This happens naturally as wind and water chip away at mountains over millions of years. The Himalaya grow more than they shrink each year, so they're getting taller. But plenty of mountains are no longer growing. The Appalachian Mountains in the eastern United States, for example, have been slowly getting smaller for about 300 million years.

# How do we know how OLD EARTH IS?

To get an idea of how old planet Earth is, scientists have to look closely at some of the oldest things around. Not animals, not plants, but rocks. By studying rocks, scientists have estimated that Earth is about 4.5 billion years old. But it wasn't easy figuring that out!

SCIENTISTS THINK THE SUN IS 4.6 BILLION YEARS OLD—ONLY "SLIGHTLY" OLDER THAN EARTH.

## IT'S ALL RELATIVE

Over the years, experts tried many different methods to figure out how old the planet might be. In 1862, an Irish scientist attempted to estimate how long it would take a ball of molten materials—how our Earth started out—to cool down to the state that Earth is in today. His answer? About 20 to 400 million years. While very old, that was nowhere near the number that scientists later arrived at!

Eventually, researchers turned to a technique known as relative dating. In this method, experts compare the various layers of rocks and settled materials, called sediment, that make up the planet. By comparing these layers to each other, scientists can figure out which layers are older or younger. Using the positions of the layers, scientists can figure out their approximate ages. By analyzing more and more sediment, the experts began to realize that the planet was actually *billions* of years old, rather than millions. However, relative dating only let the scientists figure out how old the layers probably were in relation to each other; they still didn't have a way of narrowing in on a better estimate.

## RADIOACTIVE READINGS

In the early 1900s, scientists made an interesting discovery. In nature, there are certain elements, or substances, that are radioactive. These radioactive elements are "unstable," meaning that they give off energy over time. Scientists realized that when these radioactive elements gave off energy, they broke down—or decayed—in ways that the scientists could trace. By examining how some of these elements had decayed, scientists could figure out their exact age. The scientists calculated that Earth has been around for about 4.5 billion years! This is known as radiometric dating.

## How **OLD** is the universe, and **HOW** do we know?

In the vastness of space, scientists don't always have access to elements that they can use in radiometric dating. But they do have other methods. In fact, scientists are pretty confident the entire universe is about 13.8 billion years old.

To reach this number, scientists started by studying the rate at which the universe is expanding. That's right: The universe is always expanding. Scientists believe that before the universe existed, all matter and all energy were contained in a single point. Then, about 13.8 billion years ago, an event known as the big bang sent all this matter and energy flying outward, creating the universe. And this movement never stopped; the universe continues to expand to this day.

Beginning in the 1920s, scientists using incredibly powerful telescopes discovered this expansion for themselves. By using these super telescopes to track the light from far-off stars, they also figured out how fast the universe expands. This is known as the universe's rate of expansion. Then, in the 21st century, scientists realized they could use the rate of expansion to work backward to try to pinpoint how old the universe is. For example, given how large the universe is and how quickly it is expanding, how long would it have taken to grow to the size it is now from the time of the big bang? This led them to the age we know today: 13.8 billion years.

## SUPER OLD, SUPER COOL

There's nothing on the planet that comes close to the age of Earth itself—let alone the age of the universe! But our home is still full of some amazingly old, interesting things.

» **Long-lived clam:** One clam, which scientists named Ming, was discovered to be more than 500 years old—it had been born in the 15th century!

» **Elderly tree:** Nicknamed Methuselah, a bristlecone pine in California, U.S.A., is some 4,700 years old. It was around when the Pyramids at Giza were built!

» **Super old ice:** Scientists working in the Antarctic have drilled down and found ice that has been around for nearly three million years.

» **Ancient microbes:** Scientists have discovered frozen—but living—microscopic organisms known as microbes that are millions of years old. In fact, some experts believe they have found living microbes that are hundreds of millions of years old!

EXPERTS THINK THE MILKY WAY IS "ALMOST" AS OLD AS THE UNIVERSE, AT ABOUT 13.6 BILLION YEARS OLD.

# How do SCIENTISTS predict HURRICANES?

Hurricanes aren't just regular ol' storms. They are tropical storms that form in the ocean—and to get the title "hurricane," they have to have wind speeds of at least 74 miles an hour (119 km/h). Knowing where these powerful storms are headed and when they are hitting shore is important to keep communities safe and give people enough time to prepare or evacuate if needed.

ON A SCALE OF ONE TO FIVE, CATEGORY 5 STORMS ARE THE STRONGEST—WITH WINDS HIGHER THAN 157 MILES AN HOUR (252 KM/H).

A pilot flies through the eye of a large hurricane.

## EYE IN THE SKY

A big breakthrough in hurricane prediction came in the 1960s, when the first weather satellites were launched into orbit around Earth. They constantly monitor weather from above Earth's atmosphere, giving meteorologists a better look at hurricanes forming in the ocean.

Scientists also monitor storms using weather radar, which includes remote sensing equipment that determines a storm's location, structure, and intensity. If a storm is headed toward land, hurricane hunter aircraft, which have this sensing equipment on board, fly into the storm and collect data such as temperature, humidity, pressure, wind direction, and wind speed.

## WAIT ... WHAT?

You read that right. A hurricane seems like the last place you'd want to visit by plane, but to get information about the hurricane, meteorologists and researchers need to sample the storm directly. Using either a two-prop aircraft or a jet, U.S. Air Force reserve pilots fly around or directly into a storm. Scientists on board release devices called dropsondes, which parachute down through the hurricane to the ocean, sending back data on pressure, temperature, humidity, and wind speed. The data are used in computer models that help forecasters predict how intense the hurricane will become and where and when it will strike land. The aircraft also has a radar dish to make wind and rainfall estimates. It does this by sending radio waves that bounce off raindrops in the storm before returning to the dish. Computers collect these data and map them.

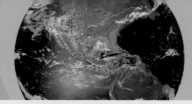

## Do **SCIENTISTS DECIDE** if a storm is a hurricane or a typhoon?

Nope! Geography does. Both hurricanes and typhoons are intensified tropical storms, but what you call them depends on where they are located. Call it a hurricane if it's above the North Atlantic Ocean or the central or eastern North Pacific Ocean. Call it a typhoon if it's over the northwest Pacific Ocean, usually East Asia. And in the South Pacific and Indian Oceans, cyclone is the correct term.

ABOUT 80 TROPICAL STORMS OCCUR AROUND THE GLOBE EVERY YEAR.

## SPEAKING OF STORMS ...

On Jupiter, there is a giant storm that behaves like the hurricanes we have here on Earth, but it is much, much larger. In fact, the storm is twice as large as our planet! Winds inside the storm reach speeds of 270 miles an hour (435 km/h). No one knows when the storm started, but it has been seen ever since astronomers began observing Jupiter, about 400 years ago.

## How are hurricanes **NAMED?**

Once a storm's wind speed reaches 39 miles an hour (63 km/h), it's given tropical storm status and is assigned a name. And there's a very strict system for what that name will be. Since 1953, the World Meteorological Organization has assigned names to Atlantic Ocean storms each year, which go in alphabetic order (skipping the letters Q, U, X, Y, and Z) and—since 1979—alternate between traditionally female and male names. Previously the names were all female.

## What does it **FEEL LIKE** in the eye of a hurricane?

It's easy to spy the eye of a hurricane—it's at the hurricane's center. While the surrounding clouds form a ring of fierce winds, the eye—which is typically 20 miles (32 km) wide, but can be as wide as 120 miles (193 km)—is strangely calm. If you were inside one, you'd experience relatively weak winds of about 15 miles an hour (24 km/h). The weather is so chill in the eye of a hurricane, you can see the sun peeping through! That calm doesn't last for long, though: As the storm moves, the eye does, too.

# Q&A

# AN INTERVIEW WITH
## EYAL WEINTRAUB

**P**lanet Earth is, on average, getting warmer. This big-picture shift in temperature is called climate change. While some climate changes happen on Earth naturally, human activity is responsible for our quickly warming world. Climate change is bad for us for many reasons, including causing extreme weather events, sea level rise, and damage to ecosystems. National Geographic Young Explorer Eyal Weintraub is a 23-year-old climate activist and co-founder of Youth for Climate Argentina. He organizes protests and works with politicians to raise awareness about the climate crisis.

climate activist

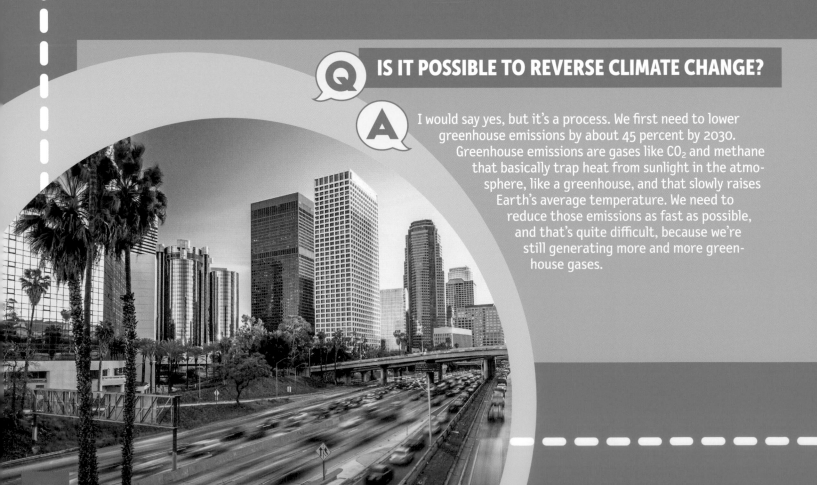

**Q** IS IT POSSIBLE TO REVERSE CLIMATE CHANGE?

**A** I would say yes, but it's a process. We first need to lower greenhouse emissions by about 45 percent by 2030. Greenhouse emissions are gases like $CO_2$ and methane that basically trap heat from sunlight in the atmosphere, like a greenhouse, and that slowly raises Earth's average temperature. We need to reduce those emissions as fast as possible, and that's quite difficult, because we're still generating more and more greenhouse gases.

## Q HOW DO WE LOWER GREENHOUSE GAS EMISSIONS?

**A** Stop using fuels that emit greenhouse gases (fossil fuels) for energy, and transition to green energies, or energies that don't emit greenhouse gases. These are energy sources like solar power (from the sun) and wind energy, for example.

## Q WHAT HAPPENS IF THINGS DON'T CHANGE?

**A** If we follow the trends that exist right now, it could become a huge problem, causing people to not have enough food to eat, safe places to live, and more.

## Q ARE YOU OPTIMISTIC ABOUT REVERSING CLIMATE CHANGE?

**A** I'm an activist, so I think it's kind of in my essence to be optimistic about it. Because of the communities that I'm a part of, I meet incredibly smart and talented people who are working on it from different angles and different fields. To succeed, we need to find ways to mix sustainability with innovation and politics and communication.

## Q WHAT CAN KIDS DO TO FIGHT CLIMATE CHANGE?

**A** Visiting local parks is a great way for kids to get involved and get to know the environment, because it's difficult to want to transform—and to want to love and protect—something that you don't know. As kids grow up, they can not only become volunteers and activists for the climate movement, they can get into the more technical aspects of studying and finding solutions—in science, politics, communication, startups, tech, and more.

## WHAT ARE FOSSIL FUELS?

Gas, oil, and coal are examples of fossil fuels. Many people use these fuels to run their cars, cook on the stove, and even turn on the lights in their homes. So, where does the "fossil" part come in? Fossil fuels aren't made from fossils, but they are made from the same things as fossils—very, very old plants and animals. Over millions of years, these prehistoric plants and animals have decomposed and been compressed deep in the earth, slowly turning into energy-rich fuels. All living things contain the element carbon, and when fossil fuels are burned, that carbon is released as carbon dioxide gas ($CO_2$), which warms the atmosphere.

# Can PLANTS HEAR?
## (Or see? Or smell? Or taste?)

At first, the answer to this question might seem obvious: No way. But the truth is that plants do sense the world around them, in many complex and cool ways.

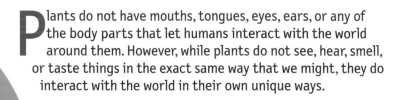

Plants do not have mouths, tongues, eyes, ears, or any of the body parts that let humans interact with the world around them. However, while plants do not see, hear, smell, or taste things in the exact same way that we might, they do interact with the world in their own unique ways.

## HEARING

Although plants do not have ears, they are able to respond to noises. Scientists believe that this is because the plants sense vibrations caused by sounds and use those vibrations to understand the world around them. In one study, scientists played a recording of the sounds of a caterpillar chewing on leaves near a plant. In response, the plant began to produce certain oils meant to fend off munching insects! In another study, scientists placed covered plants near two pipes: one with running water and the other one empty. Even though the plant had no way of getting to it, the plant still grew toward the pipe containing water. Experts think that this may be because the plant could "hear" the water running through the pipe.

## SIGHT

For many animals, eyes are an essential part of seeing. Eyes "take in" the light that bounces off the objects around us. Special cells then send this information to our brains, which sort the information into images that we can understand. Plants don't have eyes, but some scientists think that they do have special structures in their bodies that let them sense and interpret light. Does this mean that plants can "see" images of the world around them? Probably not—at least, scientists don't think so. However, it may mean that plants can use light to understand their environments in a unique way.

## TASTE

When you take a bite of something, you may be able to quickly figure out if it is sweet, salty, bitter, spicy, or something else entirely. This is thanks to tiny organs that are located along your tongue and inside your mouth, known as taste buds. When taste buds encounter different chemicals, they send messages about these chemicals to your brain. Your brain interprets these different combinations of chemicals as tastes—like a sour lemon or a sweet candy. According to scientists, plants have structures in their roots that act similarly. Does this mean that plants taste the nutrients they eat? Not exactly. Scientists aren't sure exactly how plants' sense of taste works yet, but they think it helps plants search out certain chemicals and send information between plant roots.

## TOUCH

Humans (and many other organisms) have special cells that let them feel the world around them. When these cells encounter objects or chemical reactions, they send messages to our brains that we sense as "touch." Because plants do not have these cells, scientists think that they do not feel things physically in the same way we do. However, that doesn't mean they can't respond to physical touch! Some plants, like insect-eating fly traps, have tiny hairs. When an insect touches these hairs, the fly trap reacts by snapping shut—trapping the insects for a satisfying meal.

## SMELL

Can plants smell? According to some scientists, yes they can! When you take a big whiff of a scent, small cells inside your nose are reacting to chemicals in the air. These cells then send messages to your brain, which interprets the information as different scents. While we don't know if plants interpret these chemicals or scents the same way we do, scientists have discovered that plants *can* sense and respond to them.

SOME TREES CAN USE THEIR ROOTS TO SEND NUTRIENTS TO YOUNGER SAPLINGS.

## Can plants COMMUNICATE?

According to many scientists, yes! Some studies suggest that plants can send information to each other using their roots. This may help spread news of danger, like approaching insects or forest fires. Some scientists think that this could even help plants store information, or "learn," and pass on information to younger plants around them.

# How DEEP a hole could you POSSIBLY DIG?

**Here's the unsatisfying scoop: We don't really know! But we do know how far we've already gotten.**

**THE KOLA WELL IS DEEPER THAN MOUNT EVEREST IS TALL.**

Engineers and other scientists are always trying to figure out new technologies that would make it possible to dig deeper and deeper into the earth. Does this mean that you should run out with a shovel to try to beat the current record? No, definitely not. For one thing, it can be dangerous—the sides of a hole could cave in or collapse. For another, engineers need special equipment and lots of funding to dig super deep holes.

For example, take the world's deepest hole. Known as the Kola Superdeep Borehole or the Kola Well, this hole is located on the Kola Peninsula in Russia and plunges a staggering 40,230 feet (12,260 m) underground. But it wasn't easy: The Kola Well took a massive drill, nearly 20 years, and more than $100 million to excavate. And after all that time and money, the project had to abandoned because the drill became stuck after reaching extremely hot temperatures.

**THE DEEPEST-LIVING ANIMAL EVER DISCOVERED IS THE DEVIL WORM, WHICH CAN LIVE AT 2.2 MILES (3.6 KM) BELOW THE SURFACE.**

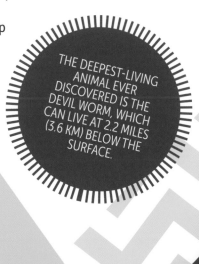

## So ... we CAN'T DIG through planet Earth?

Not with current technology. To understand the challenges facing engineers, let's take a look at the layers of the planet. Right now, the Kola Well only reaches less than half of the way through the planet's crust. Here, drills must bore through solid rock and extreme heat, running the risk of getting stuck like the Kola Well's drill did. But even if engineers could make it through the crust, things would only get more challenging.

Beneath Earth's crust lies the mantle, a layer of mostly solid, superhot elastic rock. Right now, scientists are aiming to reach the mantle—and they're having a tough time doing it! But getting through the mantle, where temperatures can reach 6,692 degrees Fahrenheit (3700°C)? Currently impossible. What if they did, though? Well, then they'd have to deal with Earth's inner, molten layer: the core. Scientists aren't sure how hot it is there, but they think it might be about 10,800 degrees Fahrenheit (6000°C).

The **CRUST** includes tectonic plates, land-masses, and the ocean. Its average thickness varies from 5 to 25 miles (8 to 40 km).

The **MANTLE** is about 1,800 miles (2,900 km) of hot, thick, solid rock.

The **OUTER CORE** is liquid molten rock made mostly of iron and nickel.

The **INNER CORE** is a solid center made mostly of iron and nickel.

## But what if we DID dig through the planet?

OK, so let's say we had the technology to make it happen— what would it be like to have a tunnel through the planet? First, it would be tough to find a spot to make it happen. For many places on the planet, if you started digging straight down to the other side, you'd end up in the ocean! Second, a person traveling through the tunnel would need to some-how be protected from the intense heat and pressure. If, somehow, all of these things were controlled, a person who entered the hole would speed through it at about 17,398 miles an hour (28,000 km/h), coming out the other end 42 minutes later.

## A WHOLE LOT OF HOLES

The Kola Well isn't the only super deep hole made by humans. Check out some of the other plunging places on the planet.

>> The South Hole: At Antarctica's Amundsen-Scott South Pole Station, researchers have tunneled about 8,000 feet (2,440 m) down through the ice.

>> Miles to go: The Moab Khotsong mine-shaft in South Africa is about two miles (3 km) deep, meaning a falling object would take about 25 seconds to reach the bottom.

>> Abandoned mantle: In the 1960s, American scientists began Project Mohole, an expedition to reach the mantle by drilling where Earth's crust was thinnest—under the ocean off Mexico. They were able to drill only about 600 feet (183 m) under the seafloor.

**Rescuers respond to a sinkhole in Los Angeles, California, U.S.A.**

## ONE MORE THING: HOW DO SINKHOLES FORM?

Even though giant holes can be quite difficult for humans to dig, some can form naturally— and suddenly—in the earth. A sinkhole is a depression or hole formed when parts of the earth collapse. They can be large enough to swallow houses or entire city blocks. Sink-holes don't happen randomly. They form when water, such as rainfall that has collected over time, wears away the rock under Earth's surface.

# A WORLD OF WATER

If you look at Earth from space, you'll notice that it's mostly blue. Even though we spend most of our lives on land, most of Earth is in fact covered in water. Oceans make up nearly three-quarters of the planet's surface. Get ready to dive into some not-so-watered-down answers to all your questions about $H_2O$!

## HOW DID EARTH GET ITS WATER?

A stream running through a meadow. Sprinklers watering a garden. An afternoon rainstorm. A cool drink on a hot day. Without water, there would be no life on Earth. In fact, an adult human is more than 50 percent water! Despite its importance, water's origin is a mystery to us. Was water always on Earth? If not, how did it get here? No one knows for certain, but one popular theory is that Earth got its water from ... outer space.

Scientists believe that when Earth formed, the planet's temperatures were much higher than they are today, and there was no atmosphere. If there was water here when the planet formed, it would have evaporated and just floated away into space. Many other scientists think that our planet didn't have water until some water-rich objects from space—comets or asteroids—crashed into Earth and brought it here. We know that asteroids in our solar system's outer asteroid belt between Mars and Jupiter contain water in the form of ice. They also contain hydrogen, carbon, and nitrogen. This means, according to many scientists, that we may have a space rock to thank for life as we know it.

## WILL WE RUN OUT OF WATER?

Water doesn't ever really go away. In fact, the water you're drinking today was around during the time of the dinosaurs! Water is constantly being recycled. It evaporates from lakes, rivers, and oceans, but then it becomes water vapor in the atmosphere. Eventually, it cools and condenses, forming water droplets that return to earth again. But even though our water supply won't go away, the demand for fresh water is increasing as the world's population grows. We need water to drink and to grow food. We need it to make clothing, to keep clean, and to flush our toilets. Making good use of the water available to us is becoming more and more important.

## WHY DOES WATER MAKE MY FINGERTIPS WRINKLY?

The sure sign of a good bubble bath is when your fingers are wrinkly when you get out. But why would water make your skin wrinkle? After a few minutes of soaking, your nervous system sends a message to your blood vessels to shrink. Thinner blood vessels cause the skin to fold over them, creating wrinkles. Scientists have long wondered what purpose wrinkly skin serves. A study from England provided some clues. Researchers tested how well people could grip an object with dry hands, with wet hands, and with wrinkled hands that had been soaking in water. Wet hands didn't grip well, but the wrinkled hands gripped just as well as dry hands. The research suggests humans might have evolved wrinkly skin after soaking in water to better grip wet surfaces.

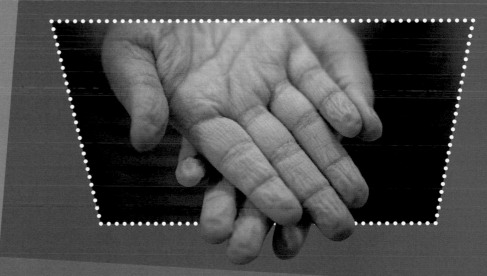

## CAN THE OCEAN FREEZE?

Ponds freeze. Lakes freeze. Even rivers freeze. But can oceans? They sure can! But they freeze differently from freshwater bodies. Fresh water freezes at 32 degrees Fahrenheit (0°C), whereas seawater freezes at a lower temperature—around 28.4 degrees Fahrenheit (-2°C). The salt in seawater keeps it from freezing at warmer temperatures. Still, at least 15 percent of the ocean is covered in sea ice at least part of the year.

## WHY DOES THE OCEAN HAVE WAVES?

The ocean is always in motion. What causes all those waves? Mostly wind, from up above. Wind-driven waves, also known as surface waves, occur when some of the energy from the wind is transferred to the water. Hurricanes, which produce powerful winds, create long waves offshore that bring about dangerous storm surges on land. Tsunamis, on the other hand, are waves created by forces like an underground earthquake or an underwater volcanic eruption. Waves are also created by objects far away—like the sun and the moon. Their gravitational pulls on Earth create tides. The moon has the biggest influence because it is closest to Earth. Its gravity pulls at Earth, creating bulges in the oceans and causing high tides. Because Earth is spinning, a beach that has a high tide in the morning will have a low tide later in the day as that spot on Earth spins away from the moon.

# How do ANIMALS AND PLANTS GET THEIR NAMES?

Did you know that many animals and plants have more than one name? There's the name you call them in conversation, and then a more formal scientific name. But it wasn't always that way.

"BINOMIAL NOMENCLATURE" COMES FROM LATIN AND CAN BE TRANS-LATED AS "TWO-NAME NAME-CALLING."

THE WORD "CAT" MAY COME FROM THE ANCIENT NUBIAN WORD FOR CAT, *KADIS*.

That faithful pooch by your side might be a dog, but it is also a *Canis lupus familiaris*. This other, longer—some might even say fancier—name is a form of organizing living things known as binomial nomenclature.

Most common names for plants and animals—such as "dog"—developed right alongside language. Historians aren't even sure where the name dog comes from! They can trace it back to the Old English word *docga,* which was used for a particular powerful dog breed. But beyond that, it remains something of a mystery.

On the other hand, the origin of binomial nomenclature is much easier to trace. In the 16th century, two Swiss brothers, Gaspard and Johann Bauhin, were working as botanists. As the Bauhin brothers studied more and more plants, they wanted an easy way to sort the plants into groups based on their characteristics. This is also known as classifying. The brothers came up with a system of classification using Latin and Greek names.

For a while, the Bauhin brothers were the only ones who used their system. But in the 18th century, Swedish botanist Carolus Linnaeus also began to use it. While studying plants and animals, Linnaeus began to organize living things into groups and subgroups based on their physical characteristics. He then gave each living thing a name to show what group it was in. Using binomial nomenclature, this name was made up of at least two parts. The first part was a larger grouping of organisms, called the genus. The second name referred to the animal's species. Thanks to Linnaeus, this way of naming animals became very popular and is still used today.

Organizations sometimes let people vote or hold competitions to name other things. A panda cub born at the Smithsonian's National Zoo was named Xiao Qi Ji, or "little miracle," after the public voted. But this can also lead to silly outcomes: The British government let the public submit ideas and vote on the name of a new boat, and it almost became known as *Boaty McBoatface*. This popular name was given to one of the boat's underwater vehicles.

## So who gets to name NEWLY DISCOVERED species?

If you go out and discover a new species, does that mean you get to name it? Pretty much! Traditionally, newly discovered species are given their names by the people who find them and introduce them to the world. This is also true of extinct species, such as dinosaurs whose fossils have recently been uncovered.

Often, the person who discovers the organism names it after themselves (who can blame them?). Sometimes, they name it in honor of a leader, a close friend, or someone they look up to. For example, the dinosaur *Sirindhorna khoratensis* was named in honor of Thailand's princess Maha Chakri Sirindhorn. Other times, scientists will give the species a name that describes it. This happened when researchers discovered a jumping spider with markings that looked like a skeleton: They gave it the species name *sceletus*.

But there are other methods, too. Some organizations allow people to choose names for newly discovered organisms in return for donations that help fund research. Others sometimes hold competitions in which members of the public can submit new name ideas. One thing is for sure: With new species being discovered each year, we'll need a lot of new names!

**ROUNDUP**

## THE MOST POPULAR NAMES

In addition to naming species after friends or historic icons, people often name them after figures from pop culture. This can range from singers to actors to fictional characters.

 *Scaptia beyonceae:* A species of horsefly was named after singer Beyoncé.

 *Dracorex hogwartsia:* One team named a newly discovered dinosaur species after Hogwarts, the magical school found in the Harry Potter series.

 *Ptomaphagus thebeatles:* Fittingly, this beetle was named after the British rock group The Beatles.

 *Daptolestes bronteflavus:* This robber fly was named in honor of Thor, a fictional superhero character. The fly's species name translates to "blond thunder."

# Population Station

**E**arth is home to a lot of people. Just how many? Well, the answer is more complicated than it seems!

## HOW MANY PEOPLE HAVE **EVER** LIVED ON EARTH?

It kind of makes you wonder … if more than eight billion people live on Earth at this very moment, how many people have lived on Earth since the beginning of time? It's tough to know the exact number, but we can probably get pretty close. First, some ground rules: By "people" we mean *Homo sapiens*—the species all living humans belong to. And to make this calculation, we have to agree on when to start counting. For this statistic, scientists began counting at 190,000 B.C.E.

At first, populations climbed pretty slowly. From 190,000 B.C.E. to the year 1 C.E., scientists estimate **55 BILLION** people had lived on Earth. But less than 2,000 years later, that number nearly doubled: By 1850, **101 BILLION** people had been born. Then things really picked up, and in 1950 that number rose to **108 BILLION**. And by 2020, more than **116 BILLION** people had walked on Earth since the beginning of time. What this means is that Earth's human population is growing like crazy—or as mathematicians call it, exponentially.

## HOW MANY PEOPLE LIVE ON EARTH?

According to clocks that keep track of this figure, Earth hit a global population of **EIGHT BILLION** in 2022. So, the answer is eight billion—easy peasy. Wait! Not so fast. This number has continued to climb—by a lot. If the population on Earth grew by 215,000 the next day, would that mean **215,000** people are born every day? Nope. People are born and die every day, but generally speaking, there are more people being born every day than dying. That's what population growth is. The day Earth's population hit eight billion, the next day it was

# 8,000,215,000.

## WHAT'S NEXT?

More people. Earth is expected to hit that big **10 BILLION** mark by 2050. Why is the human population growing so fast? A lot has changed since the time of early humans 192,000 years ago. People are healthier and safer thanks to medicine, better living conditions, cleaner water, and better nutrition, so we live much longer.

Two hundred years ago, people only lived to be about 40 years old. Today they live on average to about 72.

## WE'RE NOT ALONE

While it certainly feels like humans rule the globe, the numbers show otherwise. In fact, pound for pound, humans are seriously outnumbered by some pretty tiny creatures. If you look at the mass of all the living things on the planet, humans only make up one ten-thousandth of the total. Plants rule the planet—they make up **80 PERCENT** of Earth's biomass. Next comes bacteria, at **13 PERCENT**, then fungi, at **2 PERCENT**. Yep, that's right, humans are outranked by fungi.

## AH, RATS

But when you just look at mammals, humans are the most numerous, with one possible exception: rats. Recent studies suggest that rats are likely in the **EIGHT BILLION** range as well, but they're much harder to count than humans.

# WHAT DOES A BILLION LOOK LIKE?

Big numbers sound impressive, but it's hard to really know what they mean. What does a billion *look* like?

## VISUALIZE THIS:

» **10** apples would fill a fruit bowl.

» **1,000** apples would fill a pickup truck.

» **1 million** apples would fill a swimming pool.

» **1 billion** apples would fill a sports stadium.

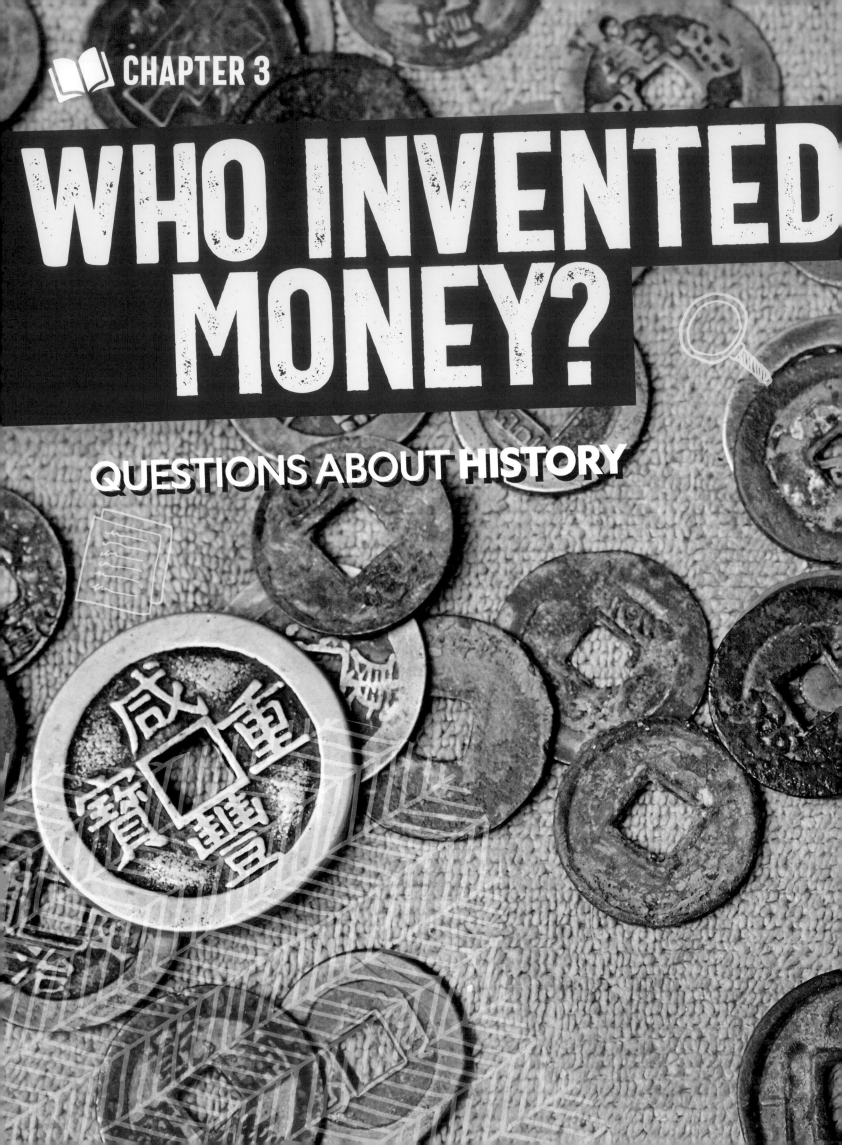

# CHAPTER 3

# WHO INVENTED MONEY?

## QUESTIONS ABOUT **HISTORY**

**Human history is full of mysteries and incredible tales.** Ever wonder how the ancient Egyptians made the enormous pyramids? Or how people discovered and harnessed fire? Or whether pirates really made people walk the plank? It doesn't matter how much time has passed, there's always more to know about the mysteries around history and archaeology—and there are more questions to ask. Get ready to turn back time and discover the answers to all your questions about the past!

# Did pirates REALLY make people WALK THE PLANK?

**YO HO HO … NO!** While this plays out time and again in movies, cartoons, and books, there's no evidence that pirates regularly made people walk the plank.

So where did this idea of walking the plank come from? Long before there were viral videos, ideas spread and got popular in books. In 1724, writer Daniel Defoe wrote a book called *A General History of the Pyrates*, in which he told tales of pirate escapades and described pirates hanging ladders out over ships and telling their captives they were free to go after they climbed onto the ladder and jumped into the sea. But of course they had to survive the swim to shore. Then, in the 19th century other writers—most famously, Robert Louis Stevenson in his book *Treasure Island*—used that same idea, but instead of a ladder, Stevenson wrote about "brave men walking the plank." And that image spread to more stories.

In J.M. Barrie's *Peter Pan*, published in 1911, mean old Captain Hook threatened his captives with walking the plank. He even sang a chantey about it:

*Yo ho, yo ho, the frisky plank,*
*You walks along it so,*
*Till it goes down and you goes down*
*To Davy Jones below!*

After books came movies about pirates and plank-walking, and what started as a fun tale in the early 18th century was passed on so many times that people assume that's really what happened on pirate ships. That's not at all to say that pirate ships were inviting places—there could certainly be cruelty on board—but "walking the plank" is more the stuff of the silver screen than actual history.

## WHAT IS A PLANK?

A plank—aka gangplank—is a removable piece of wood used to connect a ship to a dock. In a "walk the plank" scenario, the plank would be set up not to a dock, but over open water.

## Did PIRATES FLY the Jolly Roger flag?

Aye, aye! They sure did.

Pirates used a flag featuring a skull and crossbones to scare passing ships into surrendering without putting up a fight. The skull and crossbones was a symbol first used in the early 18th century that meant there was death on board a ship. It quickly became popular, including its variations—some ships used the image of a skull with crossed swords instead of bones.

Why the name Jolly, when the flag clearly wasn't a laughing matter? It's believed the name evolved from the French phrase *joli rouge*, which means "pretty red." It turns out the original Jolly Roger flags weren't black at all—they were red. The red background signified that the pirates on board didn't plan to spare a life—in other words, there would be blood (red) if anyone tried to mess with them. Shiver me timbers!

WHILE NOT EVERY PIRATE KEPT A PARROT ON THEIR SHOULDER, OCCASIONALLY PIRATES DID RAID SHIPS THAT HAD EXOTIC ANIMALS ON THEM.

## What about pirates BURYING their TREASURE? Was that REAL?

Hiding your treasure—whether it's coins or other valuables—isn't a bad idea, but burying it at some random spot on an island, as we often see depicted, doesn't seem super practical, does it? Generally speaking, pirates quickly spent the treasure they gathered from looting once they arrived at port.

And remember, not all treasure was shiny and bright. Some treasure was dry goods—like food or spices—or fabric, like silk. This kind of treasure isn't exactly going to hold up well after it's been buried in wet sand on a beach.

But there are a few examples of pirates actually burying their treasure. Probably the most famous of those is Captain William Kidd. He was wanted for piracy and murder and decided to turn himself in. But before he did, he buried gold and jewels worth millions of dollars in today's money on New York's Gardiner's Island in 1699. He was arrested in Boston, Massachusetts, U.S.A., and authorities recovered some of the treasure. Some people think he might have buried loot in other locations, which has sent treasure hunters digging holes in all sorts of suspected locations for centuries, but so far they've come up empty-handed.

# How did an ICEBERG SINK THE *TITANIC*?

On April 14, 1912, the British ocean liner R.M.S. *Titanic* sideswiped an iceberg in the North Atlantic near Newfoundland, Canada, on its maiden voyage. It wasn't a surprise that there were icebergs lurking in the water—but a collection of missteps and unfortunate circumstances led to a worst-case scenario.

## ICEBERG, RIGHT AHEAD

Before its fateful collision, the *Titanic* had received multiple warnings of icebergs in the area from other ships, but the messages weren't delivered to officers or the captain because the wireless operator receiving the messages was swamped sending personal messages for passengers. Then, in the darkness, lookouts spotted an iceberg, but it was too late to stop the ship or steer away. The iceberg sliced open the right side of ship's hull below the waterline, including several of the ship's 16 watertight compartments. These compartments had doors that could seal shut, so water could be contained if this kind of event were to happen. And if only two or three had been damaged, the ship might not have sunk, but unfortunately, at least five were ruptured. The weight of the water that rushed into the compartments meant the ship's fate was inevitable. We know how this story ends: Lifeboats were loaded, but they weren't filled, and there weren't enough to save the more than 2,000 passengers and crew on board. Only 706 survived. Within a few hours, the ship—which was almost as long as three American football fields—split in two, sank, and eventually came to rest 2.5 miles (4 km) down on the ocean floor. The *Titanic* wouldn't be seen again for another 73 years.

## CLUES FROM THE WRECK

The search was on to find the *Titanic* within days of the shipwreck. But not only does the North Atlantic have unfriendly waters (with icebergs!), the ship was miles underwater—and no one knew exactly where it went down. It was going to take 50 years for the proper

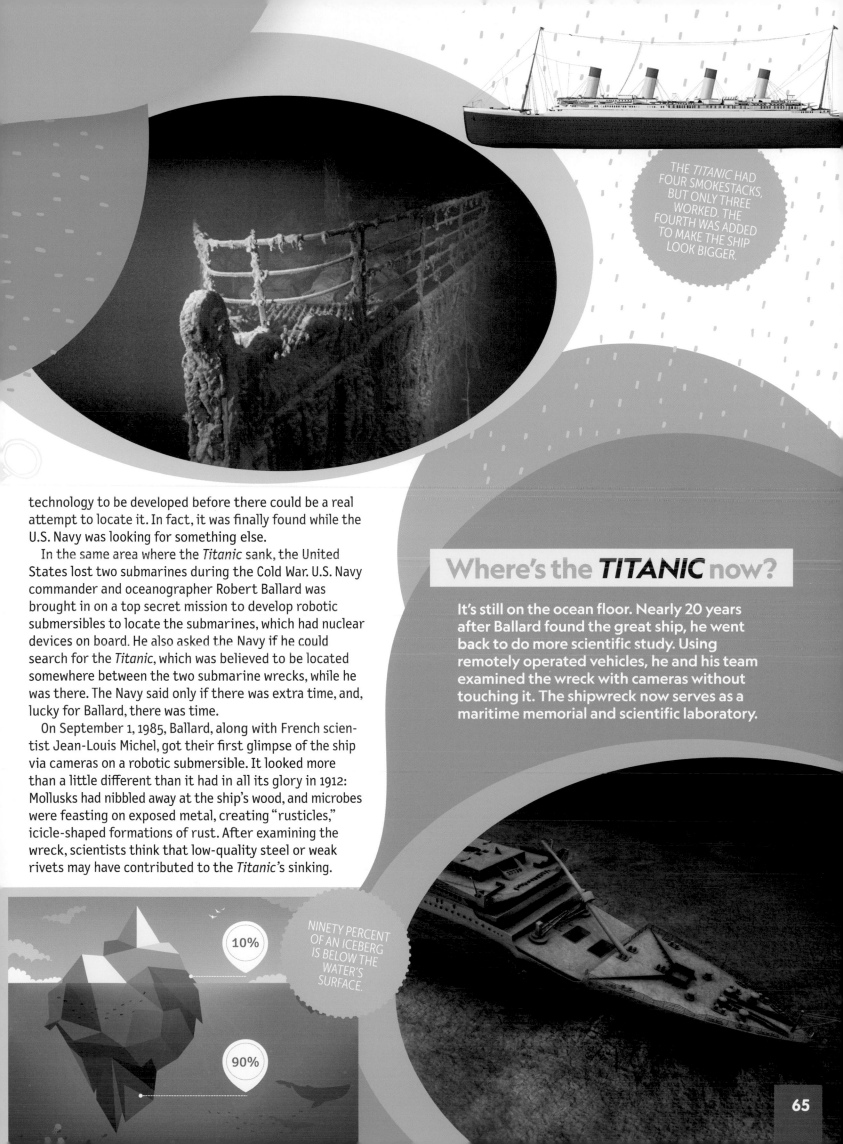

THE *TITANIC* HAD FOUR SMOKESTACKS, BUT ONLY THREE WORKED. THE FOURTH WAS ADDED TO MAKE THE SHIP LOOK BIGGER.

technology to be developed before there could be a real attempt to locate it. In fact, it was finally found while the U.S. Navy was looking for something else.

In the same area where the *Titanic* sank, the United States lost two submarines during the Cold War. U.S. Navy commander and oceanographer Robert Ballard was brought in on a top secret mission to develop robotic submersibles to locate the submarines, which had nuclear devices on board. He also asked the Navy if he could search for the *Titanic*, which was believed to be located somewhere between the two submarine wrecks, while he was there. The Navy said only if there was extra time, and, lucky for Ballard, there was time.

On September 1, 1985, Ballard, along with French scientist Jean-Louis Michel, got their first glimpse of the ship via cameras on a robotic submersible. It looked more than a little different than it had in all its glory in 1912: Mollusks had nibbled away at the ship's wood, and microbes were feasting on exposed metal, creating "rusticles," icicle-shaped formations of rust. After examining the wreck, scientists think that low-quality steel or weak rivets may have contributed to the *Titanic*'s sinking.

## Where's the **TITANIC** now?

It's still on the ocean floor. Nearly 20 years after Ballard found the great ship, he went back to do more scientific study. Using remotely operated vehicles, he and his team examined the wreck with cameras without touching it. The shipwreck now serves as a maritime memorial and scientific laboratory.

10%

90%

NINETY PERCENT OF AN ICEBERG IS BELOW THE WATER'S SURFACE.

# How were the EGYPTIAN PYRAMIDS MADE?

The Pyramids at Giza are some of the most recognizable structures on the planet. With a pair of binoculars, even astronauts on board the International Space Station can see them. That's pretty impressive for structures built 4,500 years ago without the help of any of today's construction equipment. So how did ancient Egyptians create these giant structures? Scientists are still gathering clues, but they have some ideas.

## BUILT FOR A KING

First some background: The Great Pyramid of Khufu—the largest of the three Pyramids at Giza—was built for Pharaoh Khufu, the second king of Egypt's fourth dynasty. The pyramid stood more than 480 feet (146 m) tall. It was made of more than two million tons (1.8 million t) of stone carved into 300,000 blocks. To put that in perspective, you could build a nine-and-a-half-foot (2.9-m)-tall wall around all of France with that much stone.

Khafre, Khufu's son, built a second, smaller pyramid nearby, and then Khafre's son, Menkaure, built a third smaller pyramid. The four sides of all three pyramids are perfectly oriented to north, south, east, and west.

## PLAIN ON THE INSIDE

What would you see if you ventured inside these stunning structures? It's a little anticlimactic. The Pyramids at Giza are mostly solid. Inside, there are burial chambers, but there aren't any hieroglyphic texts, and any treasuries or mummies that may have once been there were plundered during ancient times. Decoration inside pyramids—the kind we think of from King Tutankhamun's tomb—became more common centuries after the Pyramids at Giza were built, so despite being extraordinarily impressive on the outside, they were pretty basic on the inside.

THE WEIGHT OF THE MATERIALS USED TO CONSTRUCT THE PYRAMIDS AT GIZA IS 16 TIMES HEAVIER THAN THE MATERIALS USED TO BUILD THE EMPIRE STATE BUILDING.

## BUT ... *HOW?*

Still, creating such massive structures was an incredible feat. There weren't dump trucks and forklifts 4,500 years ago. Scientists and historians have been baffled about how ancient Egyptians transported materials to build these massive structures. We know the Nile River was used for transporting goods and materials, but it was miles from the pyramids. Or so we thought. In 2022, researchers discovered a previously unknown branch of the Nile that once cut through the desert. It dried up around 600 B.C.E. They believe the river likely played a critical role in moving construction materials, including enormous blocks of stone.

So, we may know how the materials got to Giza, but how were the pyramids actually constructed? Some believe workers created a wall of brick, earth, and sand, which they built higher and longer as the pyramid rose. The big stone blocks were likely hauled up with sledges, rollers, and levers.

## SPEAKING OF ANCIENT EGYPTIAN ARCHITECTURE ...

Another famous ancient Egyptian icon, the Sphinx at Giza, dates back to the time of King Khafre and is located less than a mile from the Great Pyramid of Khufu. It's one of the largest sculptures in the world, measuring 240 feet (73 m) long and 66 feet (20 m) high. It's considered to have a lion's body and a human's head. Who is its head modeled after? That is open to debate. Some say it depicts Khafre, but others say Khafre's brother had it built to commemorate their father, Khufu. The statue has eroded over thousands of years, and its nose is missing. Even so, the statue has stood the test of time. It is carved from a single piece of limestone, and estimates suggest it would have taken 100 workers three years to create it.

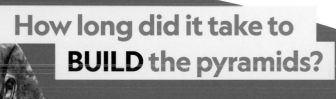

## How long did it take to **BUILD** the pyramids?

This, too, is debated. Some estimates say it took 100,000 seasonal workers 20 years to build the Great Pyramid of Khufu. Others say it took 20,000 full-time workers to get the job done.

## Why did the **EGYPTIANS** build pyramids?

The pyramids were built as tombs for pharaohs, who were believed to become gods in the afterlife. Each pyramid was built during a king's lifetime and filled with items needed to sustain him as he journeyed to the next world after death.

# How did humans THINK BEFORE there were LANGUAGES?

Way back in the early days of human evolution—before we had language—how did we think? We've learned that it might not have been all that different from how we think today.

PEOPLE WHO ARE DEAF AND HAVE COMMUNICATED IN SIGN LANGUAGE THEIR WHOLE LIVES OFTEN THINK IN A MIX OF SIGN LANGUAGE AND IMAGES.

For many people, thinking is a lot like having sentences in your head. Words move around in your mind as you process information, ponder, imagine, and develop thoughts and ideas. Even though it might seem like we are thinking in complete sentences, we are often actually thinking in a mix of words, images, and feelings. Language doesn't really take form until we put those jumbled thoughts in our head into constructed words and sentences so we can share them with others.

Think about what you did over summer vacation. Did the word "beach" or "camp" or "roller coasters" pop into your head? Or did images of these things appear? It might be a combination of the two. Studies have shown that human thought is usually divided between two modes: visual and verbal. If you were asked to think back to summer vacation, you might picture the beach. But if you were asked to describe it in an essay, you might think about it in words.

Studies also show that even when we're using verbal thinking, images still pop up in our minds, suggesting our ancient ancestors probably thought visually before language was developed in a complex way.

# INTERTWINED INFLUENCE

Complex language is one of the things that makes humans unique from all other animals, and some scientists estimate we've been having complicated conversations for at least 200,000 years. Of course humans' languages were more basic in the beginning. But as we evolved, our languages evolved too, and new languages developed. Today, there are more than 7,000 spoken languages, more than 300 sign languages, and many other ways that humans communicate. Our languages allow for an endless amount of ways for us to communicate feelings, experiences, objects, and ideas. The languages we use to communicate can even make a difference in how we think about the world. Some scientists believe that just as culture can shape our language, language can shape how we think.

Consider this: English speakers—and readers—generally view time as if it's a horizontal line, from left to right. We use phrases like "Soccer practice got moved up" or "We had to push back the pizza party." Hebrew speakers, who read text from right to left, often picture time the same way as written text. If asked to arrange objects in order from oldest to newest, they will put the oldest object in the right and the newest on the left. Mandarin speakers, who read text vertically, from the top of the page to the bottom, also think vertically. They will use the word *xia,* or "down," for something happening later. For instance, someone who speaks Mandarin would say, "Let's do that down week" instead of "Let's do that next week," as you might say in English. Greek speakers often think of time in terms of volume. A class isn't "long," it is "big." Summer vacation isn't "short," it is "small." Languages are not only a useful way to express ourselves, they influence how we think.

## Do all babies have the same FIRST WORDS?

No matter where you live in the world, and no matter what language is being spoken, babies generally say the same first words. "Mama" and "Dada" in whatever language you speak is high on the list, but also right at the top in every language is "this" and "that." Scientists say these words help babies call attention to objects that they don't have the words for yet.

## What's the most COMMON LANGUAGE in the world?

There are a few ways to look at this question. Mandarin Chinese has the most native speakers—more than one billion. But when you include people who speak more than one language, English is the most common language spoken, at around 1.5 billion. It is spoken in 146 countries.

# When did ANCIENT people learn to CONTROL FIRE?

Today, people use fire in their everyday lives. We can summon it with the strike of a match, warm ourselves by a fireplace, or turn the knob on a gas-burning stove. But many ages ago, humans used fire to change the course of history.

Fire existed long before humans discovered it. It came into existence on Earth hundreds of millions of years earlier—maybe even billions of years—as a result of lightning strikes, volcanic eruptions, and other natural events. In fact, the oldest evidence of any fire are pieces of charcoal some 420 million years old! But, unlike other animals, human ancestors learned how to control the flames and use them to their advantage.

When did this happen? Scientists aren't 100 percent sure, but they know it happened a very long time ago—even before the appearance of modern humans! Experts think that the first modern humans, called *Homo sapiens*, evolved in Africa some 300,000 years ago. However, researchers also believe that the use of fire was becoming more common around 400,000 years ago, when human relatives such as *Homo neanderthalensis* (see p. 152), *Homo heidelbergensis,* and *Homo erectus* wandered the planet.

But even those may not have been the first controlled fires. Archaeologists have discovered evidence of fire and fire-making tools at a site in Israel that may be about 800,000 years old. Another site, located in a cave in South Africa, contains remnants that suggest human ancestors could have been using fire more than a million years ago. Some experts also think that fire use may be even older than that; one researcher in Kenya believes she has found evidence of controlled fire that is about 1.6 million years old. And another researcher believes that human ancestor anatomy points to even older usage! There is fossil evidence suggesting that, around two million years ago, human stomachs began shrinking. One expert believes that this could be a result of humans getting more nutrients from cooked food, meaning they needed to eat less.

## Why was fire so IMPORTANT for early humans?

In the modern world, many humans tend to rely on electricity rather than fire. But hundreds of thousands of years ago, fire was necessary for human survival. By building controlled fires, human ancestors were able to scare away and drive off dangerous predators. In a world with little other protection, that could mean the difference between life and death. Fire also gave people light, and kept them warm during cold nights.

On top of that, humans were now able to cook their food. Until then, like most animals, human ancestors survived by eating what they caught or picked raw. Cooking plants and meat increased the nutrients in some foods. This likely gave early humans more energy and kept them full for longer, meaning they could eat less. Now, instead of spending all their time searching for food, they could do other things—like develop tools. Plus, cooking food helped make it safer by eliminating bacteria.

## When did people START using ovens?

Ovens these days can be pretty high-tech. Many rely on gas or electricity, and can be turned on with a knob or button. Ovens are nothing new, but the first ovens looked very different from today's; they were more like pits in the ground. In central Europe, researchers discovered a giant pit dating from 29,000 B.C.E. It had been used to roast a giant mammoth—sort of like a barbecue!

Over time, people began to use stone and clay to form special areas to cook. In Israel, researchers found a 23,000-year-old hearth that may have been used to bake dough. Later, these ovens became more refined. By 6,000 years ago, people in parts of Europe, the Mediterranean, and Africa were using enclosed ovens that could cook food quickly and thoroughly.

## A STRANGE MATCH

For hundreds of thousands of years, human ancestors likely ignited fire with just a few methods. They might bang a type of rock known as flint to produce sparks or rub pieces of wood together to create heat and flames. Today, we often use matches or lighters. But between then and now, there were a lot of other methods put to the test. Some worked very well, but some were, well, misfires!

» **Fire sticks:** Some of the first matches were created some 1,500 years ago in China, where one end of small sticks of wood were dipped in the chemical sulfur. When the sticks were struck or rubbed together, a spark was created.

» **Stinky starters:** The Vikings collected a fungus that could be used to start fires. The only catch? You had to boil it in pee first!

» **Jars of what?:** In the 1800s in Europe, some people would carry bottles of a chemical known as phosphorus, which could start fires. Phosphorus was first created by boiling down—you guessed it—urine.

» **Boomsticks:** In 1827, a European inventor came close to inventing easily portable matches. But because of the chemicals they were made of, they could spontaneously explode.

# TIME FOR QUESTIONS

Tick, tock, it's time to talk about clocks—and time, and everything that goes along with it. Our days are measured based on one complete rotation of Earth. But for something that seems so mathematical and exact, time can get a little confusing. Like, for instance, we add an extra day to February every four years. Why is that? And why does most of the United States change their clocks forward one hour in March and then move them back an hour come November? Only time will tell—or these answers will—if you don't want to wait.

## DO WE REALLY NEED TIME ZONES?

When you hop on a plane in California, U.S.A., and land in New York City five hours later, the clock in the airport is going to tell you that you left California eight hours ago, not five. No, your weary eyes aren't failing you. It's the time zone difference. While time zones can be confusing—and tiring!—they do serve a purpose. If the entire planet operated on one time zone, noon would be the middle of the day in some places and the middle of the night in others. After all, the sun can't shine everywhere at once. Or imagine if every city or country set its own time. As the world became more interconnected and precise, correct time became more important (consider, for example, long distance travel via trains), and a global system became necessary. A Canadian engineer proposed a worldwide system of time zones in 1878 and it stuck—in fact, it is still used today.

## WHO DECIDED CLOCKS SHOULD HAVE 12 NUMBERS, NOT 24?

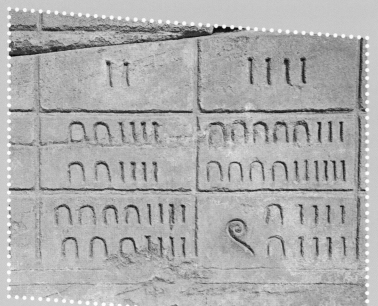

If a day has 24 hours in it, why do most of our clocks show only 1 through 12? Why don't we have a 24-hour clock? Well, for starters, it's been done this way for a long time. Some of the oldest known clocks were found in the tomb of the ancient Egyptian King Amenhotep I, who lived about 3,500 years ago. One was a sundial—which measures time by the path of the sun across the sky. The other was a water clock—which measures time through the steady, continuous flow of water from one container into another. Both clocks used a 12-hour system. One reason for the 12-hour versus 24-hour clock is that the ancient Egyptians counted in what's called "base 12"—while we might count on our fingers to 10, ancient Egyptians counted finger joints instead of fingers (each finger minus the thumb has three joints), so 12 on each hand.

For all its history, the 12-hour clock—distinguished by a.m. and p.m.—is used in only 18 countries, including the United States, the United Kingdom, Canada, Mexico, and India. The majority of the world operates on a 24-hour clock system. So instead of switching over to p.m. when the clock strikes noon, the 24-hour clock heads straight to 13:00 and on. But no matter how you tell the time (or divide the clock), we all have 24 hours in a day.

## WHY DO WE HAVE LEAP YEARS?

Even though we think of one year as 365 days, it actually takes 365.242190 days for Earth to orbit the sun—or 365 days 5 hours 48 minutes and 46 seconds. (That's one solar year.) To make things more convenient, we round the calendar to 365 days, but we need to adjust for the extra time. That's why we have a leap year every four years, adding an extra day—February 29—to the second month of the year.

What would happen if we didn't make this little adjustment? Over time (a long time), the seasons would begin to drift. After a period of about 700 years, our summers, which we've come to expect in June in the Northern Hemisphere, would begin to occur in December! So that extra day every four years is actually saving us from a lot of confusion in the years to come.

NORMALLY, YOUR CHANCES OF BEING BORN ON ANY GIVEN DAY IS 1 IN 365, BUT YOUR CHANCES OF BEING BORN ON A LEAP YEAR IS 1 IN 1,461.

## WHY DO WE HAVE DAYLIGHT SAVING TIME?

DAYLIGHT SAVING TIME BEGINS

For people living in about a third of the countries in the world, there's one day a year that they get to sleep in an extra hour. But unfortunately, there's also one day a year when they lose an hour of sleep. These people are experiencing standard time, which lasts from November to March, or Daylight Saving Time, which lasts from March to November.

There is a reason for all this leaping forward an hour and then falling back. We push the clocks forward to reflect the seasonal changes of Earth's position relative to the sun. Because Earth's axis is tilted 23.5 degrees, the amount of the time each hemisphere gets to spend in the sun varies according to where Earth is on its orbit. The Northern Hemisphere gets to enjoy long, sunny days during its summer while it's winter in the Southern Hemisphere. Then when it's winter in the Northern Hemisphere, it's time for the Southern Hemisphere to soak up the sun during its summer.

Seeking to maximize, or "save," daylight, in 1916, Germany instituted the first Daylight Saving Time during World War I to conserve resources. Other European countries and the United States soon followed. Today, all U.S. states except Arizona and Hawaii observe Daylight Saving Time, and there was a recent push by some federal lawmakers to make this change permanent—no adjustment of clocks or sleep schedules needed. But not everyone is a fan of the time change.

DAYLIGHT SAVING TIME ENDS

# How did the first person who DISCOVERED a dinosaur bone know WHAT IT WAS?

They didn't! Imagine coming across a very strangely shaped bone, and having to guess what animal it belonged to. Today, there are scientific methods and lots of technological advances that help paleontologists identify fossils. But centuries ago, people didn't have access to these.

IN ONE EXPERIMENT, RESEARCHERS CAREFULLY STRAPPED A FAKE TAIL ON CHICKENS TO STUDY HOW T. REX MIGHT HAVE WALKED.

## BEASTLY BONES

The very first person to ever discover a dinosaur bone probably lived thousands of years ago. In fact, many scientists think these ancient discoveries led to some of the legends surrounding mythical creatures that still exist today. Stories of dragons or serpent-like creatures around the globe may have been inspired by dinosaur or other prehistoric reptile fossils. Some 2,000 years ago, a Chinese historian labeled a dinosaur skeleton as that of a dragon. Similarly, historians today think that enormous fossils found across the Americas may have inspired various mythical serpent legends. And people didn't think the bones belonged only to dragons—people in ancient Greece thought that the skulls of ancient elephant relatives belonged to an enormous race of one-eyed people known as cyclops. This belief continued for many centuries: In the 1600s, a British scientist named Robert Plot concluded that a collection of enormous bones must have belonged to a human giant.

ONE DINOSAUR FOSSIL WAS SO WELL PRESERVED THAT SCIENTISTS CAN STUDY THE LAST MEAL IT ATE.

## DINOSAUR DISCOVERY

In the 1800s, scientists began to treat these discoveries differently. Paleontology, the study of prehistoric life, was gaining popularity. In 1815, British geologist William Buckland reexamined the bones that had been studied by Plot some two centuries earlier. Buckland, however, recognized that the bones were somewhat similar to those of a lizard. He named his discovery *Megalosaurus:* giant lizard. In 1822, a British fossil hunter named Mary Ann Mantell discovered what appeared to be an enormous reptile tooth. She and her geologist husband, Gideon Mantell, felt that the tooth was similar—but much larger—to those of an iguana, so they called this mysterious animal *Iguanodon*, meaning "iguana tooth."

By the 1840s, scientists were paying more and more attention to these giant, lizard-like fossils. One British scientist in particular, Richard Owen, believed that these species must be related to each other. He coined a name for them: Dinosauria, meaning "monstrous lizard." Soon, more and more paleontologists around the world were seeking out fossils to understand and learn about dinosaurs.

# How do we know what dinosaurs **LOOKED** like?

The truth is, we don't know exactly what every dinosaur looked like. With ongoing scientific and technological advances, however, we can piece together images of their appearance. Two centuries ago, people had a harder time. Many drawings of dinosaurs made by early paleontologists were based off mammals, such as hippos. Compared to what we know now, these illustrations can look pretty silly!

Over time, scientists began to compare their findings to modern reptiles. This helped them understand what dinosaurs might have looked like. But there was still a good amount of guessing. For example, many 20th-century films depicted dinosaurs as smooth and scaly. Now, based on discoveries made since then, scientists know that many dinosaurs had feathers!

In fact, modern technology has helped experts understand a lot more about dino appearance. For example, scientists can analyze fossils to try to figure out what color a dinosaur might have been. Many animals have teeny-tiny structures in their cells known as melanosomes. These structures hold melanin, something that gives coloring to skin, hair, eyes, and more. With superpowerful microscopes, scientists have discovered preserved melanosomes in some dinosaur fossils. By studying these melanosomes, experts can figure out what coloring a dinosaur might have had.

Each year, we learn more and more about what dinosaurs might have looked like, so our images of them are constantly changing!

ROUNDUP

# WHEN SCIENTISTS GUESSED WRONG!

An important part of science is making—and learning from—mistakes. Here are some of the times when the experts didn't get it quite right!

» Unicorns among us?: In the 17th century, a scientist believed he had discovered the real fossilized remains of a unicorn. Unfortunately, it was just an incorrectly assembled rhinoceros skeleton.

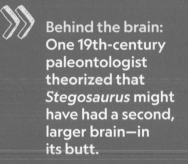

» Behind the brain: One 19th-century paleontologist theorized that *Stegosaurus* might have had a second, larger brain—in its butt.

» Nasty nickname: In the 1920s, two scientists discovered a new species of dinosaur that appeared to have died while attempting to snatch an egg from a nest. They named it *Oviraptor*, meaning "egg thief." But later scientists made a surprising discovery: The dinosaur was really a parent guarding its own eggs!

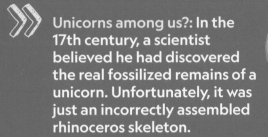

# What HAPPENED to AMELIA EARHART?

Amelia Earhart—one of the most famous American pilots in history—disappeared more than 80 years ago, and the world hasn't lost interest in finding out what happened to her.

AMELIA EARHART HAD HER OWN FASHION LINE. SHE DESIGNED PRACTICAL, WRINKLE-FREE CLOTHING MADE OF PARACHUTE SILK AND OTHER UNUSUAL MATERIALS.

## RECORD SETTER

Before her famous last flight, Earhart was already a celebrity. She was a record-setting aviator, admired for her accomplishments. She was the first woman to fly solo across North America and back, and she became the first woman to fly solo nonstop across the Atlantic. Next up, she was the first person to fly solo from Hawaii, U.S.A., to California, U.S.A. In 1937, Earhart was ready for her next challenge: circumnavigating—or going around—the globe at the Equator.

## FINAL FLIGHT

Earhart and her navigator Fred Noonan started out on their flight from Oakland, California, and traveled to Miami, Florida, U.S.A. From there they went to South America, Africa, India, Southeast Asia, and finally, Papua New Guinea. They had 7,000 miles (11,265 km) to go on their 29,000-mile (46,671-km) journey—across the Pacific—to finish their trip around the world. Their next refueling spot was Howland Island, two miles (3.2 km) long and less than a mile (1.6 km) wide, in the Pacific Ocean. After Earhart and Noonan left Lae, Papua New Guinea, they were never seen again.

Did the plane crash? Earhart's plane has not been found, so no one can say for certain that she crashed. Here's what we do know: After Earhart and Noonan left Lae, they did send voice transmissions received by the U.S. Coast Guard. She sent the messages in the area around Howland Island.

The message said they were "running north and south," probably looking for the tiny island. When they never arrived, a search was launched. The government searched for Earhart and the plane for 16 days, using ocean vessels and aircraft. Nothing was found.

## SO, WHAT *DID* HAPPEN?

There are a lot of guesses. Some people think the plane ran out of fuel and crashed in the ocean, and the search crews didn't find it before it sank. Others think Earhart and Noonan crashed but made it to shore alive on a nearby uninhabited island but eventually died. Other scenarios are little more far-fetched, including one that suggests Earhart was a spy on a secret mission. Another says that Earhart survived but didn't tell anyone, and lived out the rest of her life in New Jersey, U.S.A. Finding Earhart's plane could answer some questions, and possibly put some rumors to rest.

## Is anyone still LOOKING FOR Earhart's plane?

People have been looking ever since it went missing. But a new person has joined the search—the same person who found the *Titanic*, American oceanographer Robert Ballard. In 2019, he decided to take his search closer to Nikumaroro Island, 400 miles (645 km) south of Howland Island, in the Pacific Ocean. Ballard and his team used remotely operated underwater vehicles and autonomous surface vessels to explore the surrounding waters and search for plane wreckage, but no luck. For now, the search continues, and the mystery remains.

# Moai Math

**L**ocated on the small island of Rapa Nui (also known as Easter Island) some 2,200 miles (3,540 km) off the coast of Chile, the moai, or the "Easter Island heads," have impressed people around the world for centuries. But there is a lot more to these statues than meets the eye—including bodies buried below the ground! Read on for stunning stats about these famous marvels of engineering and art.

## WHO BUILT THE MOAI?

**Some 1,300 years ago**, Polynesian sailors settled on an island in the Pacific Ocean. They called themselves and the island Rapa Nui. Beginning around the 15th century, the Rapa Nui began carving enormous, human-like statues from the local volcanic stone. The moai were likely carved to represent island ancestors or to honor chiefs.

## HOW TALL ARE THE MOAI?

The height of the tallest finished moai is

### 32.8 FEET (10 m).

That's as tall as a three-story building! The height of the largest moai ever created, an unfinished statue known as El Gigante, is 72 feet (21.9 m).

## HOW MUCH DO THEY WEIGH?

The weight of the largest moai placed upright on an ahu, its shrine, is

### 94.8 TONS (86 t).

However, that's nothing compared to the weight of El Gigante: 200 tons (180 t). That's more than two 737 passenger airplanes!

## HOW MANY PEOPLE DID IT TAKE TO MOVE A MOAI?

**It may have taken 25 people to move one moai!** The Rapa Nui carved the moai out of volcanic rock using stone picks. Each moai was made from a single piece. Making them was likely hard, but moving them was harder. For many years, the methods used to move the moai to their final, upright places remained a mystery. The Polynesian islanders would have had no access to the engineering tools we use today. To better understand how the work was done, various historians attempted different ways of moving moai replicas. They learned that the statues were likely moved using wooden logs, wooden sledges, and ropes. Some historians even think that the statues may have been "walked" to their destinations using a lasso-like rope technique! A moai's eye holes were only carved once the statue had reached its final destination.

## HOW MANY MOAI ARE THERE?

There are approximately **1,000** moai on Rapa Nui. A finished moai would be erected on top of an ahu. However, only about 300 were successfully transported and placed upright on their ahu. Many fell down on the way, or were left unfinished where they were carved. There are 360 known ahu on Rapa Nui.

The moai are often referred to as the Easter Island heads. This is because, for many years, visitors didn't realize that the statues had bodies. They had been buried in dirt over the centuries!

# Who INVENTED MONEY?

We may never know who came up with this million (billion, trillion)-dollar idea.

PEOPLE HAVE BEEN MAKING FAKE—OR COUNTERFEIT—CURRENCY FOR AS LONG AS MONEY HAS BEEN AROUND.

IN MEDIEVAL ENGLAND, SOME PEOPLE USED TALLY STICKS—SMALL PIECES OF WOOD THAT THEY WOULD WRITE ON—TO KEEP A RECORD OF DEBTS.

Money seems to have developed around the world in many different places at different times. That's because money has its roots in one of the most ancient human practices: trading. For thousands—and likely hundreds of thousands—of years, people have traded items with one another. Often, people would trade for tools or food, but they also traded for things they couldn't get in their local areas. For example, scientists in Kenya discovered tools created some 320,000 years ago that were made with a type of rock not found in the region. This means that the tools or the stones likely came from elsewhere, possibly brought there by other traveling humans. And people have been trading over long distances for at least 50,000 years: Beads made from the same ostrich eggshells were discovered more than 1,864 miles (3,000 km) apart in parts of Africa.

However, trade could get a bit complicated. Imagine, for instance, that your friend has an apple and you have an orange. You would like to trade for the apple, but your friend already has a lot of oranges and doesn't need any more. Instead, they want a pear. Because you don't have a pear, there's no way to make a fair trade. But now, imagine that you are trading for something else that *symbolizes* value. This can be almost anything—shells, coins, or even buttons. You give your friend three buttons, and they give you the apple in return. Now, they can use those three buttons to buy a pear from someone else. In this situation, these buttons have become money, or currency.

cowrie shell

About 5,000 years ago in Mesopotamia, a civilization in what is now Iraq, people had this same thought. They began creating some of the first known metal coins, called shekels, which they used to buy and sell goods. Other people across the world also began developing metal coins. More than 2,000 years ago, various types of coins were common in ancient China, Rome, and India. However, people didn't only use coins. Before coins became popular in China, people had been using cowrie shells for more than 1,000 years. Many Indigenous nations in the Americas, such as the Chumash and several Algonquian nations, also used shells.

## PAPER ON THE SCENE

Currencies like coins and shells were becoming very common, but they had a major drawback: They could be heavy and awkward to carry. Around the eighth or ninth centuries in China, people began using money made from paper. In Europe, paper money came a little later. During the Middle Ages, people began to provide paper receipts during purchases. Eventually, these receipts became used as money itself. This caught on, and within a few centuries, governments were issuing money in paper form.

AN EARLY VERSION OF CREDIT CARDS MADE FROM HEAVY METAL SHEETS EXISTED IN THE 1800S.

# MAKING MONEY

Today, we're used to coins and paper money, and some digital forms of money, but many things have been used as currency throughout history. Check out some of the more interesting—and sometimes unusual—forms of payment here!

>> Salt: In the ancient world, salt was very valuable. Roman soldiers may have even had their wages supplemented with the mineral.

>> Squirrel pelts: That's right—some people in medieval Russia and Finland used squirrel skins as money.

>> Rai stone: For centuries, the island of Yap in the Pacific Ocean has used enormous stones as currency. (They can be as tall as a human!)

>> Knives: Some 2,000 years ago in ancient China, people used small copper knives to buy goods.

## ONE MORE THING: THE RISE OF ELECTRONIC MONEY

It might sound futuristic, but much of the money around the world today doesn't exist in physical form—it's stored as information on computers! In the 20th century, computers became common tools to track and contain data. Over time, it made more sense for many banks to use computers to keep records of how much money someone had rather than storing giant piles of cash. This practice only became more common as computers got more advanced. Soon, people could use small cards that contained digital chips to access their money, or even to buy things directly. (These cards are often called credit cards.) And after the invention of the internet, people could do their banking directly online.

# What was the FIRST CANDY EVER INVENTED?

Who can resist a sweet treat? Having a sweet tooth is nothing new. But the very first candy didn't come in a wrapper from a candy store. **Hint: There was some buzz around it!**

In most parts of the world in the ancient past, honey was the first sweet treat. Folks developed such a taste for it, they domesticated bees so that they could have honey all the time.

Candy, as we know it, started taking shape around 4,000 years ago when the ancient Egyptians preserved sweets in the form of nuts and seeds coated in honey. Fast-forward to the 17th century, and sugar plums—seeds or nuts coated in hard sugar—were popular in England. In the American colonies, maple syrup candy was the preferred sweet—and by the 18th century, it was lollipops and caramels. Milk chocolate was invented in Switzerland in 1875, and shortly thereafter came the chocolate bar.

FIVE MILLION MARSHMALLOW CHICKS AND BUNNIES AND AN ASTOUNDING 90 MILLION CHOCOLATE BUNNIES ARE MADE EACH YEAR.

## Is white chocolate ACTUALLY chocolate?

White chocolate is confusing. It doesn't look like chocolate, and it doesn't taste like it either. But it's called chocolate. So what is it? Technically, white chocolate isn't chocolate because it doesn't contain cocoa solids from cocoa beans. It does, however, contain cocoa butter, which is the fat found in processed cocoa beans. The butter doesn't give it a chocolatey flavor, but it does give it a smooth, rich taste.

## Which part of a CHOCOLATE BUNNY should you eat first?

It depends if you want to follow the crowd. Researchers surveyed more than 28,000 people, and 59 percent took a bite out of the ears first. Thirty-three percent had no preference on where they started eating their bunny, and 4 percent started with the feet or tail.

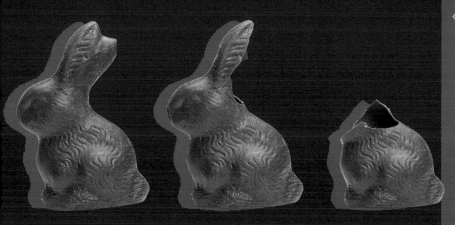

## ROUNDUP
## HISTORY, CANDY-COATED

Some of the world's most famous modern candies have surprising beginnings.

>> **Hershey's Kisses:** How'd they get their name? There are two stories. One is that the machine that produces the candy makes a "kiss" sound. The other is that when Kisses were first produced in 1907, the name for a small piece of candy was a "kiss." The only time Kisses weren't made was between 1942 and 1947, when aluminum—Kisses' signature wrapper—was rationed during World War II. The Hershey company changed its production to make chocolate rations for the U.S. military.

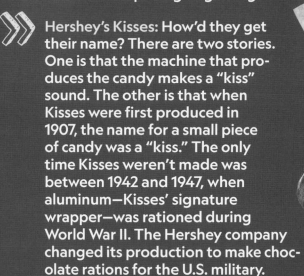

>> **Twizzlers:** The licorice candy was first produced in 1929, but it skyrocketed to popularity when American astronaut Neil Armstrong said, "I could go for some Twizzlers right now," after landing on the moon.

>> **Jelly beans:** The first known mention of jelly beans is in an 1861 advertisement, which describes them being sent to the Union Army during the U.S. Civil War. It would be nearly 100 years until their smaller cousin, the Jelly Belly jelly bean, came on the market. These jelly beans, which have unique flavors like popcorn and chocolate pudding, caught the attention of then California governor Ronald Reagan. When he was elected president in 1980, three and a half tons (3 t) of red (cherry), white (coconut), and blue (blueberry) Jelly Bellies were sent to Washington, D.C., for his inauguration.

>> **Pop Rocks:** William Mitchell, a food scientist from New York, invented Pop Rocks by accident in 1956. He was trying to find a way to make a new kind of soda by putting sugar flavoring and carbon dioxide in his mouth. The result was the crackling and popping that Pop Rocks became famous for.

# WHEN DID HALLOWEEN FIRST START?

The origins of Halloween go back more than 2,500 years, when it began as a pagan festival celebrated in Ireland, Great Britain, and other parts of Europe. Back then, the festival was known as Samhain (pronounced SAH-wen). According to tradition, Samhain was first celebrated by a group of people known as the Celts, who arrived in Ireland from mainland Europe around 3,000 years ago. However, some historians believe that the celebration may be even older, going back to the Stone Age peoples who inhabited the region before then.

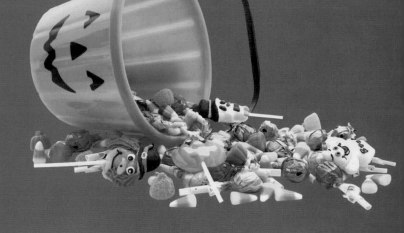

## ANCIENT ORIGINS

Regardless of who first celebrated it, Samhain started as a way to mark the beginning of the dark half of the year. During the darker seasons, the Celts believed that the barrier between the spirit world and the living world was at its thinnest. It was a time when spirits could return or when people and spirits could communicate. People celebrated by feasting and by lighting large bonfires. Many people also dressed in ceremonial costumes or covered their faces with ashes from the fire to hide from evil spirits.

## BECOMING HALLOWEEN

Several centuries later, around the year 600, Samhain was taken over by the Catholic Church, possibly in order to persuade European pagans to convert to Christianity. Then, the holiday also celebrated Christian saints and became known as All Saints' Day, or All Hallows' Day (which eventually began to fall on a separate day, November 1). People continued to light bonfires, and they began to take part in parades and dress up as saints and angels—and sometimes as devils. Eventually, the holiday made its way to the Americas along with European colonizers. There, it became known as Hallows' Eve, or All Hallows' Evening. Some colonizers, such as the Puritans, did not celebrate much of the holiday because of its pagan origins. However, other colonists did partake—and even the Puritans were said to tell ghost stories to each other.

Later, a large number of Irish immigrants helped make the holiday even more popular in the United States. In the 1840s, a devastating disease spread through much of Ireland's crops, causing what became known as the Great Potato Famine. Many starving people fled to the United States, where they hoped to make better lives. These people also brought along many of their customs, including new Halloween traditions. One such activity involved carving jack-o'-lanterns. Previously, people in Ireland had carved tiny faces into turnips and lit them with candles to guard against mischievous spirits and demons. Now, in the United States, they began to instead use the much larger locally grown pumpkins!

## Why do we DRESS UP and get candy?

Historians aren't exactly sure where the tradition of trick-or-treating came from—at least, not in the way we know it today. During the Middle Ages in Europe, many people dressed up and put on performances for Samhain. In exchange, they were often given food or drinks. This was called "mumming." Later, once the Catholic Church became involved, the tradition changed; instead of putting on performances, some people traveled from home to home and offered to pray for loved ones who had died. In return, they were given treats known as soul cakes.

However, in Scotland and Ireland, Samhain became associated with mischief-making, or a night when young people would play pranks on each other or scare people. This tradition spread to the United States with the arrival of Irish immigrants. By the 1920s and '30s, Halloween in the U.S. had become pretty chaotic! To push back against these pranks, many people in the 1900s tried to make the celebration more family-friendly and to focus on creating fun costumes—not just of angels and devils, but of anything people could imagine. Local communities began offering fun celebrations—from haunted houses to treats to costume-making—to keep young people from pulling pranks. In the 1950s, when candy companies were experiencing a boom in the United States, trick-or-treating became a holiday staple, too.

# CHAPTER 4

# WHAT DOES SPACE SMELL LIKE?

## QUESTIONS ABOUT SPACE & PHYSICS

**One thing we know about the universe is that it's big.** And that leads to some pretty big questions. Like what would it feel like to jump into a black hole? Could humans eventually set up a colony on Mars? And if so, what would that look like? What do astronauts say it feels like to be in space? And if we do go exploring outer space, will we find life? Or will it find us first? We have the scoop on these out-of-this-world questions.

# Is there LIFE IN SPACE?

We haven't found it yet, but that doesn't mean it's not there. Scientists are actively searching for life, but it's no small task. There's a lot of space to investigate. And we are still inventing the proper technology to look for it. But so far, Earth is the only place—that we know of—in the universe that supports life.

THE MARS ROVER PERSEVERANCE HAS COLLECTED ROCKS WITH ITS ROBOTIC ARM TO SEARCH FOR PAST LIFE ON THE RED PLANET.

## SIGNS OF LIFE

When scientists search for life in space, they aren't looking for the little green creatures that we've seen in cartoons. They are actually looking for liquid water, which was key to the beginning of life on Earth. All living things on this planet—including people, plants, and animals—are dependent on water. Scientists are also on the lookout for oxygen and methane—gases that living things release into the air. Finding these gases on a planet would give scientists the green light to look for life there.

Scientists also know that one reason life on Earth is successful is its location. It's not too close to the sun to make life unbearable, and it's also not too far, which would make it too cold for life to survive. So, scientists are looking for other planets with a similar location relative to their own sun—or suns (yes, there may be more than one!).

Once you take all these factors into consideration, scientists believe there are only a few dozen planets in our entire Milky Way galaxy that could check all the boxes. (Keep in mind there are an estimated 100 billion planets in the Milky Way!)

THERE ARE MORE THAN TWO TRILLION GALAXIES IN THE UNIVERSE.

## What could life on ANOTHER PLANET look like?

It's very possible it wouldn't look like life here on Earth. Remember, Earth formed 4.5 billion years ago. Two billion years ago, the first cells appeared. Animals didn't evolve until around 800 million years ago. So, if we discovered a planet that followed Earth's pattern and was younger than 800 million years old, we might not be so impressed. To find intelligent life, not only would we need to find the right planet, we'd need to find it at the right time in its history.

## THE SEARCH CONTINUES

What's next? So far, scientists have found more than 2,500 planetary systems, but that's just the beginning. Based on models and predictions, they estimate there could be tens of billions of solar systems. To say they have barely scratched the surface is an understatement!

And the search for life isn't focused only on planets. Asteroids and comets could potentially host life, too. They also orbit stars, just like the planets in our solar system, and could contain all the ingredients necessary for life.

This astronaut admiring alien flowers is purely imagined ... for now, at least.

## Could ALIENS also be searching for us?

It's possible! Scientists at the Search for Extra Terrestrial Intelligence (SETI) Institute scan the sky for signals from alien life—like radio transmissions or flashing lasers. Forty years ago, we sent out a message of our own: Two probes named Voyager 1 and Voyager 2 were launched into space, each carrying a golden record. The gold-plated copper disks also came with a needle to play each record and instructions, written in symbols that presumably can be universally understood. The records contain photographs of life on Earth; an illustration of a male and female human; architecture found on Earth, like the Golden Gate Bridge; and images of animals, like elephants. The records also include music and natural sounds from Earth, like ocean waves and thunder. And there's a detailed map of how to get to Earth. The records have left our solar system and perhaps one day will find their way to intelligent life.

This gold-plated record (right) and its cover (left) were made to explain life on Earth to extraterrestrials.

# How does GRAVITY WORK?

What's up with the force that makes you fall down? From the drip of a raindrop to the orbit of Jupiter, gravity is at the heart of it all.

THE FIRST ROCKETS WERE INVENTED IN CHINA MORE THAN 800 YEARS AGO.

SOME PLACES ON EARTH HAVE STRONGER GRAVITY THAN OTHERS.

Almost every single thing is made up of what is known as matter. Matter can be any physical substance, and it includes you—and the planet you live on. Any object made of matter creates a force, called gravity, that draws other objects to it. (Yes, even you!) Many objects are small enough that we can't detect their gravity. But the more matter something has (also known as an object's mass), the more gravity it creates. Because Earth is pretty massive, it has quite a bit of gravity. This force pulls us in so that our feet stay firmly planted on the ground, and it holds Earth itself together! Gravity also holds our atmosphere—including the air we breathe—in place around the planet.

## What would happen if gravity suddenly DISAPPEARED?

Studying gravity involves understanding some pretty complicated physics and math. However, the answer to this question about gravity is actually pretty simple: Everything would float away. Earth would keep spinning, but you—and everything on the planet not secured to the ground—would go flying into space. And we do mean everything! Not only would all the people and animals float away, so would the oceans, rivers and lakes, and even the very air you breathe. Eventually, even the planet itself would break apart with no gravity to keep it together. That is, all this would happen if gravity *could* magically disappear—which it can't!

# Why does gravity PULL Earth toward the sun?

Thanks to its mass, the sun has an incredible amount of gravity—enough to keep eight planets in orbit! But why is it that these planets move around the sun, without being pulled straight into it? The answer lies with how quickly the planets are moving. As Earth travels through space, it is moving at astounding speeds: 67,000 miles each hour (107,826 km/h), to be exact. At this speed, Earth is almost moving quickly enough to fly past the sun and escape its gravity—but not quite! Still it is moving too quickly for the sun's gravity to pull it completely into the sun. This balance keeps Earth where it is, "falling" around the sun in a wide orbit. (Lucky for us!) This is also how the moon keeps orbiting around Earth.

# Will scientists ever CREATE antigravity?

When you think of astronauts training for space, do you imagine them floating weightless in a special antigravity chamber? We're sorry to say this is not how it really happens. That's because scientists haven't figured out a way to re-create antigravity ... yet. However, they are working on it. In one experiment, experts are attempting to investigate something called antimatter. Antimatter is a rare substance in the universe that acts a lot like normal matter, except that it has an opposite electric charge. When matter and antimatter meet, they cancel each other out and create energy. So, what does this have to do with gravity? Well, the existence of antimatter makes some scientists think that there also might be a form of "antimass" out there. In theory, antimass could cancel out an object's mass, making it so that there is nothing for gravity to pull on. If this were true, scientists might be able to fashion some sort of barrier that stops gravity in its tracks. However, at this point, it's just an idea.

How do astronauts prepare for the time they will spend floating in space without using antigravity technology? The most common way is to send them for a fun flight on a fast-moving plane. When planes arc at just the right angles, the passengers inside can experience brief moments of weightlessness—similar to how it feels right at the start of a big drop on a roller coaster.

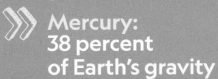
Because each planet has a different mass, it also has different gravity. Take a look to find out approximately where the different planets weigh in when compared to the amount of gravity on Earth:

» **Mercury:** 38 percent of Earth's gravity

» **Venus:** 91 percent

» **Mars:** 38 percent

» **Jupiter:** 236 percent

» **Saturn:** 92 percent

» **Uranus:** 89 percent

» **Neptune:** 112 percent

**Astronauts train for microgravity in a fast plane.**

# What would happen if you JUMPED INTO A BLACK HOLE?

**Well, it probably wouldn't end well.**

Before we get into this question, let's take a look at what a black hole is and how it forms. A black hole is a place where gravity is so strong that nothing—not even light—can escape its pull. In fact, a black hole's gravity is so incredibly strong that it distorts even the time and space around it (see p. 95).

Scientists think black holes form in different ways. Some, known as primordial black holes, may have formed billions of years ago at the same time that the universe itself formed. Others, called supermassive black holes, might form alongside—or rather, at the center of—a newly forming galaxy. This kind of black hole can be several billion times as massive as our sun!

Black holes can also form from dying stars. In each star, there is a balance between two forces: gravity and outward-pushing energy. The center of the star creates incredible amounts of heat, which push out energy. Meanwhile, the star's gravity is pulling inward. But when a massive old star runs out of fuel, it no longer has enough energy to keep up this balance. The gravity within can cause the star to

MOST KNOWN GALAXIES, INCLUDING THE MILKY WAY, HAVE A SUPERMASSIVE BLACK HOLE AT THEIR CENTER.

collapse very suddenly, sending out huge waves of energy in an explosion. This giant blast is called a supernova. Sometimes, this supernova leaves behind a black hole.

Once a black hole forms, its extreme gravity pulls matter, space, time, and light toward it. Sometimes, a disk of swirling matter even forms around the black hole. So where does all this matter and light go once it is pulled into the hole? Scientists think it stays there, forming an incredibly dense center known as a singularity.

## ON TO THE JUMPING!

Fair warning—it wouldn't be pleasant. A person or object near a black hole would have a very tough time escaping. In fact, it would be almost impossible once they passed something known as the event horizon. This is the region, or threshold, around the black hole from which even light cannot escape. Theoretically, once you've passed the event horizon, you would need to travel *faster* than the speed of light to escape.

What happens after the event horizon? Scientists think that if a person entered a black hole, they would most likely undergo a process called spaghettification. Essentially, any object falling into a black hole is likely stretched into a long, thin shape ... like a spaghetti noodle.

However, spaghettification only happens with some black holes, depending on their mass. But even without spaghettification, it wouldn't be smooth sailing. First, a person might encounter powerful and dangerous radiation or pieces of matter falling into the hole. Second, they would *almost* certainly never be able to get out again.

Why "almost" certainly? That has to do with a theory around white holes. Scientists believe that the universe may also contain the opposite of a black hole, where matter is pushed outward: a white hole. Some experts even think that black holes and white holes might be part of a pair. In that case, it's potentially possible that a person falling into a black hole might emerge from a white hole, having traveled through what is known as a wormhole—a tunnel through time and space (see p. 95). Still, it's probably best not to risk it!

A STAR MUST BE AT LEAST 20 TIMES AS MASSIVE AS EARTH'S SUN TO LEAVE BEHIND A BLACK HOLE AFTER A SUPERNOVA.

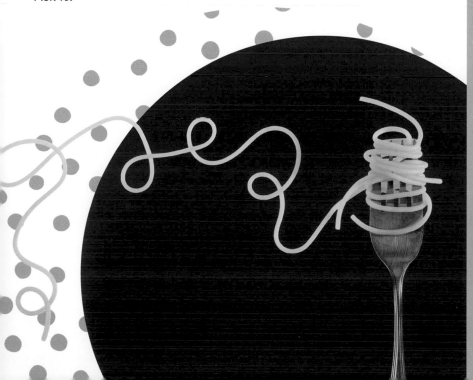

## ONE MORE THING: HOW DOES A BLACK HOLE AFFECT STARS?

If a black hole's gravity pulls in everything and anything, it only stands to reason that it would also "devour" a star that came too close. It turns out this is true—scientists have captured images of massive black holes tearing stars apart. (And after the black hole has sucked in the star? It will sometimes "burp" up gas!) But it's not the only thing that can happen. A black hole's intense gravity can briefly reignite an approaching star, bringing it back to "life."

# Will PEOPLE be able to travel BACK IN TIME?

## You won't need to pack your bags anytime soon.

IN 2009, FAMOUS PHYSICIST STEPHEN HAWKING HELD A PARTY WELCOMING TRAVELERS FROM THE FUTURE—BUT NO ONE SHOWED UP.

If you could travel back in time, when and where would you go? You might travel to ancient Egypt to see the pyramids being built, go on a dinosaur safari, or sail with the famed pirate Blackbeard. If it were possible, that is! Unfortunately, most scientists agree that time travel to the past is likely impossible and just a work of science fiction.

According to experts in the field, moving backward in time would require breaking the laws of physics. Currently, with what we know about the universe, this makes it scientifically impossible. On top of that, many theorists say that we already have proof that we will never be able to travel to the past: If it were possible, we would have already been visited by tourists from the future!

Even if we did find a way to travel back in time, there would be plenty of other problems to solve. For one thing,

the planet—and the entire universe—is constantly moving at great speeds. Scientists would have to figure out a way for the traveler to not only go back in time, but also to the correct physical location.

Time travelers would also have to make sure that they did not affect the past. Changing even small past events could greatly affect the future—or even create something called a time paradox. This would occur if a traveler created events in time that contradict themselves. For example, say a traveler went to the past and accidentally prevented the invention of the first time travel machine. If that happened, there would be no time travel, and they wouldn't be able to travel back to prevent it from happening in the first place ... which means that time travel would exist, and they would travel back, and so on and so on.

# Could people travel to the FUTURE?

Maybe! But it probably wouldn't look like the time travel of science fiction—and it would be a one-way trip, with no way to return to the past. According to some theories, people could possibly use black holes for time travel. A black hole (see p. 92) is a place where the pull of gravity is unbelievably strong—so strong that nothing can get out, not even light. In fact, a black hole's gravity even warps time itself! This makes time near the black hole move much slower compared to time elsewhere.

According to some researchers, this time difference could be used to send someone to the future. Say a spaceship were able to safely travel near a black hole. The people on the ship would experience time at a much slower rate compared to the nearby planets and stars. This might mean that when the ship moved away from the black hole to return home, its crew would find that—because time was passing more quickly elsewhere—they had traveled to the future. Of course, that's assuming that their ship could escape the gravitational pull of the black hole!

## What about WORMHOLES?

You may have seen a spaceship in a sci-fi movie travel through time using something called a wormhole. In theory, a wormhole is a connection—sort of like a tunnel—through two points in space and time. And scientists say that this connection might very well be a reality! However, using a wormhole would be incredibly difficult. First of all, it would have to be large enough for a ship to enter. Second, it would have to be stable—meaning it would have to exist long enough for the ship to pass through. But by their nature, wormholes would be very, very unstable, and would likely collapse in on themselves.

## PEERING INTO THE PAST

Even though we can't travel back in time, we can see the past. In fact, you can take a peek at the past on any clear night—just look up! The starlight we see has traveled superlong distances to reach us. Even though light moves incredibly fast, it still takes time to cover such vast distances. The stars we see sent out that light hundreds—possibly even thousands—of years ago. With powerful telescopes, scientists can see even farther back in time. In fact, experts have glimpsed light from a galaxy that existed more than 13 billion years ago!

SO FAR, WORMHOLES ARE ONLY THEORETICAL: SCIENTISTS HAVEN'T FOUND A REAL ONE YET.

# LIVING IN SPACE

**W**hether you're an aspiring astronaut, a super science fan, or just a curious kid, you've probably wondered what it's like to be in outer space. Read on to find the answers to some of the most frequently asked questions about living in space.

## WHAT DOES IT FEEL LIKE TO BE WEIGHTLESS?

Some astronauts describe being weightless as similar to the feeling you get while on a roller coaster. Others say it feels kind of like swimming or floating in a pool. However, you can't quite swim through the air, as it isn't thick enough. You might be able to change which direction you are facing, but making yourself move in one direction or another (without pushing off another object) would be extremely difficult. Weightlessness can also be tough to adjust to at first; over the first several days, some astronauts say they felt dizzy or got headaches. But other astronauts also say that once you're used to it, it's fun!

## WHAT DOES SPACE SMELL LIKE?

Space does indeed have a smell—and astronauts describe it in different ways. Some say space smells a bit like a burnt steak, while others think its odor is more similar to metal—and some have even described it as smelling like burnt almond cookies. You wouldn't be able to smell it while you were out in space because there is no atmosphere. But the scent tends to linger on space suits (and sometimes other equipment) after astronauts have returned from space walks. What causes this smell? Scientists don't know yet!

## HOW DOES FOOD TASTE IN SPACE?

Unfortunately for astronauts, food can taste a bit bland in space. This may be due to the effects of weightlessness on the human body. On Earth, the fluids in your body are pulled downward by gravity. In space, the fluids move around inside you more freely. This can block a person's sinuses, affecting the sense of taste. The blandness could also come from living in a small, cramped environment and eating the same meals over and over. This repetition of environment and food could certainly make things a bit boring! To combat this, some astronauts use lots of hot sauce.

## WHAT IS IT LIKE TO SLEEP IN SPACE?

Sleep in space can be a little tough—but not because of the weightlessness. While this might pose a problem if astronauts were allowed to float here and there willy-nilly, astronauts on the International Space Station (ISS) and other spaceships sleep strapped into their sleeping compartments. On a spaceship, however, things tend to be very cramped, as well as bright and loud. Because of this, many astronauts undergo sleep training. This includes working with doctors to train their bodies to naturally sleep on a regular cycle, no matter how bright or loud it might be.

## WHAT DOES IT SOUND LIKE IN SPACE?

The most common things heard in space (for astronauts inside a space suit or space station, that is) are the whirring and clanking of the spaceship. Of course, an astronaut might also hear other astronauts chatting, voices coming in over the radios, or music that is playing. Outside of these human-made sounds, there isn't much to hear: While many things in space—from stars to collisions to planets—do make noise, there isn't any atmosphere for sound waves to travel across.

## WHAT IS IT LIKE TO CRY IN SPACE?

Most astronauts try to avoid crying while in space—even happy tears or tears of laughter. Unlike on Earth, tears don't run down a person's face. Instead, they build up and tend to cling to the astronaut's eyes. This can get in the way or even sting a bit.

## HOW DOES SPACE AFFECT THE HUMAN BODY?

Although the day-to-day changes for an astronaut might be most noticeable at first, the biggest challenges are the long-term effects on their bodies. Without gravity to pull down on it, a person's body lengthens, making them taller (until they return to Earth, at least). While that might sound cool, gravity also keeps our muscles healthy. Each day, our bodies work against gravity, staying strong enough to keep us functioning. In space, though, there is no gravity to push or pull against. This means that a person's muscles will naturally weaken while in space. To reduce this effect, astronauts make sure to exercise—a lot!

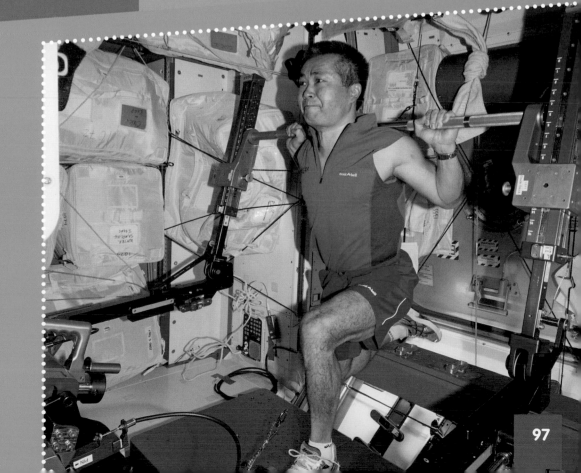

# How BIG is the UNIVERSE?

## Really big. Next question.

OK, OK, just kidding—let's get into exactly how big!
You know that the universe is huge—really huge. Really, really, *really* huge. But what exactly does that mean? As far as we know, the immediate universe around us is an enormous sphere—a 3D circle. The diameter of this universe, or the length of a line that runs straight through it from one point to the point opposite it, is about 93 billion light-years. To put that in perspective, a light-year isn't a measure of time: It is the distance that light, which travels at 983,570,400.3 feet per second (299,792,458 m/s), can cover in year. To put it another way, it would take light 93 billion years to reach from one side of the universe to the other.

However, this is not the full picture. This is the size of something called the observable universe—the extent of the universe that scientists can see and measure. The observable universe contains all the space that light has been able to reach since the universe's very beginning, the big bang. On top of that, the universe is always expanding, and has been ever since the big bang (see p. 45), when all matter was sent flying outward in an explosion of energy. That means it is only growing larger!

THERE ARE MORE STARS IN THE UNIVERSE THAN THERE ARE GRAINS OF SAND ON EARTH.

# What is BEYOND the OBSERVABLE universe?

Most scientists agree that the entire universe is larger than the part we can see. This means that there are parts of the universe that are so far away that the light traveling from those places has not been able to reach us yet. Experts aren't sure what the rest of the universe is like, how big it is, or even what shape it is—but they have some theories. This is where things start to get a bit strange, and the scope of the universe gets even more mind-bogglingly huge. Some scientists believe the universe may be flat, almost like a piece of paper. Others think it may be curved, like a piece of paper that has been partially folded. And still others think that the universe curves completely, forming a sphere. According to scientists' calculations and theories, the entire universe could be trillions of light-years across.

ONE SCIENTIST SUGGESTED THAT EVERY BLACK HOLE MIGHT LEAD TO ANOTHER UNIVERSE.

OUR UNIVERSE DOESN'T CURRENTLY HAVE A NAME BESIDES THE UNIVERSE.

# What is BEYOND the ENTIRE universe?

Many scientists agree that the universe has no edge—it is infinite. (And remember, it is always expanding.) This means that there is nothing *outside* of the universe, because the universe contains all of existence. However, that's not the only theory. Lots of researchers believe it is possible that something else exists beyond our universe: other universes. We know that many galaxies exist outside the Milky Way, so by that logic, there may be many universes in existence. This is known as the multiverse theory. In another theory, our universe doesn't exist alongside others. Rather, it exists within another, larger universe—a super universe.

## ONE MORE THING: WHAT IS THE UNIVERSE MADE OF?

The universe is made of everything in existence, from matter to energy. We experience both of these things on our home, planet Earth. However, matter and energy only make up less than 5 percent of the universe. The rest of what makes up the universe is even more mysterious to us: dark matter and dark energy. About 27 percent of the universe is made of something called dark matter. Dark matter is matter that can't be seen or detected by our current technologies. Scientists don't really know what it is! Similarly, a whopping 68 percent of the universe consists of something called dark energy. Scientists know that dark energy is a form of energy that affects how the universe expands. But beyond that, it's a mystery.

# Why does the EARTH SPIN?

Pulled by the sun's gravity, Earth makes an orbit around the sun once every 365 days. As Earth orbits, it also rotates, or spins. This isn't solely because of gravity. It has a lot to do with the way Earth first formed!

More than 4.6 billion years ago, our solar system was only a giant cloud of gas and dust. Eventually, this cloud came together to form a spinning disk. (Scientists aren't sure why or what caused this!) As the cloud spun, gravity caused gas and dust to gather at the center. In turn, this caused the disk to spin faster. Eventually, thanks to massive chemical reactions at the center of the cloud, the sun took shape. After the sun had formed, the gas and dust around it continued to spin. Bits of matter in this cloud began to crash together, sometimes sticking to each other because of gravity. These clumps grew bigger and bigger, eventually forming the planets—including Earth. And because there wasn't anything to really stop it or slow it down, Earth kept spinning. This spinning is why we experience night and day.

VENUS AND URANUS SPIN IN THE OPPOSITE DIRECTION OF THE OTHER PLANETS, AND SCIENTISTS AREN'T SURE WHY.

OVER THE PAST FEW YEARS, SCIENTISTS HAVE NOTICED THAT EARTH'S SPIN HAS INCREASED SLIGHTLY.

# Why CAN'T we feel Earth spin?

*Whee!* Flying around the sun, rotating once approximately every 24 hours—Earth seems like the ultimate roller coaster. Except for the fact that we can't feel it move! The reason for this is that we—and all the things in Earth's atmosphere—are moving along with it. To understand this, imagine being inside a fast-moving vehicle, like a plane, train, or car. If you opened the windows, you would feel the air outside rushing past. But with the windows—and your eyes—closed, it barely feels like you're moving. Earth is our vehicle, and because of its atmosphere, the "windows" are shut tight!

# What would happen if EARTH SPUN at different speeds?

Over its history, Earth *has* spun at different speeds. Billions of years ago, it was spinning much faster! Throughout human history, Earth's rotation has slowed continually, with some very minor exceptions. It happens in such tiny amounts that it isn't at all noticeable to humans—scientists estimate that Earth slows about .002 seconds every 100 years.

If this type of change happened very suddenly, it would be a different story. A sudden increase in speed could cause the ocean waters to shift toward Earth's poles, flooding lands around the world. The greater speed would also increase winds, creating powerful hurricanes. Similarly, if Earth suddenly stopped rotating, it would be a disaster for life on the planet. While Earth stopped, the things on Earth would continue to move, crashing into each other. Even if humans managed to survive that, they would then have to deal with incredibly long days and nights—about six months long each! This would be devastating for animals and plants. Fortunately, this is just a hypothetical; scientists say there's almost no way this could ever happen.

## ONE MORE THING: WHY DOESN'T THE MOON ROTATE?

The moon does rotate! However, its rotation is very slow. Scientists believe that the moon formed some 4.5 billion years ago, when a planet about the size of Mars crashed into Earth. Debris that was flung into space came together, creating a small satellite: the moon. Like Earth, the moon was formed spinning—but because of Earth's gravity, its rotation takes a long time. In fact, it is so slow that the moon's rotation matches up with its orbit around Earth. Because of this, we only ever see one side of the moon.

# Will the SUN ever BURN OUT?

Yes, the sun will eventually burn out, but it is a very slow process. (We're talking billions of years!) Read on for the details.

## THE BEGINNING

Without the sun, we wouldn't be here. Located 93 million miles (150 million km) from Earth, it is our heat, our light, and our energy. The sun has been around for about 4.6 billion years, and it has about five billion years left—so it is middle-age! The sun, which is a star, formed when a cloud of mostly hydrogen and helium—called a solar nebula—grew and grew while spinning until it collapsed from its own weight. Then it spun even faster and flattened into a disk. Most of the materials in the nebula were pulled into the center of the disk to form our sun. The other bits separated and formed everything else in our solar system.

## THE END

OK. So the sun still has a long life ahead of it. But what happens when it does eventually burn out? The sun isn't big enough to trigger a supernova, which is when a star explodes when it dies. Supernovas can become black holes, but this won't happen either in our sun's case. Our sun would need to be 10 times greater in mass to cause a supernova and 20 times greater to leave a black hole.

Once its hydrogen runs out, the sun will enter a two- to three-billion-year period of dying. It will swell in size, becoming a red giant, and swallow up Mercury, Venus, and maybe even Earth. Then it will shrink and become a white dwarf. It will still be hot, but not as hot as it is today. Eventually, it will fade and become a black dwarf, meaning it won't be very hot and won't give off much energy. What does that mean for Earth? Even if our planet survived the sun's red giant phase, it wouldn't be pretty. The oceans would burn away, and the surface of Earth would become uninhabitable.

IT TAKES EIGHT MINUTES FOR THE LIGHT FROM THE SUN TO REACH EARTH.

## How **BIG** is the sun?

In numbers, it is 865,000 miles (1.4 million km) across. But to put that into perspective, more than one million Earths could fit inside the sun if it were hollow. If you think that's big, in terms of mass, the sun is off the charts. If you were to combine all the planets in our solar system, they would make up just 0.2 percent of the sun's mass. The sun's gravity is what keeps all the planets in our solar system together. And all the planets—and moons—orbit around it.

## Is the sun **YELLOW**?

Believe it or not, no! Our atmosphere makes it appear yellow, but if you were to look at the sun from space, it would be white.

## How **HOT** is the sun?

The surface of the sun is hot: 10,000 degrees Fahrenheit (5500°C). That's about 14 times hotter than a pizza oven. But its core is where the real heat is. There, temperatures reach 27 million degrees Fahrenheit (15 million°C)!

## Where is the next **CLOSEST** sun?

Our nearest neighbor is the Alpha Centauri triple star system, which includes the red dwarf Proxima Centauri and Alpha Centauri A and B. They are more than four light-years away. How are away is that? About 25 trillion miles (37 trillion km).

## Can a planet have **TWO SUNS**?

The fictional planet Tatooine, from *Star Wars*, famously has two suns—but can a planet have two suns in real life? Yep! And astronomers have found examples. Kepler-47 is a solar system with two suns and two planets. One of the stars is about the same size as our sun, but it is only 84 percent as bright. The second star is only one-third the size of the sun and is less than one percent as bright. So you couldn't quite re-create Luke Skywalker's classic sunset scenes in the Kepler-47 system. The good news is there are likely many solar systems out there that have more than one sun—we just need to keep looking.

## What does the **SURFACE** of the sun look like?

Weirdly, a bit like peanut brittle. A video recently captured a close look at the sun and revealed cells the size of the U.S. state of Texas. The wriggling cells are made of boiling plasma, and at a quick glance could be mistaken for the candy treat.

# Q&A

# AN INTERVIEW WITH SAMANTHA CRISTOFORETTI

**H**umans evolved for life on Earth, but since 1961—when Soviet cosmonaut Yuri Gagarin became the first human in space when he circled Earth— we've been testing the limits of the human body. Italian astronaut Samantha Cristoforetti has been to the International Space Station (ISS) twice and speaks from experience about what it feels like to be in space.

astronaut

**Q** WHAT HAPPENS TO YOUR BODY WHEN YOU'RE ON THE INTERNATIONAL SPACE STATION?

**A** The very first thing you notice is what we call a "fluid shift." Much of our body is fluid—including water and blood. As soon as you're exposed to weightlessness, fluids kind of shift to the upper part of your body. You start to feel a little bit congested, like you have a cold. Some people don't taste or smell as well.

## Q WHAT HAPPENS WHEN YOU BURP IN SPACE?

A Nothing special. It's very much like burping on Earth.

## Q CAN YOU TAKE A SHOWER IN SPACE?

A We don't have showers on the ISS. A shower requires water to flow and to stay contained, and that would be very difficult. We take sponge baths for the time we're up there.

## Q WHAT WAS THE COOLEST PART ABOUT BEING IN SPACE?

A I think weightlessness, by far. The view from the window is great as well, but what I think I really enjoyed enormously was being able to float. It's a little bit like scuba diving, but without any resistance from the water. It's just this complete sense of freedom and lightness.

## Q DOES YOUR BODY FEEL FUNNY ONCE YOU COME BACK FROM SPACE?

A My sense of balance was off for a week or so. At the very beginning, in the first few hours back on Earth, I really had a hard time walking. We work out on the International Space Station, but there's something about just walking and carrying yourself in the gravity of Earth—even just sitting up straight—it requires your muscles to work together in a certain way. In spite of all of the efforts we do to work out, that seems to get lost. It comes back fairly quickly once you're home, but it definitely gets lost in space.

# ASK FOR THE MOON

Earth's moon is our trusty companion in the universe. It orbits Earth, appearing sometimes at night and sometimes during the day, sometimes as a sliver in the sky and sometimes as a bright full moon. And we aren't the only planet that has one. Moons are natural objects that orbit a planet, and there's a lot more to them than meets the eye.

## DO SOME PLANETS HAVE MORE THAN ONE MOON?

Yes! In fact, some have dozens. Mars has two moons, Neptune has 14, Uranus has 27, Jupiter has 95, and Saturn has 146! (And those are just the moons we've identified so far!) Why does Earth have one measly moon (and Mercury, none) when Jupiter and Saturn have so many? Several reasons. Mercury doesn't have any moons because it is the planet closest to the sun; it couldn't possibly compete with the sun's gravity. A moon would either smash into Mercury or go into orbit around the sun. On the other hand, Jupiter, at 300 times the size of Earth, has a stronger gravitational field and can attract more satellites. The same goes for Saturn. It even has moons that travel inside the gaps of its rings!

## CAN AN ASTEROID HAVE A MOON?

Scientists wondered for a long time if an asteroid could, and then, in 1993, the spacecraft Galileo flew by an asteroid named Idea and took images of a tiny moon! So yes, an asteroid can have a moon.

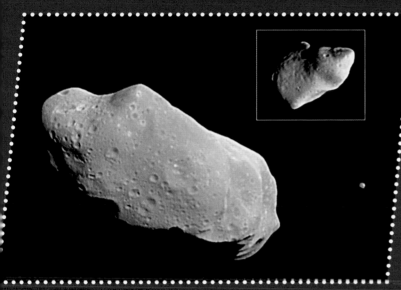

## DO ALL MOONS LOOK LIKE OUR MOON?

Not at all. Uranus's moons are cool—literally! Half of them are half made of ice. Scientists think that Ganymede, a moon that orbits Jupiter and is the largest moon in our solar system, might have an underground saltwater ocean that holds more water than all of Earth's oceans combined. And Iapetus, one of Saturn's moons, has a mountain range that runs along three-quarters of its equator and has an elevation more than twice that of Mount Everest.

## WHAT WOULD HAPPEN IF EARTH HAD TWO MOONS?

What if the moon had a twin? In theory, Earth could handle at least one other moon orbiting it, assuming the second moon was the same size as or smaller than our current moon. Researchers at the University of Texas at Arlington, U.S.A., recently did the math to see how many moons Earth could take on before they started crashing into each other—or got wonky because of gravitational interactions among them. They ran some models and calculated that Earth could maintain up to three moons with the same mass as our current moon, or around seven smaller ones. If these moons existed, they would not be in the same phase at the same time. So looking up in the night sky, we might see one full moon and two crescent moons.

## DO WOLVES REALLY HOWL AT THE MOON?

Wolves do howl when there is a full moon. They also howl when there is a crescent moon, and any other stage of the lunar cycle. It's a myth that the full moon brings out the howl in wolves. (And spoiler: Humans turning into werewolves during a full moon is a myth, too.) Wolves howl to one another as a social call. They might be letting other wolves know their whereabouts, or that a hunt is about to happen, or that this is their turf and other wolf packs should keep their distance. Wolves have individual howls, so they can identify each other. A howl can be heard as far as seven miles (11 km) away.

# How do PLANES stay IN THE AIR?

In a world where gravity is always bringing us down, planes seem a bit like magic. How does something so heavy keep from tumbling to earth? Magic has nothing to do with it.

On average, a passenger plane can weigh up to about 175,000 pounds (80,000 kg)—that's about the weight of 13 African elephants! Despite this, airplanes zip through the air, almost like birds. This is possible thanks to the balancing of different pushes and pulls, or forces, that act on a plane.

First, the plane needs to get into the air. To do this, it must overcome the force of gravity (see p. 90). This is done by creating a force that works in opposition to gravity: lift. Just as gravity pulls things down to Earth, lift pushes them up. But lift doesn't just appear out of nowhere! A plane can create lift from the air itself. For humans, air doesn't seem like much. Of course, we know we need it to breathe, but it's easy to forget that it is a gas surrounding us at all times. However, imagine that you are traveling in a car, and you stick your hand out the window. You will feel the force of air on your hand—depending on how you hold your hand, the air may even lift it up! And if you've ever done this before,

you know that this force increases the faster the car goes. Similarly, a plane can use the force of air by moving forward very quickly. But to move this quickly, it needs another force: thrust.

Thrust is the force that moves something forward. A plane uses powerful engines or propellers (or both!) to create this thrust. The engines and propellers drive the plane forward at superfast speeds. As the air flows around the plane's wings, it creates lift, raising the plane up and into the sky! However, as the plane moves through the air, the air also pushes back on the plane, slowing it down. This force is called drag. Scientists know how to overcome drag by designing planes in certain shapes that allow the air to flow around them. A shape that helps reduce drag is one that is aerodynamic. By balancing all these forces: gravity, lift, thrust, and drag, the airplane can create a lift that is stronger than the plane's weight.

THE AVERAGE PASSENGER PLANE MOVES THROUGH THE AIR AT ABOUT 575 MILES AN HOUR (925 KM/H).

## STRANGE PLANES WITH WILD NAMES

See some of the strangest planes designed to take to the skies, all named in honor of animals—including some that don't belong in the air!

>> **The Spruce Goose:** Built in the 1940s, this plane was made of wood! However, it only flew once.

>> **Pregnant Guppy:** This plane got its silly nickname from its strange shape, said to resemble a large, somewhat lumpy fish. It flew from 1962 to 1967.

>> **Stingray Planes:** Engineers have been researching ways to make planes even more aerodynamic— such as modeling them after sleek ocean stingrays, curved wings and all!

## How do helicopters FLY without wings?

A helicopter may not have wings like those on an airplane, but it does have wings. You probably know them by a different name: blades! A helicopter has multiple, spinning blades that look somewhat like a propeller turned on its side. This mechanism is called a rotor. Unlike an airplane, a helicopter doesn't create lift by moving forward so that the air can fly over its wings. Instead, as its blades quickly spin, air flows over and around them, creating lift.

HUMMINGBIRDS ARE THE ONLY BIRDS THAT CAN FLY BACKWARD AND UPSIDE DOWN FOR LONG PERIODS OF TIME.

## Could a HUMAN fly if they had wings?

Like airplanes, birds use thrust to create lift. However, unlike planes, they can't rely on handy engines or propellers. Instead, they flap their wings! This moves them forward and up. Of course, birds are also designed for flight in other ways. They have hollow bones, which keeps them light. They also have feathers, which help air easily slip around their bodies. And, of course, their wings are aerodynamic!

So, if humans had wings, could we fly, too? Unfortunately, no. We're just too heavy! We lack all those special adaptations that birds have. Our bones are solid and heavy, we have thick skulls and jaws instead of light beaks, and we completely lack feathers. On top of that, our wings would have to be enormous to create enough thrust—so large that we probably wouldn't be strong enough to flap them.

## HOW MUCH DOES A SPACE SUIT COST?

If you want your very own NASA space suit, you might need a bigger piggy bank. The suits astronauts wear cost about

# $250 MILLION

to make. Even if you could afford the price tag, you might not be able to pick your suit up. Each space suit weighs about 280 pounds (127 kg).

## HOW BIG IS THE INTERNATIONAL SPACE STATION?

The International Space Station is the largest object humans have sent into space. From end to end, it measures **356 FEET (109 M).** That's about the length of an American football field.

## HOW MUCH WOULD I WEIGH ON MARS?

Mars has less gravity than Earth, so compared to home you'd be a real lightweight if you took a trip there. If you weighed **90 pounds** (41 kg) on Earth, you'd tip the scales at **34 pounds** (15 kg) **on Mars.**

# Cosmic Calculations

## Here's a mind-blowing number:

It is estimated that there are 70,000,000,000,000,000,000,000 (or 70 sextillion) stars in the universe. Space is a big place, and it's got some jaw-dropping stats to match.

## HOW MUCH HUMAN-MADE SPACE JUNK IS THERE?

There's a whole lot of trash orbiting Earth.

## About 23,000 HUMAN-MADE OBJECTS

that are four inches (10 cm) or larger orbit Earth, and millions more smaller ones are circling it, too. How did they get there? Much of it is old satellites and leftover pieces from rockets launched into space. Space debris can stay in orbit for more than 100 years before it eventually breaks down and burns up in the atmosphere.

## DO OBJECTS FROM SPACE FALL TO EARTH?

Every day, about **100 TONS (91 t)** of space particles hit Earth. Why aren't we all wearing helmets outside to protect ourselves? Luckily, these particles are the size of sand or smaller. *Phew!* But about once a year, an asteroid the size of a car enters Earth's atmosphere, then burns up before reaching the surface. Of course, there are the rare examples when something really big strikes Earth—like the six-mile (10-km)-wide asteroid that hit Earth and led to the extinction of the dinosaurs 66 million years ago.

## WHAT'S THE HOTTEST PLANET IN OUR SOLAR SYSTEM?

It's got to be Mercury, right? After all, it is the closest planet to the sun. Wrong! It's Venus. Mercury doesn't have an atmosphere, while Venus has a thicker atmosphere than any other planet in the solar system. An atmosphere traps heat. Venus has an average surface temperature of

## 867 DEGREES FAHRENHEIT (464°C)!

# CHAPTER 5

# DO ROBOTS HAVE EMOTIONS?

## QUESTIONS ABOUT TECHNOLOGY

**It's time to get techy.** Will people one day live entirely in virtual reality? And years from now, will a vacation to the moon be as common as a weekend adventure to an amusement park? And when will we all have flying cars? You might have questions about the future, but we have answers now! From high tech to transportation, we've got everything you need to know. Onward!

# Will people ever LIVE entirely in VIRTUAL REALITY?

Plugging into a totally virtual world—and spending most of life there—is the stuff of science fiction. But could it become fact?

SOME COMPANIES ARE CREATING VR ROLLER COASTER RIDES.

Virtual reality, or VR for short, is a computer-created simulation—a computer-made world or experience that can be interacted with in three dimensions. These VR worlds can be similar to ours, or they can be fantasy lands with made-up creatures and locations. Today, people use VR for several reasons. In many video games, virtual reality can make a player feel as if they are really in the game. VR can also be used as a sort of virtual travel—after experts take 360-degree images of a real-world location, they can transfer these to a digital environment and allow people to virtually tour them.

But could a human live permanently in a virtual world? No ... and yes. Right now, to interact with a virtual world, you need the right technological accessories. This usually means a headset that lets you see 3D images of the virtual world and hear its sounds, and a controller that lets you interact with it. Some experts think that in the near future VR might be something people use on a daily basis. Even so, you'd eventually need to take a break and put down the headset—if only to use the bathroom or eat a snack! However, there may be some futuristic technologies on the horizon that would make virtual reality a little less virtual and a lot more "real."

## REMOTE CONTROL

Scientists around the world are creating ways to let humans control technology using only their minds. In fact, experts have already developed certain electronic, or bionic, limbs that can

## EVERYDAY VIRTUAL REALITY

Virtual reality often sounds like a thing of the future or an unusual experience. But check out some of the ways it is used day to day.

» **Making machines:** Some car companies are using virtual reality to create early designs and prototypes. This helps a company lower costs—and it also helps reduce waste.

» **Museum visits:** During the COVID-19 pandemic, museums across the world were forced to close. However, many of them began to offer virtual tours of their galleries that anyone could "visit" from their own home.

» **Virtual learning:** In some classrooms, virtual programs let students explore the inside of a human body or travel back in time to see what it might have been like in ancient Rome.

be controlled by the user's mind. When a person wears the bionic limb, they can make it move just by thinking about it—just like with a natural limb! Think about when you move a part of your body—like clapping your hands, smiling, or wiggling your toes. When you start to do so, your brain sends a signal to your muscles to move. "Mind-reading" bionic limbs analyze the signals a person's brain sends to their muscles. Then, they use electricity to turn these signals into movement. Scientists are developing this same concept with other technology, too. This means that in the near future, a person might be able to interact with a virtual world using just their thoughts.

## ONLINE FOREVER

Even without a controller, a person would eventually need to take a break from a virtual world. But could there be a way to stay there ... forever? According to some experts, it might be possible for us to upload our brains to a computer. However, experts aren't sure exactly what that would entail. While it might be possible to scan our brains and then transfer the data to a computer, no one knows what the result would be. Some experts think the data wouldn't be alive but more like a storage file for all the information in your mind. Others think it might be possible to make an entirely digital version of yourself—one that could stay forever in a virtual world.

ONE VIRTUAL REALITY EXPERIENCE LETS PEOPLE EXPLORE HOW OCEAN LIFE MIGHT HAVE LOOKED HUNDREDS OF MILLIONS OF YEARS AGO.

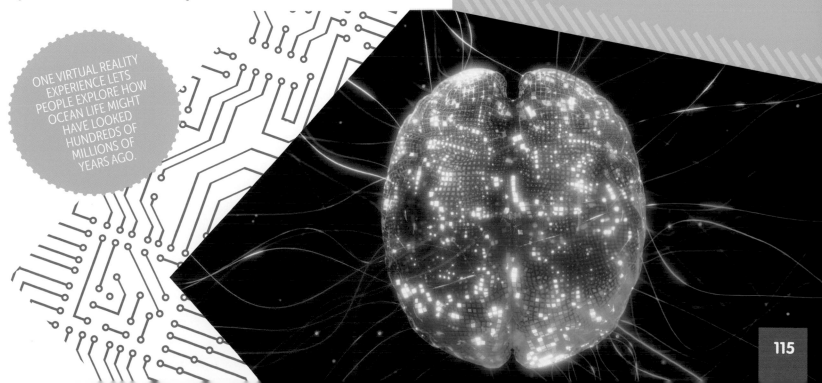

# Will we travel in FLYING CARS in THE FUTURE?

## Traffic jams could be a thing of the past.

THE FIRST "ROADABLE AIRCRAFT," INVENTED IN 1917, HAD THREE WINGS AND A PROPELLER AT THE BACK OF THE CAR. IT WAS ONLY CAPABLE OF A FEW HOPS, NOT FULL FLIGHT.

Imagine a car that scoots around roads, but if the traffic gets gnarly, it takes to the sky with the press of a button, flies up and over the congestion, and makes a safe landing at your home. We've been dreaming about this futuristic mode of transportation for more than 100 years. So when will the future arrive? It could be soon—but there are a few roadblocks.

## LOOKING TO THE SKIES

As soon as the first airplane lifted off and Ford turned out its first vehicle, people were pondering how the two modes of transportation could be combined. There were even prototypes. In 1926, U.S. inventor Sherman Fairchild made an airplane with wings that folded up like a ladybug's so it could drive down a road. Two decades later, another U.S. inventor, Robert E. Fulton, Jr., created the Airphibian, an airplane whose propeller and wings could easily be removed to turn the airplane into a car. Similar experiments were happening with car-helicopter hybrids.

Despite these clever prototypes, nothing ever really took off, so to speak, for a few reasons. For starters, learning to drive a car is one thing; becoming a pilot is much more complicated. And the consequences are greater if

something goes wrong in the sky as opposed to on the road. If you have engine trouble on the road, you can pull over. In the sky, it could very well mean a crash landing. On the road, there are lanes, stop signs, and traffic lights. Air travel requires communication with an air traffic control tower, which would likely be pretty tricky if there were as many planes in the sky as cars on the ground.

There are a lot of things to consider, to say the least—which is why we are still waiting for flying cars to become mainstream. Still, inventors continue noodling with ideas and hoping the flying car market will take off.

## PACKAGES, NOT PEOPLE

Instead of people taking to the skies in their own personal aircraft, packages are getting cleared for takeoff. One day, having a drone drop off your packages at your house might be just as common as a delivery truck pulling up to your curb. Here's the idea: You'd place an order, a special box attached to the drone would be loaded with whatever you purchased, and the drone would fly to your house. It would head to the backyard, hover close to the ground, drop the package, and leave. It's not all smooth sailing, though: Drones sometimes have issues maneuvering around objects or other aircraft in the sky, and they can only handle small packages.

ONE OF THE PROP CARS IN THE *BACK TO THE FUTURE* MOVIES "FLEW" AT THE END OF THE FIRST FILM. IT WAS AUCTIONED OFF FOR HALF A MILLION DOLLARS FOR CHARITY.

## Are there other transportation inventions that DIDN'T take off?

Yep. Have you ever heard of the traffic-straddling bus? Probably not. You don't see them zipping along highways the way engineers hoped they would. The idea was for a bus full of passengers to travel along tracks like a train, but the body of the bus was elevated so that two lanes of cars could pass underneath it. The futuristic public transit, designed in China, had a few bumps in the road—it was expensive, and it wasn't tall enough to clear large trucks. The bus never reached the on-ramp of mainstream success.

Here's another one: the one-wheeled motorcycle. Inventors have been playing with the idea of single-wheeled transportation since the 1800s, but it was more of a novelty than a mainstream way to get around town. Some of the more recent versions of the monocycle require you to sit inside the wheel. In others, you ride on top of it like a motorized unicycle. The monocycle concept isn't trending—after all, it's a bit of a balancing act to keep it rolling upright—but you'd certainly stand out in a crowd on (or in!) one.

# How do FIREWORKS WORK?

***Crack, pow!*** Colorful, dazzling fireworks are a stunning show of technology that's been around for thousands of years.

PEOPLE HAVE CREATED FIREWORKS THAT LOOK LIKE SMILEY FACES, FLOWERS, PLANETS, AND MORE.

Historians think that people accidentally created fireworks in China about 2,000 years ago, when someone tossed bamboo sticks onto a fire and the sticks exploded. Unlike today's fireworks, these bamboo sticks naturally exploded because of what's inside of them: Bamboo contains water and air. When the bamboo is heated, the water and air heat up, too. Over time, the heat causes the water to turn into gas. As the heat increases, the gases inside expand—but there is nowhere for them to go; they are trapped in the bamboo. Eventually, the bamboo explodes!

Over time, fireworks changed as new technologies were introduced. According to legend, a group of ninth-century Chinese scientists wanted to create a potion that could turn people immortal. They tried many different combinations of chemicals and substances, until they found one that created a surprising result—but it wasn't immortality. Instead, they had accidentally invented an explosive powder! This powder soon became used to make impressive fireworks, and it is still in use today.

## MAKING FIREWORKS

While experts still use explosives to create fireworks today, the process has been perfected over time. First, a designer fills two containers called shells with explosive powder (often known as black powder). These shells will be placed in the body of a firework, alongside a fuse. A fuse is a long, special type of explosive wire that can help control the timing of the black powder's explosions. To get the firework off the ground, an expert lights the fuse. This

ignites the powder in the first shell, and it explodes! As a result of the explosion, hot air pushes against the ground, and the firework flies toward the sky.

The second shell doesn't explode right away. Instead, the fuse keeps burning. The designers have timed it so that burning fuse doesn't reach the second shell until the firework is high in the sky. When it finally does, the second shell explodes, causing the impressive display you see in the sky.

## SPECTACULAR SHAPES

A firework's first explosion only has to get it off the ground, so it doesn't need to be that special. But the second explosion is meant to dazzle people watching from the ground, so designers make this one a bit differently. To create a pattern in a firework, people shape black powder into hard pellets, called stars. The stars are placed in certain patterns or designs—such as hearts—inside the second shell. To make colorful fireworks, designers add certain chemicals and metals alongside the pellets. When these pellets and chemicals erupt, they spread out in the fancy, vivid designs fireworks are famous for.

## ONE MORE THING: WHY ARE FIREWORKS SO LOUD?

It may seem obvious that fireworks are loud—after all, they are explosions! However, you might be surprised to learn that the people who make fireworks design them to burst with certain sounds. Some fireworks let out a mighty *bang*, others crackle with lots of little pops, and some even seem to whistle. Recently, some people have also begun designing quiet fireworks. These erupt with much less noise, so that animals and people nearby won't be startled.

## ROUNDUP FIREWORKS OF THE FUTURE

Fireworks have changed quite a bit from their humble beginnings as bamboo sticks—and they're still changing. Take a look at some of these futuristic fireworks displays and ideas.

» Phone fireworks: Some companies are designing fireworks that can be set off remotely from a person's smartphone. This may not seem like a big deal, but it actually makes the whole process a lot safer by keeping people safely away from the explosive materials.

» Drone works: Although fireworks are beautiful, they do involve, well, fire. This can be very bad news in dry climates, where stray sparks can cause forest or wildfires. To prevent this, some towns are switching to dazzling drone displays, where swarms of flashing drones take to the night sky in breathtaking patterns.

» Daytime display: To celebrate the Arab Museum of Modern Art in Qatar, a Chinese artist figured out a way to make rainbow explosions that could be viewed during the day.

# How does my phone KNOW what I'M SAYING?

## It's so easy to tell your smart devices what to do—literally!

MANY DEVICES CAN ALSO SCAN FINGERPRINTS TO USE FOR RECOGNITION.

SOME DEVICES CAN BE TRAINED TO RECOGNIZE VOICES SO THAT THEY KNOW WHO'S SPEAKING.

Much of modern technology is equipped with data and programs that let us give instructions just by speaking, something called "voice recognition." It seems simple—you speak to your device, and it does what you ask—but the steps are actually pretty complicated.

First, the smart device's programming lets it filter out any background noise (say, your cat meowing or a car honking). Then, once the device has zeroed in on your voice, it breaks the sounds down into little bits. This will make it easier for the device to "translate" your speech. The device now changes what you've said into digital information, which it begins to analyze. Next, the device compares this information with the information stored in its database.

What the device does next depends on what kind of device it is: For example, once a home smart device has identified key words, it will complete commands associated with those words—like playing a certain song or telling you the weather forecast. Other functions, like voice-to-text software or apps that can recognize songs, work the same way, but they use their databases to produce different results.

## How does my phone **RECOGNIZE** my face?

As with voices, a smart device can't instantly recognize a face; it needs to translate the information into something it can analyze. First, the device uses its camera to capture an image of a person's face. Then, it finds unique aspects of that person's face. However, what might seem unique to one person looking at another—the person's eye color, for example—isn't necessarily what will catch a computer's attention. Instead, the device focuses on things like the distances between facial features, such as the distance between a person's eyes. Using this information, the computer makes a digital map of the person's face. This is known as a facial signature, or a "faceprint." When a person opens their phone and uses face recognition, the phone "reads" their face and compares the data to the faceprint it has on file.

## ONLINE SAFETY TIPS

While devices safely store data through encryption, it's still important to be careful when sending information online. Here are some tips for staying safe online.

» Make sure you have a guardian's permission when going online.

» Never share passwords with anyone else, online or in person.

» Never post or send pictures of yourself or other personal information such as your address or where you go to school.

» Don't download or install any programs without a guardian's permission.

## How do devices **KEEP** information?

From passwords to bank codes to faceprints, smart devices such as phones store a lot of important information. And experts have designed ways of keeping all this information safe. One of these methods is called encryption. When information is encrypted, it is changed into a secret code that can't be decoded without special information, called a key.

## Are computers always **LISTENING?**

The truth is, experts aren't sure! The technology that allows smart devices to hear and see us is relatively new. People are still trying to figure out how to put rules in place to limit devices from listening in when we don't want them to. Some experts say that current technology does allow computers or phones to listen in on us. Others say that these devices can only truly listen when they are actively recording. One way to be sure? Turn off device microphones and cameras when not using them.

# Do ROBOTS have EMOTIONS?

## Don't be fooled by a human-sounding voice and big, cute eyes.

THE WORD "ROBOT" COMES FROM A SCIENCE-FICTION NOVEL WRITTEN MORE THAN 100 YEARS AGO.

SOME COMPANIES ARE DESIGNING ROBOTS THAT WILL HELP SOOTHE PEOPLE TO SLEEP.

A robot is a machine that is programmed to carry out actions—especially actions that help humans—on its own. This includes some of the simple, automated machines you might see in everyday life, like robotic vacuum cleaners, robots in factories, and robotic toys. These robots can only process the information they have been programmed to process and can only act in ways this programming tells them to.

However, more advanced areas of robotics—such as artificial intelligence—can get more complicated. Artificial intelligence, or AI for short, combines many different technologies to imitate how humans learn, solve problems, and even display and recognize emotions. Recently, researchers have begun developing robots that use AI to figure out what a person might be feeling. They do this using facial recognition technology and other programming cues that let them uncover a person's emotions based on context, facial expression, tone, and more. The robot's programming then lets it select an appropriate response or action. What's more, some robots have even been designed to mimic these emotions themselves—a robot might be designed to look sad, laugh, or even seem angry. However, is the robot really experiencing these emotions? Experts say no. While the robot's ability to analyze feelings or copy them might seem incredible, it is all the result of complex programming.

So, will AI ever be able to truly experience emotion? After all, it's one of the main ideas explored in science fiction! Researchers aren't sure, but they think it is probably impossible. This might have something to do

with what causes emotions in humans: different chemical messages sent to the brain. Right now, the technology to translate these chemicals into programming just doesn't seem to exist.

## MADE FOR A PURPOSE

If true emotions are out of reach for robots, why do humans bother making it seem like they can feel? Or why on earth would a robot need to know what a human is feeling? Well, the truth is—it's for us! Robots that can analyze a human's emotions might be able to provide better service or do their job better. For example, more and more artificial intelligence is being used in hospitals and other healthcare facilities around the world. A robot that can analyze a person's feelings may be able to give better care or even make the patient feel better.

Plus, we like it! Humans are drawn to things that express emotion or make us feel emotions. This could be very helpful in something like a robotic pet, for example—a "pet" for people who are allergic or who would prefer less responsibility but still want an emotional connection. Robots that show emotion can also act as companions for people who are feeling lonely or even help out in places like nursing homes. Even if the robot can't feel emotions, we can!

## ONE MORE THING: WHY ARE SOME ROBOTS SO CUTE?

Over the past few years, some robots have been making headlines. Not for having advanced programming or new features, but simply for being absolutely adorable. From buglike, automated delivery robots to a robotic companion seal to fan-favorite robot science-fiction characters, cute creations keep going viral. Why are so many robots designed to be adorable? To put it simply, humans love cute things! We are hardwired to adore big eyes and big heads. This is likely a trait that evolved over time to make sure we dote on our young. But now, we also dote on really cute bots! Companies design their robots this way on purpose. For one thing, it helps us accept the robots into society. For another, it grabs our attention!

## What is LOVE?

If a robot could feel love, what would it be feeling, anyway? It might seem like a simple question, but the truth is that there is no one right answer—and the answer will likely change depending on who you ask! According to scientists, the feeling of love—in humans—is associated with certain chemicals released by the brain. These chemicals, such as serotonin, oxytocin, and vasopressin, create feelings of happiness and attachment. This may have helped our ancestors survive, as it encouraged them to protect and care for each other. However, love isn't always straightforward—in fact, sometimes it's completely illogical. Scientists (and poets and artists and philosophers!) have been trying to understand what love truly "is" for centuries. Today, we understand more about what is going on in our brain when we experience love. But we may continue to debate its true meaning for centuries to come!

MANY ANIMALS EXPERIENCE MUCH OF THE SAME ACTIVITY IN THEIR BRAINS THAT HUMANS DO WHEN FEELING LOVE.

# TINY TECH

**A**s people create newer, groundbreaking technology, they also aim to make the tech different in other ways. This often includes making it run more quickly, making it more affordable for everyday people, and often, making it smaller. How small are we talking? Take a look and see!

## HOW SMALL CAN DRONES GET?

Imagine that you're sitting outside, minding your own business, when out of the corner of your eye you see something whiz by. Is it a small bird? Or maybe a bug? No, it's a tiny drone! There is a drone with a diameter of about .87 inch (22 mm). This makes it about as large as a U.S. quarter.

## WHAT IS THE SMALLEST COMPUTER?

If you look around, you will likely see computers everywhere, from phones to tablets to toys and cars. But soon there might be some you don't see. Engineers have created an itty-bitty computer that's less than .01 inch (0.3 mm) long. That's small enough to sit on the tip of a grain of rice!

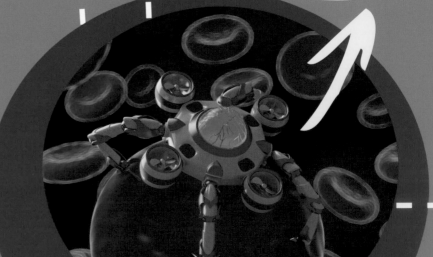

IMAGES NOT TO SCALE

## WHAT IS THE SMALLEST ROBOT?

Get out your magnifying glass, because one of the world's tiniest robots is just .02 inch (0.5 mm) wide. How small is that? Well, this crab-shaped robot is tinier than a flea. On top of that, it's remote controlled!

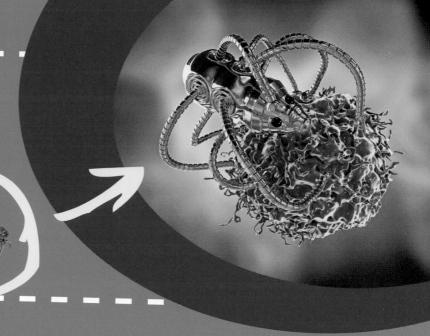

## HOW SMALL CAN TECH GET?

All these tiny machines might make you wonder: Can technology get even smaller? You bet! Scientists are working to create microscopic machines, known as nanobots. These machines would be just one to 100 nanometers. What does that mean? Well, you'd need a microscope to see them: They'd be smaller than the cells in your body.

## HOW BIG WERE THE FIRST COMPUTERS?

These days, computers can be so small you hardly notice them. However, this wasn't always the case. In fact, the first computers were downright enormous. One of the world's earliest functional computers stretched more than 50 feet (15 m)—about the length of a large school bus. And it weighed even more: At five tons (4.5 t), the computer was heavier than a hippo!

## WHAT CAN TINY TECH ACCOMPLISH?

Itty-bitty technologies aren't just cool—they can also do important jobs that big machines can't. For example, scientists are hoping that nanobots will help keep humans healthy. After safely injecting nanobots into a person's body, a doctor could then direct them to fight harmful diseases or help repair the body's cells. But it doesn't stop there: Experts are working to design robots and other technology that could make it easier to clean teeth or to travel through a person's bloodstream and even into their brain.

SCHOOL BUS

# Will we ever VACATION on THE MOON?

## What's one place you see just about every day, but you've never visited? The moon!

Apollo 11 astronauts first stepped foot on the moon on July 20, 1969. They took bounding steps in their space suits, and they a planted U.S. flag there. A year and a half later, Apollo 14 astronaut Alan Shepard hit a golf ball on the moon. During the Apollo 15 mission, astronauts drove around in a lunar buggy collecting samples and bouncing along the moon's bumpy surface. Sound like fun? Even though it's been more than half a century since astronauts made the moon look like a pretty fun playground, the rest of us Earthlings have had to wait for a chance to visit. NASA has plans to send astronauts back to the moon as soon as 2024, but it will still be a while before the everyday person

will get there. Launching rockets into space is pricey. As private companies have started using reusable launch vehicles, the cost could come down—a little. For the fore-seeable future, though, a ticket to the moon would not be a bargain, if moon tourism ever becomes a thing at all.

## DESTINATION: SPACE

So, let's say you *did* go to the moon on vacation. What should you expect? Well, for starters, you'd need to prepare for a long journey. The distance between Earth and the moon is

THERE WERE A FEW THINGS LEFT ON THE MOON THAT YOU MIGHT NOT WANT TO FIND IF YOU VISIT ONE DAY, INCLUDING FOOD PACKAGING, WET WIPES, AND PACKAGES OF URINE AND POOP.

about 240,000 miles (386,000 km), and it would take a spacecraft about three days to get there.

Once you arrived, you'd be in for a trip like no other. The moon doesn't have beaches (no oceans!), and it doesn't have roller coasters—although taking a spin on a lunar buggy could be a wild ride—and checking out everything other astronauts left behind would be like visiting a museum (more on that later). The moon is very rocky and dotted with craters, thanks to comets and other objects smashing into it. And there's not a lot of variation in scenery. Then there's the weather: Looking to vacation someplace hot? Someplace cold? The moon has both! The average temperature on the moon ranges from minus 298 degrees Fahrenheit (-183°C) at night to 224 degrees Fahrenheit (107°C) during the day. That's because the moon doesn't have much of an atmosphere to help regulate its temperature. It's kind of hard to figure out what clothes to pack!

## MOON MUSEUM

What exactly did astronauts leave behind on the moon? For starters, if you were to visit, you would still see the first astronauts' footprints. Because there isn't much atmosphere, there isn't any wind. That's why those famous first steps haven't been swept away. But there's more. To save weight for the return flight back to Earth, astronauts dumped a lot of stuff on the moon—including those lunar buggies, their boots, tools, and television equipment. This freed up space to bring back 850 pounds (385 kg) of moon rock and soil. And the golf balls that Alan Shepard hit? They're still there. Astronauts also left six U.S. flags and a gold replica of an olive branch.

a photo from the Apollo moon landing

## Did the APOLLO MOON LANDING change everyday life on Earth?

Yes, it absolutely did. Firefighters got safer uniforms thanks to the Apollo missions. A type of material that could withstand extreme heat was made for the astronauts and later used to protect firefighters on Earth.

Without the technology related to the missions, we wouldn't have the Dustbuster cordless vacuum. The company that makes it worked with NASA to create a cordless drill for the astronauts. Then that same technology went into the portable vacuum. And backpackers have astronauts to thank for their freeze-dried meals. NASA came up with the technology to create lightweight food that could be stored for a long time. Companies later began marketing freeze-dried food for backpackers who don't want their food to go bad on overnight trips when refrigeration isn't available.

SIMPLE KITCHEN
freeze-dried
BLUEBERRIES & YOGURT
real fruit snacks!

# THE UPS AND DOWNS OF ROLLER COASTERS

Sometimes tech is just for fun! The most thrilling coasters in the world almost seem to defy the laws of physics—but there's a lot of science behind the screams.

## WHAT'S THE FASTEST ROLLER COASTER?

What makes the world's fastest roller coaster seem even faster? Modeling it after a race car driving along a speedway. Passengers on the Formula Rossa roller coaster at Ferrari World Abu Dhabi in United Arab Emirates sit in a Ferrari-style car that goes from zero to 149 miles an hour (240 km/h) in just 4.9 seconds. The car races along a 1.3-mile (2-km) track, reaching a height of 170 feet (52 m) and then drops, giving its passengers an intense adrenaline rush.

## WHAT'S THE LONGEST ROLLER COASTER?

When it debuted in 2000—the Year of the Dragon on the lunar calendar—the Steel Dragon 2000 was the fastest, tallest, and longest roller coaster in the world. Today, it is still holding on as the longest. Riders of the Steel Dragon, located in Mie Prefecture, Japan, travel 1.5 miles (2.4 km) on an out-and-back track that takes about four minutes to cover.

## WHAT'S THE TALLEST ROLLER COASTER?

What goes up must come down— and in the case of the Kingda Ka, it comes down very fast. Located in Jackson, New Jersey, U.S.A., the Kingda Ka goes from zero to 128 miles an hour (206 km/h) in 3.5 seconds, carrying thrill seekers to the peak of the 90-degree angle track, 45 stories high. The Kingda Ka is the tallest roller coaster in the world and the fastest in North America. Once you're there, it's back down again into a 270-degree spiral that lasts another 50 seconds.

## WHY DO PEOPLE LIKE ROLLER COASTERS?

Terrifying twists, turns, drops, and climbs that leave you feeling queasy don't exactly sound like fun, but a lot of people walk away from a roller coaster ride wanting more. What is it that makes them so enjoyable? Researchers think the good or bad feeling you experience while riding a roller coaster may have something to do with differences in brain chemistry. People who have higher levels of a brain chemical called dopamine may be more prone to enjoy sensation-seeking experiences—like roller coasters, bungee jumping, or parachuting.

## WHY AREN'T ROLLER COASTER LOOPS PERFECT CIRCLES?

There's science behind that—and some trial and error. If a roller coaster has a perfectly circular loop, the cars go really fast near the bottom of the circle and too slow at the top. The speed near the bottom puts too much force on the passengers, and the slowdown at the top, when riders are upside down, causes them to fall out of their seats. None of these things are the makings of a successful roller coaster. In fact, in the late 19th and early 20th centuries, some roller coasters had circular loops, leaving some passengers injured. So these days, a teardrop-shaped loop is the preferred way to send roller coaster enthusiasts upside down.

## WHAT'S THE RECORD FOR LONGEST ROLLER COASTER RIDE?

American Richard Rodriguez set a roller coaster marathon record by riding on two roller coasters in the UK for 405 hours 40 minutes in 2007.

## WHAT WERE THE FIRST ROLLER COASTERS LIKE?

When you think of a roller coaster you probably imagine cars zipping along tracks at an amusement park on a bright sunny day. In fact, roller coasters were inspired by 15th-century giant sled rides. In Russia, wooden slides up to 70 feet (20 m) tall and 100 feet (30 m) long were covered with ice in the winter. A block of ice with a straw seat was used as the car, and passengers would cruise along the slide at speeds of up to 50 miles an hour (81 km/h)! Catherine the Great had one of these rides made with wheels that fit into wooden rails so it could be ridden during the summer—an early version of the roller coaster that would become popular in Europe in the late 18th century.

Montagnes de glace sur la Neva

# What TECHNOLOGY could REPLACE PHONES?

We can't tell the future, but experts have some good guesses as to what could eventually take the place of our beloved smartphones.

Some 30 years ago, telephones were home appliances that had to be connected to a power outlet and a phone line. Today, they are tiny computers, cameras, televisions, and more—that we carry around with us! But is there anything that could replace our current phone technology, or totally transform it? As it turns out, several companies are already working on it, using something called augmented reality, or AR for short. Augmented reality—which means improved or expanded reality—would involve merging computer technology with our everyday lives. This would likely mean wearing a small computer and screen on your face, likely in the form of glasses or something similar. The computer would then project a virtual screen in front of the user. For example, instead of a looking at their phone for directions, a person might see directions displayed directly in front of them, superimposed over the real world. Or another person might watch a video tutorial while teaching themselves to play the piano, with notes projected onto the keyboard! And, of course, the AR would also allow people to make calls or video chat with each other.

## NO PHONE, NO PROBLEM

Some experts think that advances in technology won't stop with wearable computers. One day, people may even have small computers implanted in their bodies. Some researchers are working to develop brain implants that would allow people to interact with real-life computers or other

2:25
Monday
July 23

$ ATM
Low withdrawal fees       15m

🏨 HOTEL
★★★★★                75m

🛒 Groceries
★★★★☆            10m

☀ 32° Sunny,
light showers in 3h

🍕 Pizzeria
★★★★☆         20m

electronics using their minds instead of their hands and fingers. Is it possible? Probably! Technology that can "read" a person's brain and then translate the messages into actions that control electronic devices already exists (see p. 114). Turning that tech into a brain implant would be just one step further. And a step beyond that? Implanting technology that would allow people to call others and speak to them—with no phone.

But what about the screens, you say? Well, there may be a solution for that, too. Several companies are working on designs for wearable contact lenses that would let people take photos or even stream images and videos they are seeing to nearby devices. Eventually, the contacts might be able to host AR technology, allowing the wearer to view videos, receive directions, store information, and more.

And that's still not all! Scientists are also working on skin implants that can do other things cell phones do, such as storing personal data. This way, instead of reaching for a phone or credit card, a person with an implant would be able to pay for an item using their finger—and the implant inside. Skin implants could also potentially be used to unlock car or home doors, pass security checks, and more.

# HELLO TO HOLOGRAMS

In lots of science-fiction films, characters in the far-off future interact with holographic images, or even communicate with miniature holographic versions of each other. As it turns out, the future is now—because scientists are developing this technology!

A hologram is an image—often 3D—made up of beams of light created by lasers. Several companies are currently developing ways to apply this technology to phones, so that video calls include holographic representations of the people speaking. Other companies are using the tech in more subtle ways, such as creating phones that have holographic features instead of physical or digital ones. But phones aren't the only uses for holograms. Experts are already designing holographic versions of celebrities for concerts, representations of historical figures for tours, and even holographic animals. What's more, scientists are experimenting with ways that people can "touch" a hologram—or at least make it feel like they are—using small jets of air.

(see p. 114)

## ONE MORE THING: WILL WE BE ABLE TO TELEPORT?

Forget the phone—wouldn't it be better to just instantly transport some place when you need to talk to someone? Unfortunately, this is one area that may remain out of grasp. For one thing, teleportation would require enormous amounts of energy. For another, it would be immensely difficult. Every living thing is made up of teeny building blocks called atoms. These small building blocks make up slightly larger ones called cells, which make up our bodies. To teleport someone, a device would have to take apart these materials and then send them over long distances. Then, at the destination, it would have to put them back together again!

SOME COMPANIES SELL "HOLOQUARIUMS"— AQUARIUMS THAT FEATURE HOLOGRAPHIC FISH INSTEAD OF REAL ONES.

SOME TOUCH-SCREEN PHONES CAN FOLD IN HALF.

## Q&A

# AN INTERVIEW WITH CAS HOLMAN

toy designer

Have you ever considered that toys are a type of technology? It's true! And as technology changes and grows, so do the things kids love to play with. In fact, many people dedicate themselves to designing new, innovative toys and games.

Meet one such person: Cas Holman is an American toy designer and the founder of Rigamajig, a company dedicated to creating open-ended building and machine kits. Read on to learn about the future of toys.

### Q HOW DID YOU BECOME INTERESTED IN CREATING TOYS FOR KIDS?

**A** As a kid, I loved to make my own fun. I noticed that a lot of toys come with the stories built into them; there's not much room for imagination. In designing Rigamajig, I wanted to create something that allows kids to create from their imaginations and play out their own stories. I also didn't see many toys that encouraged kids to make things together with their friends. I think it's important that we have toys that allow for creative teamwork.

### Q WHAT DOES IT TAKE TO DESIGN A NEW TOY?

**A** Imagination. Curiosity. Some pens, paper, and cardboard help, too. These are all things that kids have! I hope that kids are making their own toys as often as playing with mine.

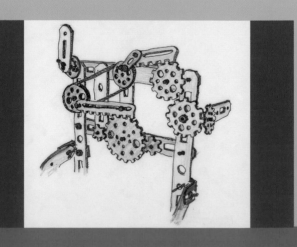

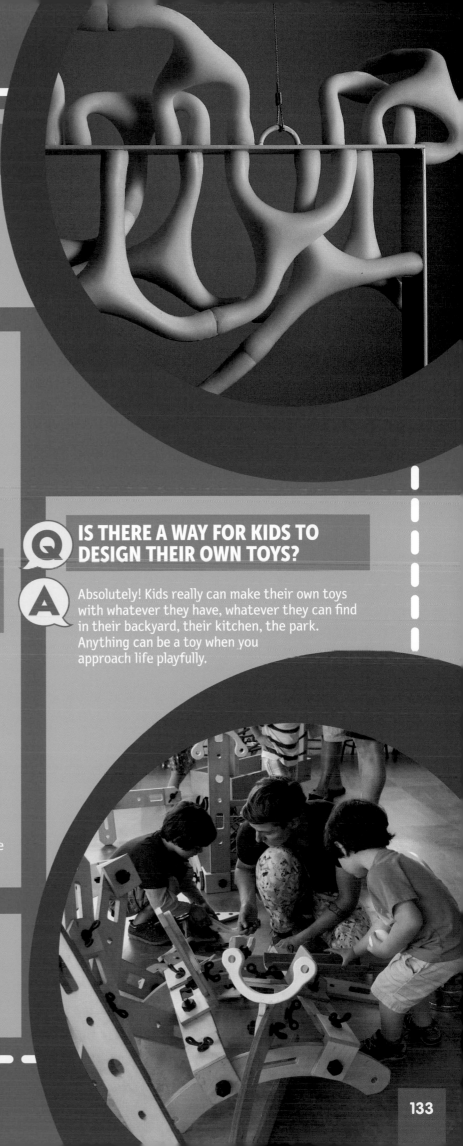

## Q: WHAT KINDS OF TOYS DO YOU THINK WE WILL SEE IN THE FUTURE?

**A:** With how much information kids have available to them now, I think we'll see more open-ended toys that allow kids to create anything that they want—maybe like Minecraft [and other open-ended video games], but in the physical space. We'll have more toys that encourage creative, independent thinking.

## Q: HOW WILL TECHNOLOGIES LIKE VIRTUAL REALITY CHANGE THE WAY PEOPLE PLAY IN THE "REAL" WORLD?

**A:** I consider the virtual world to be "real"—it's just experienced much differently than the physical world! In designing toys and play for kids, I work with companies to figure out where digital and physical come together. It's challenging because the materials are very different. But I think having a curiosity for and comfort with both digital and physical tools is super important for kids. It makes them more confident and adaptable as they navigate the rest of life. One thing that really excites me about the virtual world is that it makes it easier for kids to create from their imaginations. A kid may not have the physical materials or the technical skills to make something, but what they can do is create a virtual prototype.

## Q: WHAT'S YOUR FAVORITE WAY TO PLAY?

**A:** With my dogs, Wiley and Knuckles! They're also my favorite play partners.

## Q: IS THERE A WAY FOR KIDS TO DESIGN THEIR OWN TOYS?

**A:** Absolutely! Kids really can make their own toys with whatever they have, whatever they can find in their backyard, their kitchen, the park. Anything can be a toy when you approach life playfully.

# What's the FASTEST way TO TRAVEL?

## Do you have a need for speed?
### Buckle up for an out-of-this-world answer.

The fastest human-made object is one that can jet you straight off the planet. NASA's Parker Solar Probe, a spacecraft the size of a small car, has clocked 330,000 miles an hour (532,000 km/h)—faster than any other object built by humans. That's fast enough to circle Earth 13 times in one hour. It set that record in 2020 during its mission to study the sun. It skimmed the sun's atmosphere and used the sun's gravity to reach its top speed. But while the Parker Solar Probe has the record for fastest human-made object, it didn't have any humans on board.

Right now, the fastest way for humans to travel is aboard the International Space Station. Floating around at 220 miles (355 km) above Earth, astronauts zip through space at speeds of 17,500 miles an hour (28,165 km/h). They make a complete orbit of Earth every 90 minutes—this means the sun rises and sets 16 times in one day for astronauts!

There are also some pretty speedy means of travel here on Earth. Japan's Shinkansen bullet trains travel as fast as 200 miles an hour (322 km/h), carrying millions of people

**an imagined train of the future**

## Can HUMANS travel faster than the speed of light?

According to Albert Einstein's theory of special relativity, nothing moves faster than light. It travels at 186,000 miles per second (300,000 km/s). Light can go from Earth to the moon in just over one second.

For humans to travel even a fraction of the speed of light, we'd need a lot of energy. Currently, rockets use rocket fuel to launch into space. This isn't very efficient, and it doesn't have enough oomph to get to the next level of space travel. Engineers are exploring electric and magnetic forces, along with nuclear fusion, the same process that powers the sun. Speaking of the sun, researchers are also investigating solar. The thought is you could attach thin sheets of plastic to a spacecraft, and the energy from the sun would push the vehicle—like wind in a sail. It's possible that by using this method, spacecraft could travel 10 percent of the speed of light.

throughout the country every year. The trains get their power from an overhead wire system, making them far more eco-friendly than airplane travel. The bullet trains use 12.5 percent of the energy that planes do, and they produce about 92 percent less carbon emissions per seat.

Someday the bullet train might need to move to the slow lane. A new form of transportation called a hyperloop, which is three times faster than the bullet train, is in development. By some estimates, taking a ride on a hyperloop would mean sitting in a magnetic pod that levitates inside a tube and travels at more than 760 miles an hour (1,223 km/h). It could go from Los Angeles to San Francisco, California, U.S.A., in 45 minutes—and it would be a smooth ride. Magnets on the bottom of the pod would repel the material the tube is made of, causing it to levitate. No bumps in the road!

## What is a LIGHT-YEAR?

A light-year is the distance light travels in a year: about six trillion miles (9.7 trillion km). If humans could travel at the speed of light, it would take us between 323 and 423 years to get to Polaris, aka the North Star. We're 2.5 million light-years from Andromeda, our closest neighboring galaxy. And we're 13.4 billion light-years from the oldest galaxies we've ever found.

# Could technology from SCIENCE FICTION COME TRUE?

Flying around in spaceships, bringing back prehistoric animals, "beaming" from one place to another instantly—if only all that stuff in science fiction were real, right? **Well, some of it is!**

Captain Kirk's communicator on *Star Trek* was ahead of its time.

The gadgets and technology of sci-fi books, movies, TV shows, and games have inspired inventors to make them a reality. And sometimes the writers of fiction get their ideas from up-and-coming science and make them seem real before they actually are.

## TO BOLDLY GO

The stuff of fiction can be the start of a very good idea. The TV series *Star Trek,* which began in the 1960s and led to several spinoff series, along with multiple movies, inspired some pretty familiar technology. For instance, the communicator used by Captain Kirk when he was away from his ship and needed assistance from his crew had a flip antenna that started working when he opened it. Sound familiar? Decades later, the flip phone was introduced and did the same job—right here on Earth. *Star Trek: The Next Generation,* which debuted in 1987, introduced a keyboard without keys—the characters on the show touched the screens of computers and handheld devices. Two decades later came the iPhone, then the iPad, which did the same thing.

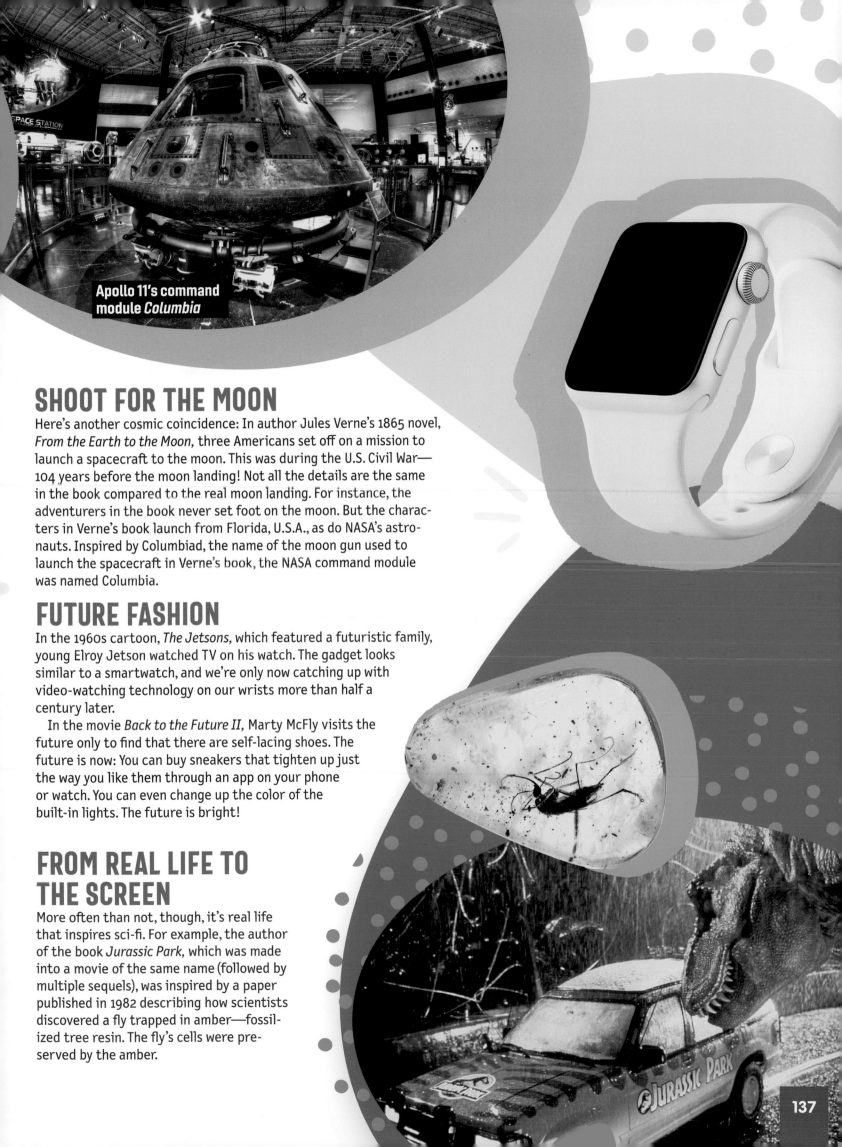

Apollo 11's command module *Columbia*

## SHOOT FOR THE MOON

Here's another cosmic coincidence: In author Jules Verne's 1865 novel, *From the Earth to the Moon,* three Americans set off on a mission to launch a spacecraft to the moon. This was during the U.S. Civil War—104 years before the moon landing! Not all the details are the same in the book compared to the real moon landing. For instance, the adventurers in the book never set foot on the moon. But the characters in Verne's book launch from Florida, U.S.A., as do NASA's astronauts. Inspired by Columbiad, the name of the moon gun used to launch the spacecraft in Verne's book, the NASA command module was named Columbia.

## FUTURE FASHION

In the 1960s cartoon, *The Jetsons,* which featured a futuristic family, young Elroy Jetson watched TV on his watch. The gadget looks similar to a smartwatch, and we're only now catching up with video-watching technology on our wrists more than half a century later.

In the movie *Back to the Future II,* Marty McFly visits the future only to find that there are self-lacing shoes. The future is now: You can buy sneakers that tighten up just the way you like them through an app on your phone or watch. You can even change up the color of the built-in lights. The future is bright!

## FROM REAL LIFE TO THE SCREEN

More often than not, though, it's real life that inspires sci-fi. For example, the author of the book *Jurassic Park,* which was made into a movie of the same name (followed by multiple sequels), was inspired by a paper published in 1982 describing how scientists discovered a fly trapped in amber—fossilized tree resin. The fly's cells were preserved by the amber.

# CHAPTER 6

# WHY DO WE DREAM?

## QUESTIONS ABOUT BEING HUMAN

**Have you ever tried to tickle yourself?** Go on, try it. We'll wait. No luck? There is, in fact, a reason! Humans are pretty cool, and there's some cool science behind how we tick. Like, why do we dream? Or forget? Or cry? Humans are complicated, and scientists are still trying to figure out a lot of the answers to these questions. But that doesn't mean we can't keep asking: Why do we get the hiccups? And is there a miracle solution to make them stop? And the answer to the question we all want to know: If you sneeze with your eyes open, will your eyeballs fall out? Hold that sneeze and read on!

# Why do WE FORGET THINGS?

Have you ever studied for a spelling quiz only to find the next day that you've completely forgotten how to spell a word? There could be a good reason for that.

Forgetting things happens to everyone. But why does it happen? Is it just a glitch in our brains? Researchers used to think that's what it was—a little blip that happens from time to time. But it might be more than that. In fact, forgetting things might not be a problem with our brains—it might actually be helping them.

There are four main types of memory. Short-term memories are brief, lasting minutes or a few hours. For example, if someone tells you their phone number, you'll likely forget it in a few minutes if you don't write it down. Long-term memories, like opening a favorite birthday present, can last years. Working memory lets us remember something by repeating it over and over—like memorizing a phone number. And then there's sensory memory—this lets us remember specific sensory information after an experience. Have you ever twirled a sparkler, and you saw a circle of light? That's sensory memory. The sparkler wasn't actually making a circle, but your eyes couldn't process the motion fast enough, so what you saw was a light trail, thanks to sensory memory.

There are a lot of things buzzing around us all the time, and our brains have to sort out what to remember and what to let go. Researchers think that forgetting some things might help people think more clearly, make better decisions, and even be more creative. So forgetting things once in a while isn't the end of the world.

## Is there such a thing as PHOTOGRAPHIC MEMORY?

There's no proof that it exists! Photographic memory is the ability to recall something you've seen in perfect detail, as if it were a photograph. But testing this ability is difficult in a scientific study, and it has never been proven. Scientists think it might have less to do with memory and more to do with some people being able to take in information better visually, as opposed to, say, hearing information.

## Why don't I have any MEMORIES from when I was a baby?

Think back. Do you remember learning to walk? Or eating your very first slice of birthday cake? These are pretty exciting events in a little kid's life, but most of us don't have any memory of them. Why?

Most people don't remember much before age three or four. And sometimes it's hard to know if you remember it or just saw it in a photo or video and convinced yourself it is a memory.

Babies' and little kids' brains are still developing, which likely plays a part in why we can't remember much from these important times of early brain growth. But there's more to the story. Language is still developing during the period when we don't have a lot of memories—which means we don't have the words to reinforce what we are learning. We aren't repeating things back and replaying our memories with our words. All this means we might not hold on to a memory the way we do once we have the words to describe it.

## Why is WHAT I REMEMBER sometimes wrong?

Have you ever been at the same place at the same time with someone and they remember something completely differently about something that happened there? For example: You and your best friend are talking about a birthday party you both went to one year ago. You remember a classmate being there and that you all played in the bounce house together. You friend remembers being in the bounce house, but they have no memory of the classmate being there. How can two people have different memories of the same event? It's possible you had what's called a false memory. That's a recollection of an event that never happened. For instance, the party happened, but your memory of the classmate being there might be wrong. How does that happen? The human brain is complex, and we're still learning about how it works. Scientists think we sometimes create false memories by taking one memory and combining it with another one. Maybe you saw the classmate at a different event, not at the birthday party.

# Why CAN'T you TICKLE YOURSELF?

Have you ever had someone pretend like they were going to tickle you and without them even touching you, you become all squirmy and giggly?

When the mere suggestion of being tickled makes us laugh, why can't we tickle ourselves? If you haven't tried it, give it a try. Tickle your ribs, the bottom of your feet. Nothing, right? What gives?

## NO PAIN, NO GAIN

Let's start by going into why we're ticklish in the first place. After all, being ticklish is kind of silly. Does it serve any purpose at all? It sure does! British scientist Charles Darwin, who analyzed plants and animals during the 19th century, thought tickling was linked to a person's sense of humor. But other scientists disagreed—after all, a lot of people laugh when they are being tickled, but they don't actually enjoy it. We've learned that being ticklish was an important part of evolution.

Our bodies are covered in tiny hairs. And when something—like a bug—touches those hairs, we notice and flick it off. As we evolved, people who were more sensitive to things landing on them—especially dangerous things, like poisonous insects—were at an advantage. But they were also more ticklish. So we evolved to be ticklish because it serves us well to be extra aware of danger. But what makes us let out a giggle when we're tickled? This might have to do with evolution, too. Scientists believe early humans might have learned that laughing, even when they felt nervous, made a tense situation lighter and prevented them from getting hurt.

## BRAIN KNOWS BEST

You can be ticklish anywhere on your body, but for most people, the top spots to get a laugh are your armpits, rib cage, and the bottom of your feet. But tickle yourself all you want, and you likely won't squeak out a giggle. The reason? You know what your body is going to do before it does it, and your brain anticipates it. Your brain then backs off its typical sensory response.

## SPEAKING OF GIGGLES ...

Laughter isn't all fun and games. It also helps relieve stress. Laughing stimulates our hearts, lungs, and muscles—and our brains release chemicals that produce a positive feeling. After a good laugh, we feel more relaxed and less stressed.

## ONE MORE THING: ARE ANIMALS TICKLISH?

People used to think that only humans were capable of being ticklish, but then some scientists decided to test that theory. Imagine what a fun job those scientists had tickling different animals to see if they were ticklish. Great apes are ticklish, and chimpanzees even chase after and tickle each other. They don't always tickle with their fingers; sometimes they "play bite" in the same way to get a giggly reaction. Scientists compared the sounds great apes make when tickled to humans' sounds and found them to be very similar, leading scientists to conclude that we share a common ancestor that giggled. This suggests that laughter is at least 30 to 60 million years old.

Other animals are ticklish, too—including rats! Scientists tickled the rodents and found they made high-pitched chirps that humans can't hear. And the rats made the same sound when they were playing with each other. When the researchers

realized that rats were ticklish, they wondered about other animals. Lo and behold, they found owls, dogs, penguins, dolphins, and camels react with a noise when tickled.

# WHY do we DREAM?

Every night when we close our eyes and hit the hay, our minds unravel stories that we sometimes remember—even if only for a few seconds—and sometimes don't remember at all.

Why do we go to dreamland when we sleep? From a purely physical point of view, you generally dream during rapid eye movement (REM) sleep. This is the stage of sleep when your brain appears to be in an active state but you're actually sound asleep. Research has revealed that during REM sleep the emotional center of the brain is super active, while the logical center of the brain is slowed. This might be the reason why dreams, especially during REM sleep, are emotional and fantasy-like.

## COGNITIVE CLEANUP

We know a little bit about what is happening in the brain during sleep, but *why* do we dream at all? Scientists aren't sure. It doesn't make a lot of sense from an evolutionary point of view—after all, when you're dreaming, you aren't aware of your surroundings. Back when we were vulnerable to predators in the wild, REM sleep would have been a pretty risky time for humans. Do dreams serve a purpose that makes deep sleep worth the risk? The best guess is that dreaming is an important process of sorting through information and processing data in our brains. In addition, people report feeling more refreshed after dreaming.

STUDIES HAVE FOUND THAT SOME OF THE MOST COMMON THEMES OF NIGHTMARES INVOLVE ANIMALS, FALLING, AND BEING CHASED.

Night terrors aren't technically dreams because they don't occur during REM sleep. A night terror is a sudden fearful event that happens during a transition from one sleep phase to another—usually two to three hours after you go to bed. Kids are more likely to experience them than adults. Your parents might tell you that you were kicking and yelling in your sleep. Unlike when you have a nightmare, you probably won't remember a thing—that's because night terrors happen in a phase of sleep that we don't remember.

## SCARY STUFF

As you probably know all too well, not all dreams are refreshing. A nightmare is like a scary movie—but it's playing out in your sleep, and you feel like it's actually happening to you. Bad dreams and good dreams probably serve similar functions in your brain. Researchers believe nightmares are often linked to something stressful that's going on in real life and, like dreams, are a way the brain is working through it in REM sleep. And some sleep scientists think dreams are a way of reorganizing and storing memories that happened during the day.

## FORGET ME NOT

Scientists have some strong theories about why we dream. But, in the end, dreams are still mysterious. And a lot of people don't remember most of their dreams. Why? Since our dreams are scenarios that we've made up, our brains don't log them in the same way as real-life events. So dreams generally leave our memory quickly. Usually, we only remember the very last dream we have right before we wake up. One thing we do know is that when we are stressed, we are more likely to remember our dreams, possibly because we are also likely to wake up more frequently when we are worried and anxious.

## What happens if you DON'T get enough sleep?

"Get a good night's sleep" is about as common a piece of advice as "eat well" and "brush your teeth." Why is sleep so important? For a lot of reasons, actually. If you don't get enough sleep—for school-age kids that's nine or more hours a night—your brain doesn't process what you learned during the day as well. Plus, you'll have difficulty remembering it later. Moral of the story: If you stay up too late studying, it's actually not going to help you do better on a test. Sleep is also important for other parts of your body. A lack of sleep can increase your blood pressure and can give you headaches. And it can increase your likelihood of getting sick. So it turns out getting a full night's sleep is pretty solid advice!

# How do we KNOW that we're all seeing the SAME COLORS?

## Here's the thing: We don't!

Let's pretend two people are shown a picture of a tree. They're both asked what color the tree is. They both say it is green. Does that mean both people are seeing the exact same color? What if what both people are calling "green" is actually two different colors?

There are a couple things to break down here: We don't all necessarily see colors the exact same way—but how could we know since we can't see through one another's eyes? And, is a tree green just because we say it's green? Let's get into it!

THE WORLD IS MORE COLORFUL TO HUMMINGBIRDS THAN TO HUMANS. THEY HAVE AN EXTRA COLOR CONE IN THEIR EYES THAT ALLOWS THEM TO SEE A BROADER RANGE OF COLORS THAN WE CAN SEE, WHICH HELPS THEM FIND FOOD MORE EASILY.

## SEEING IN COLOR

When you look at a picture of a tree, you are seeing it through your eyes. There are physical differences between one person's eyes and another's. Our eyes' job is to sense light. And light is made up of different wavelengths. Of the light we can see, the shortest wavelengths are violet and the longest wavelengths are red. The wavelengths in between are the rest of the colors in the rainbow, which we know are orange, yellow, green, blue, and indigo. The backs of our eyes are covered in cells, known as "cones," which are sensitive to light. Most people have three kinds of cones, and each cone has a role in helping us distinguish colors. But people have variations in their cones, which affects how they perceive color. One person's eyes might be slightly more sensitive to red, and the next person's might not be. The difference might be very slight, but that tiny difference could wildly change the way someone sees, say, red versus orange. To one person, a yellow traffic light is bright yellow. To another, it might be orangish yellow.

Instead of having three kinds of cones, some people have two kinds. People with two kinds of cones are considered "color-blind." This doesn't mean they see the world in black and white, but rather that they usually have difficulty seeing the difference between certain colors. A person with typical color vision can see up to one million shades of color. But a person who is color-blind might see just 10,000 colors. People who are color-blind commonly can't distinguish between red and green (both colors appear more brownish to people who are color-blind).

And then there are people who are the opposite of color-blind—they have super color vision. Instead of two or three cones, the rare individual—oftentimes female—has four cones. Instead of being able to see one million shades of color, they can see 100 million shades!

## WHAT'S IN A NAME?

The names of the colors that we have assigned to those different wavelengths—red, orange, yellow, green, blue, indigo, and violet—are just that: names. Back to the tree. Let's say when you were little, your mom pointed at the tree outside your bedroom window and said, "The tree is green." You assigned the word "green" to the color of the tree. But that's just a word you were told was a certain color. What if instead your mom told you the tree was purple. That would mean you'd say grass, broccoli, and frogs were purple, too! This is an extreme example, but it's a way to explain that the names we give the colors of the rainbow are just words. They don't necessarily accurately reflect exactly what each of us is seeing—because we see the world through our own eyes, and we use words to describe it through our own experiences.

These images are examples of what the world might look like with three cones (left), compared to two (right).

THERE ARE SEVEN COLORS IN THE RAINBOW, BUT MANY MORE NAMES FOR COLORS THAN THAT! CRAYOLA CRAYONS, FOR EXAMPLE, HAVE 120 DIFFERENT NAMED COLORS.

## What does purple SOUND like?

Wait, colors have a sound? For some people, they do! It's a trait called synesthesia, and it's when you experience one sense through another sense. Researchers think that people who have synesthesia, which is experienced by less than 5 percent of the population—have a response in their brains that automatically pairs up senses, like sound and taste, sound and colors, and letters and colors. But it's more complicated than reading the word "grass" and suddenly smelling grass. People who experience synesthesia usually have unexpected couplings. For instance, when someone walks on grass and breathes in through their nose, they might smell purple, meaning the smell of grass might be associated with purple. And the same is true of sounds. The sound of flutes playing might be indigo blue. So what does purple sound like? To some people purple sounds "strong." But everyone who experiences synesthesia has different experiences!

# Does the HEART have anything to do WITH EMOTIONS?

Heartache, heartbroken, loving with your whole heart—so many phrases make it seem like emotions come from the heart.

WHEN A PERSON GETS HUNGRY, THE CHANGE IN CHEMICALS IN THEIR BODY CAN MAKE THEM FEEL ANGRY—OR AS IT'S CALLED, HANGRY!

In reality, when it comes to feelings, your brain reigns supreme. Day after day, your brain is processing lots of information. This can be in the form of physical information, conversations you have, things you see—the list goes on and on. While it sorts this information, the brain often reacts by sending messages to your body. Some of these messages can be physical reactions, like increasing your heart rate or causing you to blush. Some messages are sent in the form of chemicals. Different combinations of these chemicals cause the emotions you feel.

## THE HEART OF THE MATTER

The idea that the heart is the center of emotion has existed for more than 6,000 years. In ancient Mesopotamia (in what is now Iraq), people believed that the heart controlled most of the body. Similarly, people in ancient Egypt believed that the heart was so important that it would be weighed in the afterlife to judge whether a person was good or bad. They thought the brain was fairly unimportant—they even threw it away during mummification! Later, in ancient Greece, several famous philosophers also argued that the heart was in control. Over time, the heart came to serve as a symbol for emotions. When a person referred to their heart, they weren't necessarily talking about the organ in their body, but rather their emotions as a whole.

But why this focus on the heart in the first place? It actually makes a lot of sense when you think about it—after all, the heart pumps blood throughout the body. Doctors in ancient times knew this and came to the conclusion that because the heart was driving blood flow, it was also controlling a person's feelings. In fact, ancient people may not have been completely wrong. When a person is experiencing a strong emotion, they often feel physical sensations in their chest. Recently, scientists made an interesting discovery that may help explain this: The heart contains many of the same kind of special cells that make up the brain—neurons. Neurons are cells that can send and receive messages. Because of this, the heart and brain may send many messages back and forth. Scientists aren't yet sure exactly what this means, but the heart may actually be involved in emotions after all!

## ONE MORE THING: WHY DO PEOPLE CRY?

Most of the time, tears are something your body uses to get rid of tiny, irritating objects in your eyes or to keep your eyes moist. But sometimes—like if you've gotten some sad news or watched an emotional movie—tears are expressions of your emotions. When you cry because of emotions, your tears are different from the ones that keep your peepers from getting too dry. They contain certain chemicals, known as stress hormones. They also contain other special "painkiller" hormones that make us feel good and reduce any pain we might be feeling.

On top of making us feel better physically and emotionally, scientists think that emotional tears might help us better connect to other humans. When we cry, we are communicating our feelings to other people who can help us.

## Why do we have
## EMOTIONS in the first place?

Scientists think that emotions may have developed to help humans react quickly in different types of situations. For example, anger can help animals in the wild survive. When the brain encounters a dangerous or difficult situation, it may react by sending chemicals that cause the animal to feel aggressive—or angry. For many animals—including our human ancestors—this might help them defend themselves or chase off dangerous predators. On the other hand, when people experience pleasant situations, the brain often releases "happy" chemicals that make a person feel nice. This may have encouraged human ancestors to seek out safe and healthy situations. On top of that, emotions may also serve a social role. Feelings can help humans bond, work together, and protect each other.

THE EXPRESSION "CROCODILE TEARS" IS OFTEN USED TO REFER TO INSINCERE EMOTION. IT LIKELY COMES FROM AN OLD MYTH THAT CROCODILES CRIED TO LURE THEIR VICTIMS.

HUMANS ARE THE ONLY ANIMAL KNOWN TO CRY AS AN EMOTIONAL RESPONSE.

# Why am I RIGHT- (OR LEFT-) HANDED?

Most humans—and some kinds of animals, too—have a natural preference for using their right or left hand. In humans, this is especially strong when writing or using scissors. However, scientists aren't totally sure why that is!

Today, most scientists believe that being right- or left-handed is determined by your genes. Genes are the things that determine your traits—in other words, the unique characteristics that make you *you*. For example, genes are responsible for things like how you look—from your hair color to your eye color to whether you have freckles—as well as for some of the ways you act and even some of your likes and dislikes.

But what exactly are genes? Your body is made up of tiny building blocks known as cells. In each of these cells, you have microscopic, threadlike structures called

chromosomes. Chromosomes are made up of DNA: deoxyribonucleic acid. DNA is what makes up every single living thing. DNA is grouped into units within your chromosomes. There, these units serve as the instructions for making a type of molecule called a protein. Proteins are your body's building blocks. Larger sections of these DNA units are called genes. Genes tell the proteins what to build and how. That may sound like a lot of info—and it is! But all this is to say: Whether you are right- or left-handed may be controlled by information stored in your body!

MOST PEOPLE ALSO HAVE A NATURAL PREFERENCE FOR EITHER THEIR RIGHT OR LEFT FOOT—AND IT CAN BE THE OPPOSITE OF THEIR HAND PREFERENCE.

## Where do I get my GENES?

Genes come from a person's biological parents. This is why biologically related people can often look alike. Each human cell usually holds 46 chromosomes. These chromosomes are grouped into pairs, meaning every cell usually has 23 chromosome pairs. For every pair of chromosomes, one chromosome comes from the female parent while the other comes from the male. One of these chromosome pairs determines a person's biological sex. The other pairs determine your other traits.

Genes are what are responsible for what your facial features look like, your height, your coloring, and so much more. They can even influence what foods you like (see p. 178). Since your genes come from your biological parents, you might look more like your biological mother or more like your biological father. Or, maybe you look like a mix of both—or neither! This is because genes can combine in surprising ways. Different combinations of genes can give people different traits, such as having curly or straight hair. In fact, some scientists calculate that about 70,368,744,177,664 combinations of genes exist for all humans—much more than the number of humans who have ever lived!

On top of that, genes can express themselves differently—meaning that they can "turn on" or "turn off." For example, maybe you grew up having straight hair, but it started to get curly once you got older. For this reason, even people who are biologically related don't always look alike. Siblings can receive different genes from different parents or have genes that express themselves differently. This difference in gene expression can even happen with identical twins!

SCIENTISTS THINK REDHEADS MAY BE MORE LIKELY TO BE LEFT-HANDED.

(see p. 178)

# IT'S IN YOUR GENES

Genes are complicated—in fact, scientists are still learning exactly what your genes can determine. Take a look at some of the more surprising traits your genetics can influence!

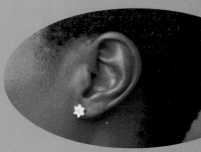

>> The shape of your earlobes

>> Whether you get motion sick in vehicles

>> How long you tend to sleep

>> Whether you have natural musical talent

>> Whether you have a fear of heights

>> Whether you have a fear of public speaking

# WHAT HAPPENED TO NEANDERTHALS?

Humans began evolving from a common ancestor ape more than six million years ago. Over the ages, many different kinds of primitive humans appeared and disappeared. Some 2.4 million years ago, a new group of humans began to appear. The different species in this group all shared the same genus—a way of organizing closely related species that have evolved from a recent common ancestor. Scientists call this genus *Homo*. Over time—around 300,000 years ago—modern humans, known as *Homo sapiens*, evolved. However, they weren't alone. Another type of species known as *Homo neanderthalensis,* or the Neanderthals, existed at the same time.

SOME SCIENTISTS THINK THAT NEANDERTHAL DNA CAN INFLUENCE WHETHER A PERSON PREFERS SAVORY OR SWEET THINGS.

# MEET THE NEANDERTHALS

Neanderthals are our closest known human relatives. In fact, they looked a lot like us! However, they tended to be shorter and to have slightly sturdier bones—including a larger brow ridge above their eyes.

For many years, scholars thought that Neanderthals must have been somewhat primitive, or less advanced than *Homo sapiens.* In pop culture, they were often portrayed as grunting cave people. However, recent discoveries have shown that this was not true at all. Neanderthals were sophisticated people who made complex tools, created art, and even may have had domesticated dogs for pets. They also fashioned clothing, wore jewelry, used fire, and carefully buried those who had died.

# A DISAPPEARING ACT

These human "cousins" of ours appeared on the scene around 400,000 years ago, across much of Europe and Asia. But then, around 40,000 years ago, they disappeared. What happened? So far, scientists don't know for sure. However, they have several theories.

For many years, scientists thought that Neanderthals must have been driven extinct by *Homo sapiens*—perhaps through direct fighting, or by competition for food and living places. However, evidence shows that the two human species coexisted for tens of thousands of years.

Other scientists think that disease may have wiped out the Neanderthals. It is possible that Neanderthals and modern humans had different kinds of immune systems; an illness that was deadly to Neanderthals might have been one that *Homo sapiens* could survive. Other scientists think that, over the years, Neanderthals had a harder time surviving the world's changing climate.

Either way, scientists are certain of one thing: Neanderthals didn't disappear *completely.* This is because modern humans and Neanderthals sometimes interacted and had children with each other. In fact, many people today have Neanderthal DNA!

ON AVERAGE, NEANDERTHALS HAD LARGER BRAINS THAN MODERN HUMANS.

# ONE MORE THING: DID MODERN HUMANS INTERACT WITH OTHER HUMAN RELATIVES?

*Homo neanderthalensis* was not the only other human species that shared the planet with modern humans. In what is now Indonesia, a species called *Homo floresiensis* lived from about 100,000 to 50,000 years ago. This species was much smaller than modern humans, only up to about 3.5 feet (106 cm) tall. However, there is no evidence as to whether this species ever met or interacted with modern humans (or Neanderthals)!

# Why do we HAVE FINGERPRINTS?

## Those whorls and loops on your fingertips are one-of-a-kind ... and pretty useful!

IDENTICAL TWINS DON'T HAVE MATCHING FINGERPRINTS.

You are unique. Of all the eight billion people on the planet, there is no one like you. Yes, you might look like other people, and you might have been born on the exact day, hour, minute, and even second as someone else. But there is still no one exactly the same as you. And there is no one who has exactly the same fingerprints. Those little squiggly lines on the tips of your fingers are way more complicated than they look.

Fingerprints are tiny ridges of skin that we're born with. They don't change as we grow or age. If you get a cut on the tip of your finger—or a minor burn— the new skin that grows back duplicates the original pattern.

## HELPING HAND

There are a few theories for why we have fingerprints. One is that they help prevent us from getting blisters. We are less likely to get blisters on our fingertips than other places. Having blisters on their fingertips would have made early humans' lives more difficult, and we might have evolved fingerprints to protect us from that. Another theory is that they increase sensitivity to touch, helping us feel specific details on objects. When we run our fingers over a piece of fabric, for instance, there are vibrations in the skin that our nerves detect. Fingerprints increase these vibrations by 100 times.

# How do fingerprints SOLVE crimes?

No two people have the exact same fingerprints. So when detectives check for fingerprints on, say, a stolen car, they can try to the match the fingerprints they find with fingerprints they already have in their computer system. But fingerprints aren't always accurately read. A study found that 0.1 percent of fingerprint analysts make false positive matches—meaning they wrongly identified prints as belonging to someone. That's a pretty small number, but it still means it's not a perfect identification system.

# Do other ANIMALS have fingerprints?

Two other types of animals have fingerprints: great apes and koalas. Koalas? Yep, koalas have fingerprints that look just like a human's. But let's start with the great apes: Species closely related to humans like gorillas, chimpanzees, and orangutans have fingerprints that look a lot like those of humans. And just like with humans, no two animals have the same fingerprints. Humans belong to the same group as these other great apes, so that makes sense. But where do koalas fit in?

You almost can't tell the difference between your fingerprints and a koala's. Humans' and koalas' last common ancestor lived more than 100 million years ago, and a lot of things have changed between our two species since then—but not fingerprints. Why? Scientists have a hunch that the added sensitivity that fingerprints provide works well for koalas. Their favorite food is eucalyptus leaves ripened to a very specific age. Having sensitive fingers might help them find exactly what they're looking for.

## TOTALLY UNIQUE

Not all animals have fingerprints, but many have other traits that make individual animals unique. Check out some of these wild examples:

» Dogs and cats: Dogs and cats—even big cats!—have unique whisker patterns.

» Whale sharks: Each of these giant sharks has a one-of-a-kind pattern of spots.

» Humpback whales: These whales have special markings on the underside of their tails.

» Zebras: No two zebras have the same stripes!

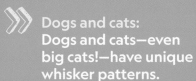

# HEAD TO TOE— HUMANS ARE WEIRD!

O ur bodies can be pretty complicated! Check out these answers to questions about our wonderfully weird human bodies.

SOME SPIDERS ARE ATTRACTED TO THE SMELL OF STINKY FEET.

## WHY DO MY FEET STINK?

Feet smell thanks to a combination of sweat and bacteria. Much of your body is covered in tiny organs, known as glands, that produce sweat. You are also covered in microscopic, harmless bacteria. When sweat dries, bacteria on your body feasts on it, producing a smelly waste. But why are feet extra stinky? Because feet are covered in extra sweat glands— and they're often in the dark, moist conditions that bacteria love.

## WHY DO I GET GOOSEBUMPS?

Goosebumps are an involuntary reaction, which means that it happens without you meaning for it to. When you are cold, tiny muscles in your skin squeeze and relax to help create warmth. This makes your hair follicles—the places where your soft body hair grows—stand up. If you were a furry kind of animal, this would help you warm up by trapping a layer of air between your hair and your body. For modern humans, it doesn't do as much. The same probably goes for the goosebumps you get when you're afraid. For our furry ancestors, having fluffier hair would have made them look larger and more intimidating, potentially scaring off threats. For us humans, it's mostly just a leftover trait.

THE SCIENTIFIC NAME FOR GOOSEBUMPS IS CUTIS ANSERINA.

## WHY DON'T I HAVE A TAIL?

Animals that spend all or most of their time on all fours often have tails to help them balance. In fact, long, long ago, human ancestors likely had tails, too. But as our ancestors slowly evolved to walk upright on two legs over the years, they no longer needed a tail for balance. Over time, the tails of human ancestors got shorter and shorter—until they disappeared altogether. Now, the only reminder is in the form of our tail bone!

## WHY DO HUMANS LOSE BABY TEETH?

When they are young, kids grow super quickly. They grow taller and larger. However, because teeth can't grow along with a person's skull, they need to be replaced. The new teeth are bigger and stronger— and there are more of them!

## WHY DON'T HUMANS HAVE FUR ON THEIR BODIES?

Scientists don't really know! Some scientists think that, over time, humans may have lost their body hair to stay cool. This may have occurred about two million years ago, when human ancestors moved from cool, shadowed forests in Africa to hot open savannas. Losing all their hair would have helped them stay cool. However, other scientists think that they may have lost their body hair because it helped get rid of body parasites.

## WHY DO HUMANS HAVE ONLY FIVE SENSES?

Who says humans have only five senses! For many years, it was popular to categorize how people experience the world into five different senses: sight, smell, hearing, taste, and touch. But many scientists today think that humans have a sixth sense: the ability to tell where all our body parts are in space without looking at them. This sense is called proprioception. Want to try it out? Try clapping with your eyes closed!

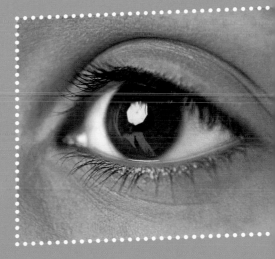

## WHY DO I GET MORNING BREATH?

Bacteria are to blame for your stinky feet, and you have them to thank for morning breath, as well! When we eat, bacteria in our mouths break down the food left over on our teeth and gums. In the process, the bacteria also create chemicals that stink, causing bad breath. In the morning, we've gone so long without brushing our teeth, eating, or drinking that the bacteria have had lots of time to create stinky smells.

# How do you STOP HICCUPS?

**Pretty much everyone who's experienced hiccups has also tried to make them go away. Which tricks work the best? Read on!**

*A FETUS IN THE WOMB CAN GET HICCUPS.*

Hiccups sound exactly like their name. Your body makes a *hicc-up* sound every few seconds until someone asks, "Did your hiccups go away?" and you realize that, in fact, they did! But what exactly are hiccups?

## ACTING UP

Hiccups start in the diaphragm, which is a muscle located under your rib cage that helps with breathing. When you take a breath, aka inhale, the diaphragm pulls down to let air into your lungs. When you breathe out—exhale—the diaphragm relaxes, and air flows from your lungs and heads back out through your nose or mouth.

That's when everything is running smoothly. But sometimes your diaphragm acts up, and during the stage when it pulls down to let air in, it does it in a jerky way that makes the breathing process happen too fast. When the air hits your esophagus, your vocal cords close quickly, causing that signature *hic* sound.

We know what is going on when we get the hiccups, but why does our diaphragm decide to pitch a fit every so often? Researchers aren't certain, but they think it might have to do with nerves leading to the brain stem that become irritated.

## THE CURE ... KIND OF

There are a few ways to dodge the hiccups before they start. Eating and drinking more slowly can help you avoid them, as can avoiding eating too much. Carbonated beverages can cause the hiccups, and so can stress.

But what if you already have them? There's no miracle cure. Popular remedies include:

**Drinking from the "wrong" side of the glass might relax the diaphragm.**

>> Holding your breath and counting to 10: Scientists say this increases carbon dioxide levels in the lungs, which might help the diaphragm relax.

>> Drinking from the "wrong" side of a glass of water: This might just be a good distraction from the hiccups, causing you—and your diaphragm—to relax.

>> Taking small sips of cold water: The temperature change might help them stop.

>> Someone jump-scaring you: In theory, making you gasp and "scaring" away the hiccups.

>> Sometimes the best approach for getting rid of the hiccups is simply waiting them out.

## SPEAKING OF PERSISTENT HICCUPS ...

Charles Osborne of Iowa, U.S.A., had the hiccups for 68 straight years! In 1922, Osborne had an accident while butchering a hog. He fell and burst a blood vessel in his brain. According to his doctor, this damaged a small part in the brain stem that inhibits the hiccup response. This meant his body was incapable of stopping the hiccups. He has the world's record for longest attack of the hiccups, and it is estimated that he hiccuped 430 million times before he died at the age of 97.

## How **LONG** do hiccups last?

Usually, hiccups last only a few minutes to a few hours. Anything over a few days is called persistent hiccups, and that's when you should go see a doctor. Long-lasting hiccups are very rare.

## Can my **DOG** get the hiccups?

Yes! Your cat can, too. Scientists think most mammals get the hiccups, and they're commonly seen in dogs, horses, and humans. But birds, amphibians, and reptiles are lucky enough to not get them.

# Will too much SCREEN TIME DAMAGE MY EYES?

It's definitely not good for your eyes. Between computer time at school, TV time at home, and fun time on a tablet, it's likely your eyeballs have logged a lot of screen time.

## TIRED EYES

When you're looking at a screen you tend to blink less. Instead of blinking the typical five to seven times per minute, people often blink every 15 to 20 seconds. And all the images moving on a screen—even the scrolling words while you're doing your home-work—makes it harder for your eyes to focus.

What are the consequences? It can cause something called eye strain. Tired eyes can give you head-aches and double vision, which means seeing two of one thing. Because you aren't blinking as much your eyes can get dry. After too much time on a screen, you might find that objects in the distance look a little fuzzy. And, in extreme cases, too much screen time can cause long-term damage of your retina (the back of your eye), and potentially lead to loss of eyesight.

HUMANS CAN SEE GREEN BETTER THAN ANY OTHER COLOR.

THE FIRST EYEGLASSES WERE INVENTED IN THE 13TH CENTURY BY ITALIAN MONKS—THE FRAMES WERE MADE OF EITHER WOOD, IRON, OR ANIMAL HORN.

# PROTECT YOUR PEEPERS

Experts say there are some things you can do to help your eyes. For starters, adjust the brightness on your screen. Your screen shouldn't be brighter than the rest of the light in the room. (This means when the lights are out in the room, the brightness level on your screen shouldn't be too high.) Adjust the room's lighting and your screen's brightness so they even out.

The standard rule for looking at a screen is that after 20 minutes, you should look away at an object 20 feet (6 m) away—about three lengths of your bed—and blink 20 times for 20 seconds. This helps your eyes by letting them rest and refocus.

Sometimes whatever is on our screen is so engaging that we want to get super close to it. It's better to keep your distance. Experts say you should keep your screen two feet (0.6 m) away from your eyes, and you should be looking slightly downward at the screen.

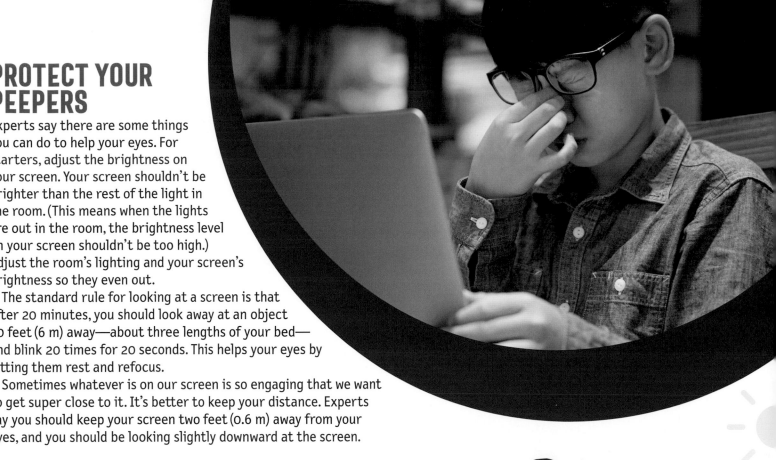

SHARKS' EYES HAVE ALMOST THE EXACT SAME STRUCTURE AS HUMANS'.

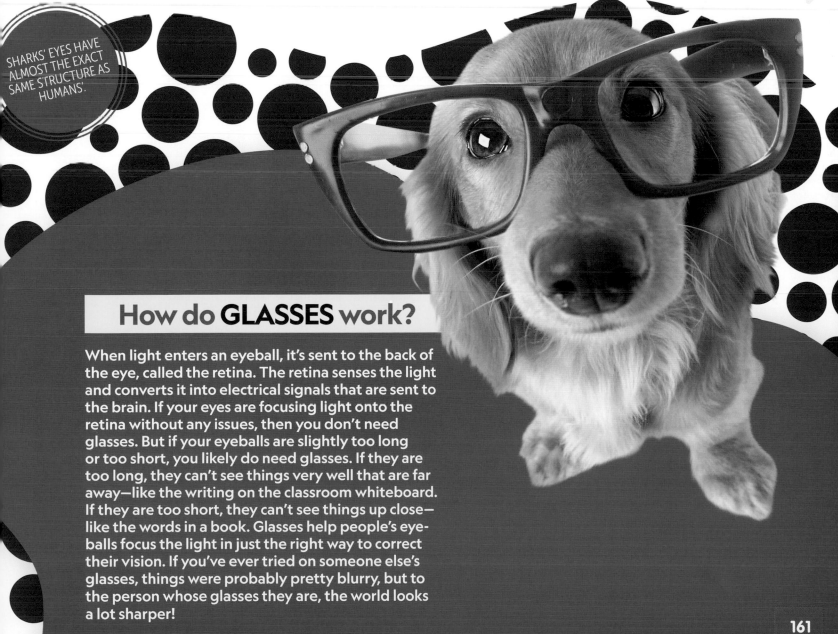

## How do GLASSES work?

When light enters an eyeball, it's sent to the back of the eye, called the retina. The retina senses the light and converts it into electrical signals that are sent to the brain. If your eyes are focusing light onto the retina without any issues, then you don't need glasses. But if your eyeballs are slightly too long or too short, you likely do need glasses. If they are too long, they can't see things very well that are far away—like the writing on the classroom whiteboard. If they are too short, they can't see things up close—like the words in a book. Glasses help people's eyeballs focus the light in just the right way to correct their vision. If you've ever tried on someone else's glasses, things were probably pretty blurry, but to the person whose glasses they are, the world looks a lot sharper!

# MYTHS BUSTED

# WOULD SNEEZING WITH MY EYES OPEN MAKE MY EYEBALLS FALL OUT?

If you've ever tried keeping your eyes open when you sneeze, you'll know it's not easy to do. This is because your eyes tend to automatically close when you let a sneeze rip. But why—is it because they would otherwise pop out of your head? (Spoiler alert: No, it isn't.)

## SNEEZING 101

Sneezing is a way for your body to protect itself. After all, your nose is very important—it's your body's main air passageway. The air you breathe contains the oxygen you need to live—and sometimes foreign objects that can irritate you or make you sick. This means your nose has the tough task of letting in the good stuff while keeping out the bad. One way your body does this is by relying on your nose hairs—and mucus. The tiny hairs inside your nose can trap germ particles, dust, or other irritants. The same goes for sticky snot. But these aren't your only defenses; your body also has an automatic response that can shoot out invading bits of pollen, dirt, or more—sneezing!

## AND THE EYES?

Scientists aren't completely sure why, but your eyes tend to automatically close when you sneeze. This might be to help your body focus on driving out the irritants, or else to stop irritants from getting into your eyes. But what would happen if you didn't shut them? Not much. A really, really unusually powerful sneeze can cause some pain, but it can't produce the kind of pressure behind your eyes to make them pop out. Plus, the same muscles that let you look all around, up and down, and side to side, keep your eyes snugly in your head. Still, experts say it's better to let your body do what it does naturally—and to focus instead on sneezing into a tissue and not on those around you.

## SINUS SECURITY

In addition to nose hairs and mucus, a person's nose is also home to many cells. Some of these cells help capture and analyze scents. Others respond to physical touch. And others respond to certain chemicals. These cells all send your brain messages, which help you understand what you are feeling or smelling. But sometimes, when these cells come across an irritant, they send a different message to the brain: There's something in your nose that's not supposed to be there.

When this happens, a person's cells alert the part of the brain that controls sneezing. The brain then sends messages of its own. These messages automatically make certain muscles move in what's known as an automatic response. First, your eyes close. Then, your tongue usually moves to the top of your mouth. Next, the muscles in your chest, throat, and around your lungs start squeezing. These squeezes put pressure on your lungs, causing air to suddenly and forcefully shoot out of your nose—hopefully, along with whatever was bothering it.

SOMETIMES PEOPLE SAY "GESUNDHEIT!" AFTER SOMEONE SNEEZES. THIS IS GERMAN FOR "HEALTH," AND LIKELY CAME TO THE U.S. WITH GERMAN IMMIGRANTS.

ANOTHER WORD FOR SNEEZING IS "STERNUTATION."

A SNEEZE CAN TRAVEL UP TO 100 MILES AN HOUR (161 KM/H).

# WHY DO
## SOME PEOPLE SAY
# "BLESS YOU"
# WHEN YOU
# SNEEZE?

In the United States, it's quite common to say "Bless you!" after someone sneezes. You may even have said it without really thinking about it—it's just considered polite. But why? The answer may have something to do with superstition. "Bless you" is short for "God bless you," which is often meant as a wish of good health. Historians think that people once considered sneezing to be dangerous or a sign of bad health. In the early Middle Ages in Europe, some people thought that sneezing was an early symptom of deadly plague (it's not!). In response to someone sneezing, it was kind to wish good health upon that person in case they were sick. Other people believed that sneezing could allow evil spirits to enter a person's body (again, not the case). However, saying "God bless you" could ward away these spirits. Today, while beliefs have changed, the saying remains.

# CHAPTER 7

# HOW WERE SPORTS INVENTED?

## QUESTIONS ABOUT
## ART, FOOD & CULTURE

**To be human is to ask questions.** And our culture—including where and how we live, what we eat, how we express ourselves, and how we play—is a big part of what makes us human. Why do people like different types of art and music? Why does music sometimes make us feel emotional? Why are there so many different languages? Why does every country in the world choose to have a flag? These are complicated questions, but then again, no one ever said humans were simple!

# What was the FIRST EMOJI?

**Whether you love them, or love to hate them, emojis are part of modern communication. And they might be older than you think!**

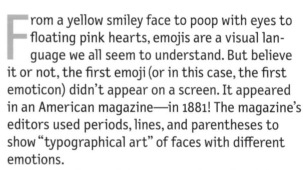

From a yellow smiley face to poop with eyes to floating pink hearts, emojis are a visual language we all seem to understand. But believe it or not, the first emoji (or in this case, the first emoticon) didn't appear on a screen. It appeared in an American magazine—in 1881! The magazine's editors used periods, lines, and parentheses to show "typographical art" of faces with different emotions.

A hundred years later, a computer scientist proposed using :-) in computer chat rooms so people knew if something was a joke, not something serious. Japanese emoticons took this to the next level, adding more characters to make more intricate expressions, like 「^_^」.

## EMOTICONS VS. EMOJIS

Emoticons are the ancestors of the emojis we know and love today. The difference is pretty simple: If you create an expression using a keyboard—like a sideways smiley face—it's an emoticon. If it's a little cartoon figure, it's an emoji.

## THE FIRST EMOJIS

In the mid-1990s, teenagers in Japan began to send emojis—like cartoonish hearts—to each other's pagers, which send or receive simple alerts and messages. But the types of emojis we're familiar with today were created in 1999 by a Japanese artist named Shigetaka Kurita. He created

176 emojis in just six colors: red, orange, lilac, grass green, royal blue, and black. The emojis were highly pixelated and included objects for the weather, like the sun; transportation, like a car; and of course, a red heart.

## THE EMOJI ALPHABET

In 2008, a nonprofit group called the Unicode Consortium, which works to maintain global software standards, created a uniform emoji alphabet. Not long after, words and phrases got shortened into emojis. Love became ♥ and "LOL" became a 🤣, and just as language changes over time, the emojis we use to express ourselves do, too. Emojis have become so accepted that 😂 became Oxford Dictionaries' "word" of the year in 2015.

Since the early days of emojis, designs have gotten a lot more sophisticated and specialized. There are now thousands, and new ones are being added as emoji language evolves.

## Who decides what EMOJIS get added?

The Unicode Consortium. Members meet to decide which new emojis to approve. In 2022, they added 31 to the emoji alphabet, including a pink heart, jellyfish, and melting smiley face. Anyone can submit a proposal for a new emoji, but you do need to explain why your emoji should be considered and what exactly it would look like. It takes several years for an emoji to go from consideration to appearing on your phone.

## SPEAKING OF FACES ...

In a forest in Oregon, U.S.A, a smiley face emoji is revealed every fall. How did it get there? More than a decade ago, the lumber company that owns the land planted deciduous larch trees among the evergreen Douglas firs. The larch trees' needles turn yellow and drop in the fall while the Douglas firs that surround them—and make up the eyes and mouth—stay green. From an aerial view, a smiley face 😄 looks out from the hillside.

## What are the MOST POPULAR emojis?

There are some category favorites and then there are overall most popular emojis. In the transportation category, the rocket ship 🚀 rules. In the body parts category (excluding hands), strength wins—the flexed bicep 💪 is most popular. The most common animal emoji is a butterfly 🦋. And a person doing a cartwheel 🤸 is the most popular person-sport emoji. The emoji can also be used to show happiness. The top overall emojis are less specific but say plenty without using words. In 2021, for example, the top emojis worldwide, from most popular to less popular, were:

# Why are there SO MANY LANGUAGES?

Many people on the planet speak or understand lots of languages—in fact, some people might know more than 50. But no human has ever come close to speaking every language on Earth.

THE FIRST KNOWN REFERENCE TO SIGN LANGUAGE WAS WRITTEN MORE THAN 2,000 YEARS AGO IN ANCIENT GREECE.

It's no wonder: There are more than 7,000 languages spoken around the world! This is because languages change along with the people who use them, especially when people move to different places or communities separate. Over time, people rely on different words and invent new ones, as well as new slang and new phrases. Slowly, the way one community speaks becomes different enough that it is considered a totally unique language.

## HUMBLE BEGINNINGS

Scientists aren't sure what the first language was—or even when language first happened. Many think that spoken language may have been developed relatively recently—within the past 300,000 years or so—as earlier human relatives may not have had the right vocal structures to form words like we do. However, vocal communication likely existed long, long before spoken language. After all, most animals communicate using some form of vocal sound.

Like animals, early humans may have used noises, grunts, and cries to interact, along with body gestures and movements (see p. 68). Over many years, they may have begun to form words and, eventually, grammar—the rules that define a language. Some historians think this may have happened in one location and then spread around the world as humans migrated. Others believe that different people in different places likely created languages independently.

## FORGOTTEN WORDS

Every language around the world changes over time. Check out these words that were once widely used in the English language that now may make you giggle.

>> **Groak:** To watch someone eating and desire their food

>> **Jargogle:** To confuse or trick someone

>> **Slubberdegullion:** A person who slobbers or drools

>> **Gorgonize:** To mesmerize or charm someone

>> **Houppelande:** A cloak

## ALWAYS EVOLVING

Human language is a tool people use to communicate and to explain the world around them. Because of this, language changes right along with people and their experiences.

Languages tend to change when people from different cultures meet and trade. When this happens, humans tend to borrow words from each other. Some changes are quick; for example, think of the words people used to think were cool and compare those to the slang of today. Other changes, like changes to grammar, happen over longer periods of time. Languages also change when people move away from each other. Over time, separate groups develop different speaking habits. And these habits can become entirely new languages.

Humans also like—and sometimes even need—to invent new words and meanings to describe things they haven't seen before. This especially happens when we invent things. For example, the bicycle didn't exist until the 19th century ... and neither did the word "bicycle"! Other times, people create new phrases that catch on and become popular. And in the same vein, some words and sayings can fall out of favor and stop being used. For example, you probably don't use the word "groovy" very much—but people in the 1960s did!

TODAY, PEOPLE OFTEN REFER TO CELL PHONES JUST AS THEIR PHONES. BUT A FEW DECADES AGO, THEY WERE KNOWN AS CELLULAR PHONES OR MOBILE PHONES.

## Why do languages DISAPPEAR?

A language that is no longer spoken is referred to as a "dead" language. This can happen when one language morphs into another—or into several others. For example, the ancient Roman empire, which united many lands, had an official language, Latin. However, after the empire fell, its people were no longer united. Over time, the way Latin was spoken in certain places changed from the way it was spoken in others. Now, instead of Latin, many people who live where the former Roman empire was speak Spanish, Italian, or many other languages—and very few people speak Latin itself. Other times, languages can disappear when large populations are killed, whether through conflict or disease. And sometimes, younger generations stop learning the language or languages of their ancestors. This can happen because of colonialism, or because younger generations choose to speak a language more common around the world.

# Will people someday LIVE in UNDERWATER CITIES?

The answer may surprise you: It's not impossible!

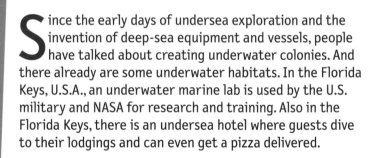

S ince the early days of undersea exploration and the invention of deep-sea equipment and vessels, people have talked about creating underwater colonies. And there already are some underwater habitats. In the Florida Keys, U.S.A., an underwater marine lab is used by the U.S. military and NASA for research and training. Also in the Florida Keys, there is an undersea hotel where guests dive to their lodgings and can even get a pizza delivered.

## HOW TO LIVE UNDERWATER

Even though creating an underwater city is much more complicated than creating a single structure, architects and planners are considering how it could be done. Big concerns include planning for emergency evacuation systems and controlling air supply, temperature, and humidity. As far as air supply goes, fresh air would be collected at the surface and pushed into the habitat in tubes. Habitats might also have plants growing in them to generate fresh oxygen.

Food—including fish and plankton—would be all around underwater, and canned or preserved food brought from land could be stored inside the city. A special desalinization machine—which removes the salt from seawater—could be used to make the ocean water safe to drink.

And then there's the pressure. At sea level, air presses down on our bodies at 14.7 pounds per square inch (1.03 kg per sq cm). But as you dive into the ocean you feel more pressure the deeper you go. At the deepest point in the ocean, the Mariana Trench, the pressure is more than 16,000 pounds per square inch (1,125 kg per sq cm)—that's the weight of 50 jumbo jets

NASA USES UNDERWATER HABITATS TO TRAIN ASTRONAUTS FOR LIFE IN SPACE. MOVING AROUND IN THE WATER WITH SCUBA GEAR IS SIMILAR TO THE WEIGHTLESSNESS OF BEING IN OUTER SPACE.

pressing down on you! Habitats likely wouldn't be built deeper than 1,000 feet (305 m) because of the pressure. And don't forget light: It gets dark quickly underwater. Keeping the underwater habitat well-lit would be a must.

Building an underwater city wouldn't be cheap or simple. But then again, neither is space exploration, and the ocean is right here on planet Earth.

## WET-TROPOLIS

Taking all of these factors into consideration. architects in Japan want to build underwater cities they've dubbed "Ocean Spirals." The first Ocean Spiral would sit off the coast of Tokyo. For energy, turbines stationed on the ocean floor would collect power from the ocean's waves, tides, and currents, and send it up to a sphere-shaped underwater community housing 5,000 people. The community would include homes, business, and hotels—and a big price tag. It's estimated it would cost $26 billion to build and about five years to construct.

## What about ATLANTIS?

The Greek philosopher Plato wrote about Atlantis more than 2,000 years ago, and people are still talking about it. This utopian land was supposedly founded by people who were half human and half god. It was full of wealth and exotic animals, but, according to Plato's writing, the people became greedy, and the gods punished them by sending fire and earthquakes that caused the city to sink to the bottom of the sea. It has inspired modern-day fiction, including comic books and movies, and adventurers are still trying to find it.

# WEIRD UNDERWATER STRUCTURES

Humans might not quite be ready to live permanently underwater, but we've been putting things on the seafloor for a long time.

>> Sea sculptures: Off the coast of Cancún, Mexico, there is an underwater museum located in the Manchones Reef. Underwater sculptor Jason deCaires Taylor created an exhibit of 400 sculptures, many of people. The museum can be reached by divers and snorkelers and draws 750,000 people per year.

>> Underwater post office: Just off the coast of Vanuatu, an island nation in the South Pacific, snorkelers and divers can mail waterproof postcards from a post office located 10 feet (3 m) underwater.

>> Lucky kiss: A sunken statue near a scuba shop in Grand Cayman, one of the Cayman Islands, has been named the Guardian of the Reef. If you kiss it, the scuba shop owner says, it will bring you good luck.

# WHY do countries have FLAGS?

A piece of cloth with symbols and patterns on it can carry a lot of meaning.

UNLIKE THOSE OF OTHER COUNTRIES, THE FLAGS OF SWITZERLAND AND VATICAN CITY ARE SQUARE.

Flags were originally used in warfare as a way of showing leadership and to indicate whether a group was a friend or foe when entering a new area. Varying in design and purpose, flags have been used by countries for thousands of years.

## ANCIENT HISTORY

The first people to use flags were likely the Chinese. More than 2,000 years ago, the founder of the Zhou dynasty had a white flag carried in front of him. Flags were also flown on chariots in battle and displayed on walls of cities after they had been captured. In India, flags were historically flown on chariots and carried on elephants. In Europe, national flags became popular in the Middle Ages. A leader would often use the flag of their patron saint, or heavenly protector, to represent their country. For instance, in the 13th century, the Cross of St. George was included on England's national flag, and it is still on this flag today!

## FLYING COLORS

Today, countries use flag colors to communicate their national values. While a white flag is universally seen as a symbol of truce, researchers in Denmark who studied the flags of countries around the world found that other colors don't share the same meaning across cultures. First, they discovered that blue and red are very common colors incorporated into national flags. All countries but 10 have blue or red in their flags. Those countries are Jamaica, Ireland, Mauritania,

Ivory Coast, Niger, Nigeria, Cyprus, Saudi Arabia, Bhutan, and Pakistan.

But even though many countries have color crossover, the colors don't always hold the same meaning. Yellow might symbolize mineral wealth in one country and generosity in another. The most common meaning for red in a flag is blood. Blue often refers to the sea, but it also represents justice and truth in some countries. Green is often tied to nature and the land. And while white does mean truce, in national flags it can also mean peace, purity, and harmony.

## IT'S SYMBOLIC

Besides color, one of the most noticeable parts of a national flag is its symbols. A third of the world's 195 countries have a religious symbol on their flag—from a cross representing Christianity to an Islamic star and crescent. The Cambodian flag shows Angkor Wat, a temple located in the country that is associated with both Hinduism and Buddhism. And the blue chakra at the center of India's flag has symbolic meaning for both Hindus and Buddhists. Israel's flag includes the Jewish Star of David, and its white-and-blue-striped background represents a traditional Jewish prayer shawl. Japan's flag includes a rising sun, which represents spiritual roots to Shintoism, and Uruguay and Argentina's national flags include golden suns, symbols of the Inca sun god, Inti.

NICARAGUA'S AND DOMINICA'S FLAGS FEATURE A COLOR RARELY SEEN ON NATIONAL FLAGS: PURPLE.

## SPEAKING OF SYMBOLISM ...

Of all the 195 present-day national flags, only one doesn't have four sides. Nepal's flag is two triangular-shaped pennants of different sizes, and they have very specific meanings. The triangles represent the Himalaya, which are in the northernmost region of Nepal. They also represent the country's two major religions: Hinduism and Buddhism.

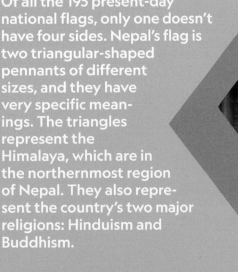

# Are elite athletes BORN with NATURAL TALENT?

## Yes ... and no.

If a girl was born with athletic genes—say both her parents were Olympic track stars—it's reasonable to assume she inherited some physical traits that would put her on the path toward being a top track athlete herself. But being a top track athlete takes more than having long legs or the right build. Her parents put in countless hours of practice and training. Perhaps they developed exceptional mental strength, which helped them gain a competitive edge and overcome adversity, like losses and injuries. They might have found the right teammates who encouraged them, and coaches who knew when it was time for a rest or to have an injury looked at by a doctor. And does the girl even want to run in her parents' footsteps? Just because she inherited some genes that might give her an advantage in track, doesn't mean it's her thing.

Researchers think that athletic performance is influenced by both genetic and environmental factors. We're all born with our own individual DNA structure that makes up our body type. Michael Phelps, who has won 23 Olympic gold medals, has a long torso, large hands, and big feet. His torso has been compared to the long hull of a canoe, which helps him glide through water, and his hands and feet are like paddles. These certainly gave him an advantage. But they didn't automatically make him an Olympian. He only went into swimming because his two older sisters joined a swim team, and even though he was nervous in the water, he decided to give it a try. He happened to be in the right environment for things to fall into place. And then he started training, found the right coach, and developed his skill.

## Is it ever too late to discover your **NATURAL TALENT?**

It's true that a lot of elite athletes started their craft when they were young, but there are plenty of stories of people finding their sport later in life and excelling. Take two high jumpers: Stefan Holm, 2004 Olympic gold medalist, started training at age six to stand on the podium at the age of 28. Then, at the 2007 World Championships, he got silver. The person who got gold at those championships, Donald Thomas, had been high-jumping for only eight months! He was previously a college basketball player with good jumping skills, and a friend challenged him to try the high jump. Moral of the story: It is possible to rise up through the ranks quickly if you (or a friend!) discover your talent.

## Do you have to be **TALL** to play in the NBA and WNBA?

You don't have to be, but most professional basketball players are taller than the average person. An average American man is five feet nine and a half inches (1.8 m) tall, compared to the average NBA player, who is around six feet seven inches (2 m). The same holds true for women. The average American woman is around five feet four inches (1.6 m), while the average WNBA player is almost six feet (1.8 m) tall. The hoop has always stood at 10 feet (3 m) for men and women, but as players get taller—the average NBA player in 1947 was six feet two inches (1.9 m)—the height hasn't been adjusted. According to former WNBA coach Michael Cooper, height doesn't matter. He once said that having talent and knowledge of the game are what's important, and if you have those, height requirements are less relevant. WNBA guard Shannon Bobbitt is five feet two inches (1.5 m), and the shortest player in NBA history, Muggsy Bogues, was just an inch (2.5 cm) taller and was known for his passing and stealing.

# WHERE DID PAINT COME FROM?

Today, people usually buy paint online or from stores. But paint itself is much, much older and was around long before there were even stores at all. Historians think that the first paints were created at least 100,000 years ago. Back then, people made paint from the colors they found in the world around them. These natural colors, known as pigments, could be collected from many different substances. Black pigments were often found in charcoal; yellows and oranges were taken from clays and soils; and whites were made by grinding up certain rocks and minerals. Then these pigments may have been mixed with spit or animal fat to form a fluid paint.

## What did prehistoric humans paint?

Over the millennia, humans have used paint to decorate important and sacred places, their homes, clothing, and even themselves. Some of the oldest surviving paintings were made some 45,000 years ago, in what is now Indonesia. There, people painted large images of boars and other wild animals. Around the world, people used different methods to create these masterpieces. Sometimes, they used their hands to paint. Other times, they may have used early versions of paintbrushes made from moss or hair. And on some occasions, they sprayed paint by blowing it through hollow bones or reeds. One stunning example of this can be found in Argentina, where some 9,000 to 13,000 years ago, artists covered the walls of a cave in sprayed tracings of their hands.

## How has paint changed?

As people continued to paint, they developed new methods for creating art. In ancient Egypt, Rome, and Greece, painters began covering walls in a coating known as plaster. Then, they would paint directly on the plaster, creating what are known as frescoes. The plaster gave the artist a smooth surface to paint on and helped keep a fresco looking fresh—sometimes, for thousands of years!

With these new art styles came a desire for new paint colors. One special paint, a shade known as lapis blue, came from grinding up a precious and rare gem called lapis lazuli. The gem was so valuable that it was worth more than gold! And it wasn't the only unusual paint ingredient. A shade called Indian yellow was made from the urine of cows that had only eaten mango leaves. Another shade, a red known as carmine, was created by crushing up a type of insect known as the cochineal bug. The main ingredient in the first purple dye? Sea snails.

Today, most paints are created in laboratories and factories. However, that hasn't stopped scientists from searching for ways to make new colors. Recently, a paint color made headlines when its creators claimed that it was the blackest paint to ever exist. Who knows what colors will appear next?

## ONE MORE THING: WHY DID CAVE PAINTERS TRACE THEIR HANDS?

Historians aren't completely sure why early artists traced their hands onto cave art, but they have some theories. This practice may have been a way for artists to sign their art, like many painters do today. Or, it may have been a way for ancient humans to communicate with one another. In fact, some historians think that these depictions of hands may have been an early form of sign language. To communicate different meanings, artists may have folded down different fingers before tracing their hands.

# Why do different people have DIFFERENT LIKES AND DISLIKES?

From music to food to art and more, people tend to like and dislike many different things. This can be a great thing—it adds variety to the world, after all! But *why* is it a thing?

SOME PEOPLE HAVE A GENE THAT MAKES CILANTRO TASTE LIKE SOAP.

CATS CAN'T TASTE SWEET THINGS.

The truth is, many humans may be born liking different things—because it's in their genes! Genes are the traits and characteristics passed on to you by your biological parents. Scientists believe that some things, such as food preferences, are at least partly controlled by our genetics. For example, scientists have discovered differences in genes that can turn some people into "super tasters." These people develop taste buds—tiny organs found on a person's tongue that help them taste things—that are much more sensitive than other people's. That means that certain things might taste different to them, or that they taste certain flavors more strongly. For example, to some people, celery tastes super bitter!

## ANCIENT TASTES

Even though humans have different tastes in lots of things, there are also many things that the majority of people enjoy. For example, many people like both salty and sweet things. And many people also like soft things, like soft, cozy blankets.

As it turns out, some of your preferences may come from your human ancestors. Scientists think this is what causes our natural love for sugary or salty snacks. Sugar and salt are both

Maybe you used to hate spinach, but now you can't get enough of that good stuff. Or maybe you used to be obsessed with sweet things, but have recently begun to prefer salty snacks. Either way, it's totally normal for your tastes to change. As you age, your body itself continues to change. As kids, humans tend to have very sensitive taste buds. This can make some bitter foods taste a bit too strong. Kids also need lots of energy to grow. This can lead them to develop a sweet tooth, as sugar provides tons of energy! However, as humans age, their taste buds become less sensitive. This means that they may start enjoying foods that they previously weren't fans of.

And it's not just your taste buds: Your mind changes as you grow, too. As people are introduced to new and different foods, they can become accustomed to things they once thought were "odd" or "gross"—and even start to like them. This even goes for things that aren't food related, like styles of music, reading subjects, and more. The more you experience, the more you may find new things to enjoy!

important for humans to survive. In prehistoric times, however, neither would have been very easy to get—at least, certainly not as easy as visiting the corner store. Experts think that cravings for salt and sugar could have been good for human health, because they would have caused humans to search out foods that contained these ingredients. Similarly, both humans and other animals may enjoy cuddling with soft things because it helped them develop. For example, an animal cuddling with its mother or siblings would likely have been somewhat safe and secure—and warm! Today, our brains continue to send us messages of safety and security when we cozy up to a nice soft blanket.

## TASTEMAKERS

Does this mean you are automatically born liking or disliking everything? Definitely not. While your ancestors and your genes influence some of your tastes, a lot of your preferences also come from where—and how—you were raised.

Have you ever noticed that things that seem "normal" in one country can seem unusual in another? This is because over time communities around the world developed different customs and habits. A lot of the foods you were introduced to as a child will be ones that you like, while new ones you come across later on may take more time to get used to (although you might also enjoy those right away!). Studies have also shown that young children who are given a lot of new foods tend to be less picky as they grow—probably because they are exposed early on to different flavors and textures.

The same thing is often true of many other kinds of preferences, from movies to music to clothing. However, at the end of the day, your preferences are up to you!

# How were SPORTS INVENTED?

Sports have existed for a very long time—in fact, they've been around for at least 15,000 years ... and probably a lot longer.

HOPSCOTCH STARTED AS A TRAINING EXERCISE FOR ANCIENT ROMAN SOLDIERS.

PROGRAMMERS HAVE USED AI TO CREATE A BRAND-NEW SPORT.

While historians can't be sure what the first sport was, they think that it was likely something that required no equipment, such as wrestling or running. Archaeologists have even discovered ancient paintings, created some 15,300 years ago in France, that show people doing both these things.

## GAMES WITH A GOAL

Experts think that some of these sports, such as running, may have gotten their start in hunting. Others, however, like wrestling, may have started as training exercises for warriors and soldiers. As people trained and formed armies around the world, these kinds of exercises became more popular. In fact, soccer began in ancient China for this very reason: Soldiers practiced a training drill called *cuju*,

meaning "to kick the ball." This exercise was meant to help them stay healthy and fast. Over time though, it morphed into the modern-day game of soccer.

## CEREMONIAL SPORTS

Other sports began as important rituals or ceremonies. In Central and South America, several cultures played a version of a game that's now called the Mesoamerican ball game. The game, which involved players attempting to shoot rubber balls through hoops without using their hands, had religious importance. And while the game of lacrosse may have had its origins as a training session for young warriors of several Indigenous nations across northern North America, it was also likely played during religious ceremonies.

Of course, many sports were simply played for entertainment or for fun. In ancient Mesopotamia, in what is now Iraq, participants used their bare hands to box with each other in front of audiences while musicians played. In ancient Egypt, contestants sometimes jousted in the Nile River by balancing on boats and trying to knock each other off with long poles while spectators cheered.

## CHANGING THE GAME

Over many years, sports can change into new, slightly different versions of themselves as people add or change rules. For example, baseball and softball are similar games played with slightly different rules and equipment.

Sports also tend to change and appear along with new inventions or discoveries. Some equipment-based sports, such as skiing and surfing, have been around for many thousands of years. Others have changed over time. Sledding, for example, has existed for thousands of years in snowy places across the globe. However, it wasn't until streamlined sleds called luges were built in the 1800s that luge racing became a sport. And other sports, like car racing or air stunts, didn't exist until the 20th century—thanks to the relatively recent inventions of the automobile and the airplane.

## Are NEW SPORTS still being invented?

Absolutely! Some of the most popular sports today are actually pretty recent inventions. Basketball was created in 1891 in Massachusetts, U.S.A., when a college athletic director wanted to find a way to keep his students active indoors during cold weather. Experts think that football was created shortly before that, when two college sports teams decided to play a game combining soccer and rugby. Even today, people love to create new games and sports. One such game is underwater hockey—or octopush. Started as a training exercise for divers, the game is now recognized by the Olympics.

STRANGE SPORTS

All sports can be a bit strange if you really think about it—but they sure are fun! Take a look at some of the more unique sports played around the world.

>> Bog snorkeling: In this sport, invented in Wales in the 1970s, players must snorkel their way through the dank, murky waters of a bog as quickly as possible.

>> Cheese rolling: Believe it or not, people in England have been partaking in this sport since the 15th century. The goal? To chase a wheel of cheese to the bottom of a steep hill.

>> Toe wrestling: Also found in England, this competition revives a classic with a new twist: Competitors wrestle each other ... using only their toes.

>> Cow chip tossing: Based in the United States, the object of this game is for contestants to fling cow "chips" as far as they can. What's a cow chip, you ask? A patty of dried cow poop!

## ONE MORE THING: WHAT COUNTS AS A "SPORT," ANYWAY?

That's a great question, and not everyone agrees on an answer. The consensus around the globe (and in most dictionaries) is that a sport is a competitive activity involving physical skill. However, exactly what this means is open to interpretation. For example, do you think of bowling as a sport? What about e-sports, or electronic sports played online by gamers? Many people claim these are not real sports, but others believe they are. For this reason, many official sports organizations, such as the Olympics, have committees to help determine which activities qualify as sports. Outside of that, though—it's up to you.

# Who CREATED WRITING?

Writing has been around for thousands of years—maybe even tens of thousands of years—but it looked a lot different from how it looks now.

THE KHMER LANGUAGE FROM CAMBODIA HAS THE LONGEST ALPHABET IN THE WORLD, WITH 74 LETTERS.

The very first kinds of writing did not use an alphabet. Instead, people developed writing using something called pictograms, or pictographic writing. An alphabet uses symbols to represent individual sounds. A pictogram, on the other hand, used symbols to represent whole words or ideas.

Some of the oldest pictograms we know of were invented in two separate places around the same time: ancient Egypt and Mesopotamia (modern-day Iraq). People in Mesopotamia began recording things some 5,000 years ago, using a system of symbols we call cuneiform. While writing itself would change human history, the first things written down weren't all that exciting—they were often storage records. About the same time in ancient Egypt, another writing system, known as hieroglyphics, appeared. Like cuneiform, hieroglyphs could be read as symbols for objects and things. However, they could also sometimes be read as symbols for sounds, like an alphabet.

THE PHOENICIAN ALPHABET HAD 22 LETTERS.

Character-based writing began to appear in other parts of the world as well. In China, a system of writing that used characters to represent objects, items, and sounds began to develop by 3,000 years ago. Around the same time, pictographic writing systems also began to appear in Central and South America. By 2,000 years ago, the Maya had developed their system into a series of glyphs, or picture-based characters.

## Who **CREATED** the alphabet?

Just like there is no "one" language, there is no "one" alphabet—there are many. In some places around the ancient world, people began to record things in different ways. Around 3,000 years ago, people living in Phoenicia—parts of modern-day Lebanon and Israel—began using some hieroglyphic symbols in a new way. Instead of representing ideas and things, they modified the hieroglyphs into simple symbols that represented sounds. Put together, these sounds would form words.

Experts believe that most of the alphabets in the world come from the Phoenician alphabet. Over time, however, that alphabet changed in different places. Some people added different symbols—now known as letters—and others got rid of some. The way the letters looked also changed. Today, many alphabets look and sound completely different from one another, even though they may have started in the same place.

## Who **DECIDES** if a word goes in the dictionary?

Dictionaries have existed for thousands of years. However, until somewhat recently, these were often just an individual person's or record keeper's collection of words. In fact, for much of written history, people spelled many of the same words—and even names!—with lots of variety. There was no one "correct" way of spelling. This could be very frustrating for people trying to read. Around the 12th century in Europe, some people began trying to fix this by making larger and more complete dictionaries. However, it wasn't until the 18th century that dictionaries started to really catch on and become "official."

Today, there are several well-established societies and organizations that keep dictionaries of various languages. However, languages are always changing (see p. 168)—and as a result, so are dictionaries. The editors of a dictionary make it their job to pay close attention to words that become commonly used. If it seems enough people are using a word for a long enough period, they add it to the dictionary. And while it may seem like the editors are making the call, it's actually the people who use the language. Some recent examples? Photobomb, selfie, and smartphone.

## ROUNDUP — UNWRITTEN LANGUAGES

Not every language has a written version. Over time, people have developed other ways to communicate their ideas or to keep records without a written language.

» Quipu: Some ancient Andean cultures in South America, including the Inca, used a recordkeeping system known as quipu. This method used portable quipu, a collection of strings and knots, to communicate dates, numbers, ideas, and more. Many people still use quipu today.

» Wampum: For centuries, Haudenosaunee people in North America have used wampum belts to record events and stories. These belts are expertly crafted using wampum beads made from shells.

» Oral tradition: Used by many peoples around the world for thousands of years, oral tradition is the practice of passing information from person to person—and generation to generation—by speaking. Speakers often rely on rhyme, tales, chants, or songs to recall and communicate long stories.

to be best
point of view
**Selfie** [sɛlfiː] n
self-portrait p
hand-held di

# Why does MUSIC make me FEEL EMOTIONAL?

Have you ever listened to a sad song and felt like crying? Or maybe you've listened to music that made you feel so happy you just had to get up and dance!

Music can influence us to feel a wide range of emotions—or even help us focus on tasks or help us recall certain memories. To understand how music influences humans, we need to take a closer look at one special part of the human body. No, it's not our ears—it's our brain!

For human beings, the brain is one of the most important organs. Your brain helps you move, breathe, think, remember, feel, and much, much more. The human brain is made up of billions of special cells known as neurons. These neurons help control your entire body by sending and receiving messages. When your neurons receive information from the rest of your body—for example, the things you are seeing, feeling, or hearing, they can then interpret these signals to understand what is happening in your body. The neurons also send signals back out to instruct your body what to do—whether that's squeezing a ball, writing a word, or digesting your food.

Scientists have divided the human brain into three major parts: the cerebrum, cerebellum, and brain stem. These areas help control different functions. What do these regions have to do with music, you ask? As it turns out, music can cause a reaction in certain parts of your brain. When you are listening to music, cells in your ears are sending information to the neurons in your brain. In particular, they tend to send a lot of information to a region in your brain known as the limbic system. This is an area located under your cerebrum that helps control how you are feeling. If that all sounds complicated, think of it this way: Music can activate the regions of your brain that influence your emotions!

## How else does music AFFECT ME?

Thanks to the way it influences your brain, music can move you emotionally. And it can also make you want to move—physically! Scientists have discovered that music activates more parts of the brain than just those that are responsible for emotions. It also influences parts of the brain that trigger happiness as well. Some of these "happiness areas" are connected to parts of the brain that help control movement. This might link our feelings of happiness to wanting to move around—especially when those areas are "lit up" by music. On top of that, music also directly stimulates a different part of our brain that relates to movement and coordination.

But music does much more than this. In fact, scientists aren't totally sure just how much music affects the human body. Studies have shown that listening to music can help people—and even animals—feel calmer and more relaxed. In some studies, people listening to music were even able to study and learn new information more easily. And in other studies, listening to music helped activate people's memories to recall certain events.

MUSIC CAN INFLUENCE HOW MUCH MILK A COW MAKES.

LIKE HUMANS, SOME PARROTS DANCE ALONG TO MUSIC.

## Why do I like some sounds BEST?

Scientists have studied many ways music affects the human brain. But the truth is, some parts of music and sound remain a mystery. Experts think that many of the reasons you prefer certain songs to others may be the same as why you have favorite foods (see p. 178). Some of it may have to do with your genetics. Other reasons likely include what music you grew up listening to and what you find familiar. But scientists have no idea why certain sounds sound "good" to humans, and certain sounds sound, well, bad! For example, which would you rather hear first thing in the morning: a bird singing or a dog barking? Most people would prefer birdsong to barking, simply because it just sounds nicer. But as to *why* people think it sounds nicer, scientists have yet to figure that out.

# FOOD FAQs

**D**id you know that an average American spends about 70 minutes a day eating and drinking? And that doesn't include shopping for food, preparing it, and cleaning up after a meal is done. Food is a big part of our day!

## WHY DO ONIONS MAKE ME CRY?

Don't be sad—you did nothing wrong to cause those tears! When you slice into an onion, you kick-start a whole scientific process. The onion releases a chemical irritant the moment you start chopping. This chemical goes into the air, causing glands in your eyes to release tears. (It's our body's way of protecting our eyes from irritants.) Is there anything you can do to avoid crying your way through a recipe? Yes! There are a couple things that might help: Some onion varieties like sweet onions tend to burn people's eyes less. Freezing or refrigerating onions can also help slow that chemical reaction. And if you can keep them from fogging up, some people find wearing goggles helps!

## ARE TOMATOES FRUITS OR VEGETABLES?

If you use tomatoes to make spaghetti sauce and BLTs, how can they be fruits? Get ready to rethink everything you know about fruits and veggies. Any produce with a seed or seeds inside—like tomatoes, cucumbers, peppers, and pumpkins—are fruits! Another way to define a fruit is whether it grows from a flower on a vine. A vegetable is any edible part of a plant that isn't a fruit, including the roots and leaves—like lettuce, asparagus, and broccoli.

## CAN EATING TOO MANY CARROTS MAKE ME TURN ORANGE?

Yes—but it would take a lot of carrots to turn your skin orangish. Here's what's going on: Carrots and other orange-colored fruits and veggies, like squash, sweet potatoes, mangoes, oranges, and apricots, are rich in beta-carotene. Beta-carotene is a pigment that causes some fruits and vegetables to turn orange, and when humans eat it, the pigment is converted into vitamin A by cells in our small intestines. But when we eat too much, not all the vitamin A gets converted and instead it circulates in our bloodstream. This is when skin can take on an orangish color, especially on the palms of the hands, soles of the feet, and the tip of the nose. Remember: It's best to eat all the colors of the rainbow, not just one, to get the best nutritional benefits.

## WHY DO APPLES TURN BROWN AFTER I CUT THEM?

When you slice up apples, you are actually doing a science experiment. The moment a knife cuts into an apple, the inside of the apple is exposed to oxygen, triggering a chemical reaction called enzymatic browning. Different apple varieties contain different amounts of enzymes and antioxidants, so the browning can't be compared, er, apples to apples. Red Delicious and McIntosh apples turn brown quickly, while Granny Smiths take longer to turn brown after they're sliced.

## WHAT'S THE DIFFERENCE BETWEEN JAM AND JELLY?

Jam and jelly are used pretty interchangeably in conversation: "Do you have jam on your hands?" "Yeah, I had a peanut butter and jelly sandwich at lunch." The gist is, you have had a sticky, fruity spread with your peanut butter. But are jam and jelly the same thing? No, but they are very similar. The difference is in the fruit. Jelly is made by crushing up fruit and tossing out all the chunky extra bits. This leaves fruit juice, which is mixed with pectin and heated to make a nice clear jelly that is very easy to spread. Jam, on the other hand, while also made from crushed fruit, includes the fruit solids—and seeds. It's chunkier and has more texture. (In the end, though, jelly and jam are equally sticky.)

## WHY DOES CILANTRO TASTE LIKE SOAP TO SOME PEOPLE?

Do you take your tacos with cilantro, or do you refuse one topped with the herb? The answer depends on your genetics. Some people find cilantro, which is the name used for the stems and leaves of a coriander plant, to be delicious. To others, it tastes like a mouthful of soap! These people have a smell-receptor gene that lets them perceive the soapy-flavored compounds in the cilantro. Perhaps not surprisingly, in regions where cilantro is popular, like Central America and India, fewer people have the gene that allows them to taste the soapiness.

## WHY DOES MY PEE SMELL FUNNY AFTER I EAT ASPARAGUS?

Have you ever had asparagus for dinner, and then, the next time you peed, thought to yourself, Well, that smells weird. This is the result of a special acid found only in asparagus that comes back to remind you that you ate it. When you eat asparagus, asparagusic acid breaks down into sulfur by-products. If you pee around 15 minutes after you eat asparagus, the sulfur by-products will evaporate and you can smell that unique odor. The catch here is that, while it can cause a funky smell, not everyone will smell it. There is a specific genetic modification in people who can't smell sulfur by-products. For the people who can smell it, the fragrance is notable in your pee for up to 14 hours after munching on the vegetable.

## MYTHS BUSTED

# COULD A WATERMELON REALLY GROW IN MY STOMACH?

If you've ever swallowed a watermelon seed, don't worry—it's not going to sprout in your stomach! Seeds are hardy, but they're still not strong enough to survive your digestive system. In fact, your body starts to digest that seed before you've even swallowed it. Saliva, or spit, contains substances called enzymes. These enzymes start breaking down, or digesting, food as soon as it enters your mouth.

But let's say the seed slipped past your pearly whites unscathed—what then? After that, you would swallow. Your tongue would help do this by pushing the seed and any other bits of watermelon to the back of your throat, where it would enter a pipe called the esophagus. Muscles in your esophagus would then squeeze the food down toward your stomach, completing the swallow.

Now, even if the seed had reached your stomach whole, its journey would end there. In your tummy, stomach muscles and a strong substance called gastric acid would dissolve the seed into liquid mush. Goodbye, seed! The mush would then enter your small intestine. Your organs would now create special juices to help your body absorb nutrients from the mush. From there, any leftover waste would move on to your large intestine. And now, for the (former) seed's last stop: It would move on to your colon and eventually come out as poop.

# MORE FOOD MYTHS, BUSTED!

Over time, there have been a lot of interesting beliefs about food—many of which aren't true. Read on to discover some of these food myths.

**APPLE SEEDS ARE POISONOUS:** This myth comes from some true science, but don't worry— eating a few apple seeds accidentally won't hurt you. There are tiny substances called cyanogenic glycosides in apple seeds and some other fruit seeds. In your stomach, these can turn into a poisonous chemical known as cyanide. However, the traces of this chemical are so super tiny that it does absolutely no harm, and just moves through your digestive system. How many crushed apple seeds would it take to be dangerous? At least 150, and maybe even thousands!

**TOMATOES ARE POISONOUS:** You've probably never heard anyone say this, but for centuries, people across parts of Europe believed that tomatoes were deadly. The fruit, which is originally from the Americas, was introduced to Europe in the early 1500s. At the time, wealthy people ate on fancy lead plates, and we now know that lead can be dangerous to humans. Normally, the plates were fine to eat from because the lead was contained inside them. But when acidic tomatoes were placed on top, the lead leached out, making people very sick. And, without understanding what was going on, they blamed the tomatoes.

**ORANGE JUICE CAN CURE A COLD:** Because orange juice has lots of vitamin C, some people think it can zap away colds, pronto. This is just a myth, unfortunately. Once a cold has taken hold, vitamin C isn't much help. However, studies do show that getting enough vitamin C before a cold sets in can make it shorter and more mild.

BUSTED!

BUSTED!

BUSTED!

189

# CHAPTER 8

# IS AREA 51 REAL?

## QUESTIONS ABOUT ALL THINGS WEIRD AND WILD

It's time to get to the really weird, really wacky questions you've always wanted to know the answers to but were afraid to ask. Questions like, Do zombies exist? Are mermaids real? What really happened at Area 51? Find out what scientists have to say about spirit encounters. Then hear from an expert who has taught brain cells to play video games. Let's go get some answers!

# Do ZOMBIES EXIST?

**Humans don't need to fear a zombie apocalypse. But we've got bad news for some other animals ...**

The answer to whether zombies exist depends on what kind of zombie you're talking about. A mindless former human raised from the dead? Nope—those only exist in fiction. But real zombies do exist in the wild—even if they don't go around moaning about brains!

In nature, some organisms have the ability to take over the minds of others and force them to do certain actions. One such organism is a type of fungus known as *Ophiocordyceps unilateralis,* or cordyceps. To reproduce, cordyceps sends out small cells known as spores. For humans, these spores are harmless. But, wanderings ants—watch out! After a cordyceps spore comes into contact with an ant, it infects the ant's body. At first, the ant may appear unaffected. But deep inside, cordyceps is growing around the ant's muscles. Within a few days, the fungus takes control of the ant's movements. It forces the ant to climb to a high place on a nearby plant, staking out a place and staying there—until it dies. Once the ant is dead, the cordyceps sprouts from the ant's body, before sending out spores to start the cycle all over again.

CORDYCEPS AREN'T HARMFUL TO HUMANS; IN FACT, SOME PEOPLE DRINK THEM IN TEAS OR TAKE THEM IN VITAMINS.

**ladybug and aphid**

**parasitic wasp**

## THE MORE THE MERRIER

Want to meet more zombie-makers? Say hello to several different species of wasp. Don't worry, though—these wasps don't target humans. Instead, they zombify other insects and creepy-crawlies.

The first of these, the jewel wasp, has a pretty name ... but some pretty chilling behavior. Jewel wasps turn cockroaches into zombies by stinging them in their brains, where the wasps then inject a type of mind-control venom. After that, a wasp leads the zombie roach to its burrow, where the wasp will lay an egg. When it hatches, the larva, or baby wasp, will feed on the cockroach.

Other parasitic wasps exhibit similar behavior. One, the tiny *Dinocampus coccinellae*, targets ladybugs, zombifying them with a special venom and using them as bodyguards for their larva. Another kind of wasp forces spiders to spin webs around their larva, and yet another zombifies caterpillars.

## What about VAMPIRES— do they exist?

Vampires from horror movies—that is, undead humans who drink the blood of others to survive and sometimes turn into bats—definitely don't exist. But there are plenty of animals that survive by drinking blood.

One of the most famous of these is the vampire bat. Found in parts of Mexico, Central America, and South America, these small, furry mammals feed mostly on the blood of birds or livestock such as cows, pigs, and horses. Vampire bats are nocturnal, meaning they are most active at night. To get a tasty meal, a bat lands on or near an animal and uses its sharp teeth to make a small cut. Then, it uses its tongue to lap up the blood. A special substance in its spit makes it so the wound doesn't heal right away, keeping its meal flowing. However, vampire bats don't drink enough to harm the animal—in fact, most don't feel a thing!

Because of their, well, *unusual* eating habits, vampire bats are feared by many people. Bats can also sometimes spread harmful diseases. However, they are very important to local ecosystems. Many bats help keep insect populations under control, and others help spread plant seeds that grow new trees. Scientists are even studying the chemicals found in vampire bats' spit to help make new medicines.

## ROUNDUP — VARIOUS VAMPIRES

Vampire bats may be some of the world's best known vampires, but they aren't the only blood-drinking animals around. Check out some of the other real-life "vampires" that call this planet home.

» **Mosquito:** The female mosquito uses its long mouthpart to slurp up blood. Its saliva can leave behind an itchy red bump.

» **Lamprey:** The lamprey is a type of jawless, eel-like fish that's been around since the time of the dinosaurs. It feeds by using its many teeth to attach to another fish and drink its blood.

» **Vampire finch:** Found in the Galápagos Islands, this small bird uses its sharp beak to drink the blood of much larger birds.

A VAMPIRE BAT BABY, CALLED A PUP, DOESN'T DRINK BLOOD—IT DRINKS ITS MOTHER'S MILK.

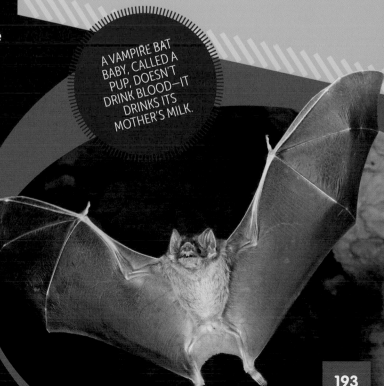

 Q&A

# AN INTERVIEW WITH DR. HON WENG CHONG

In this book, you've read a lot about the differences—and similarities—between computers, artificial intelligence, and humans. But what if there were a way to merge biological human intelligence with artificial intelligence?

It sounds like something out of science fiction, but it might become a reality. Just ask Dr. Hon Weng Chong. Hon is the founder of Cortical Labs, a company dedicated to studying the fusion of AI and biological intelligence. Recently, Cortical Labs created DishBrain: a fusion of living human brain cells on a computer chip. What's more, they taught DishBrain to play a simple, tennis-like video game called Pong!

company founder

**Q HOW DOES WORKING WITH INDIVIDUAL BRAIN CELLS HELP EXPERTS UNDERSTAND THE HUMAN BRAIN AS A WHOLE?**

**A** Learning how the brain works is like learning a language. For most people, the first thing they learn in a language is the alphabet. Then, by putting different letters together, we can make words, sentences, and eventually, paragraphs. The same concept applies to understanding brain cells. First, we understand how brain cells work individually. Then we can understand how groups of cells work in networks, like letters do in sentences. Finally, we can understand how masses of cell networks, called organoids, work. This helps us start to understand how the brain is put together.

**Q WHAT ARE SOME KEY DIFFERENCES BETWEEN COMPUTER-BASED AI AND BIOLOGICAL AI?**

**A** Computer-based AIs are digital in nature. What this means is that everything is represented as a series of 0s and 1s. Our brains, on the other hand, are analog. This means they use varying kinds of signals in different times and measurements. Another difference is that computer-based AI runs on electrical energy while biological AIs run on sugar energy that can be found in food. This makes biological AIs use much less energy than computer-based AIs. They also produce almost little to no heat, as opposed to computer-based.

CONTROL PANEL ∧

Spike Decay Period: 6 sec
1 sec ▬▬▬▬ 10 sec
Max Amplitude: 27.5μV
0μV ▬▬▬▬ 54.9μV

ELECTRODE INFO ∧

Electrode Number: 6279
Electrode Coordinate: 28, 119

 **WHAT OUTCOMES WOULD YOU LIKE TO SEE FROM THIS TYPE OF RESEARCH?**

 The most important use of this research is to help us create new ways to treat people with brain conditions. This research may also be able to help us know if taking a medication will affect your thinking. This will help people avoid medications that slow their thinking and instead choose the right medication that doesn't. And, since we started with teaching the brain cells in the dish to play a simple video game, I would love to see the cells learn to play more complicated games. That way, we will always have someone to play with.

**HOW DID YOU DECIDE TO TEACH THESE BRAIN CELLS PONG?**

Lots of people probably agree that video games are fun. We decided that the first thing we wanted these brain cells to do was have fun by learning how to play a video game. For this, we chose the first video game ever created: Pong. Pong has also traditionally been used as the first skill taught to AIs. Pong is an excellent game for this purpose, as the rules and controls of the game are simple.

**DO YOU HAVE ANY ADVICE FOR KIDS WHO WANT TO WORK IN BIOLOGICAL INTELLIGENCE?**

 The field of biological intelligence is brand-new, so most universities and colleges won't have any courses designed specifically for it. That might sound challenging, but it also makes this a fantastic time and opportunity to get into a brand-new field of science! If you want to get started, a good solid background in (bio)chemistry, cell biology, and physiology would be perfect starting points for the biological parts of this field. To cover the intelligence part, having a good grasp of mathematics would be beneficial. Being able to program with high-level computer languages would definitely help, too!

# Could scientists "BRING BACK" DINOSAURS?

**Maybe—only time will tell. Right now, we don't have the technology to do it. But that doesn't mean we never will.**

To bring back dinosaurs, scientists would most likely need to create a dino clone from real dino DNA. To imagine how that might happen, let's first take a look at what cloning is. Cloning is making a copy of a living thing—a copy with the exact same DNA, or genetic material, as the original. Right now, scientists do have cloning technology and have in fact been able to clone living things from individual cells to an entire animal.

However, to clone something, you first need DNA. And there has never been a confirmed discovery of dinosaur DNA. DNA tends to break down over time, even when it's been fossilized—and dinosaur DNA would be millions of years old!

OK, but what about finding DNA in another way ... say, in the blood found in a mosquito? After all, that is the plot of one very popular movie series! In the first film, *Jurassic Park,* experts are able to get DNA from dinosaur blood, millions of years old, found inside a fossilized mosquito. Well, that *might* work ... but first, paleontologists

SOME SCIENTISTS THINK THAT THEY MAY HAVE FOUND PRESERVED DINOSAUR DNA IN FOSSILIZED DINOSAUR TISSUE, BUT THEY'RE NOT YET CERTAIN.

In the Jurassic Park books and movies, scientists have brought dinosaurs back to life.

IN 2013, SCIENTISTS ANNOUNCED THEY HAD FOUND A BLOOD-CARRYING FOSSILIZED MOSQUITO FROM ABOUT 46 MILLION YEARS AGO.

would have to find a well-preserved mosquito that had been fossilized since the time of the dinosaurs. On top of that, the mosquito would have to have a belly full of its bloody meal—and that meal would have to be dinosaur blood, and not the blood of one of the many other animals that lived during the time.

That's tricky enough, but there's more! Scientists would then need to successfully collect the DNA from the insect and use it to make a clone. However, cloning technology is still in its early stages—and a lot could go wrong. So, while it's not impossible, it's very, *very* unlikely.

## CONSIDERING CLONING

While bringing dinosaurs back is currently out of the question (sorry!), cloning does exist. However, even if no extinct animals are involved, it's still a very tricky area of science. For one thing, cloning is not a magical duplication machine like you might see in science fiction. Although a clone will receive all the same DNA as the original, it won't have the same memories or experiences—it will be its own being. On top of that, clones can also end up looking different from their original. This is because even though the genes might be the same, they can turn on and off—or "express themselves"—at different times or in different ways (see p. 151). Plus, cloning raises important questions about whether science can be harmful. Making a human clone could be harmful to the clone—not just physically, but also emotionally and psychologically. Because of this, scientists do not try to clone humans. However, they are learning more about how to clone healthy human cells to help treat illnesses and diseases.

SCIENTISTS HAVE USED CLONING TO SAVE SOME ENDANGERED SPECIES, SUCH AS THE BLACK-FOOTED FERRET.

## ONE MORE THING: COULD WE CLONE WOOLLY MAMMOTHS?

Hold on to your seats—the answer for this one might be yes. Some scientists are on a mission to bring back the woolly mammoth—or at least a very close version of it. Because woolly mammoths lived much more recently (until about 4,000 years ago!), their DNA is much better preserved. In fact, scientists have found frozen woolly mammoth bodies that still contain preserved flesh and blood. Some experts want to find a way to combine woolly mammoth DNA with that of one of their relatives—an Asian elephant. If it worked, the animal still wouldn't exactly be a woolly mammoth, but it would be something very close ... a mammophant!

# Could MERMAIDS be REAL?

Legends of mermaids—half human, half fish creatures that swim in the sea, and sometimes sit on rocks and sing eerie songs—have been told for thousands of years.

Ancient lore in Asia describes mermaids as the wives of powerful sea dragons that delivered messages between the sea dragons and the ruling emperors on land. But there's an even older nod to mermaids—magical female mermaid-like creatures first appeared in cave paintings tens of thousands of years ago. Is there something to all the mermaid myths? Could they be real?

## NOPE!

According to the U.S. National Oceanic and Atmospheric Administration (NOAA), they are not. NOAA made an official statement in 2012 after a science-fiction TV show suggested the body of a mermaid had been found on a beach. The statement: "No evidence of aquatic humanoids has ever been found."

## MERMAID MUSES

So, there you go. But why all the stories then? Sailors—including one of the most famous sailors of all time, Christopher Columbus—reported seeing

At Weeki Wachee Springs Park in Florida, U.S.A., you can watch mermaids swim in an underwater show. Wait, how is that possible if mermaids aren't real? It takes a fancy tail and good breath control!

For the show, synchronized performers don fake mermaid tails and swim routines set to music and narration. The show takes place in a swimming hole with large windows for the spectators in an underground auditorium. The "mermaids" breathe air through hoses, which lets them stay underwater for extended periods of time. It's clear that mermaids never really go out of fashion—the shows have been running for 70 years!

mermaids during their travels. In 1493, Columbus was sailing near the Dominican Republic when he claimed he saw three mermaids, which he described as "not as beautiful as they are painted."

Yet a lot of the lore is based in some form of reality. Sailors were likely seeing manatees or seals. Manatees and their look-alike cousins, dugongs, belong to the scientific order Sirenia, named after the sirens in Greek mythology, and are believed to be the origin of the mermaid myth. Not exactly Ariel from *The Little Mermaid*!

## ONE MORE THING: WHAT ABOUT THE KRAKEN?

If there's one thing we know about early seafarers, it's that they had a lot of mythology surrounding the sea. Historians think that's partly because the long days, months, and even years at sea could make a person see things that weren't really there. It's also because the sea has some pretty out-of-this-world creatures that sailors might have imagined were even more fantastical than they really are.

Take the kraken: Based on illustrations, this gigantic ocean creature could have belonged in the same family as squid and octopuses. It originated in Scandinavian folklore, and stories say the kraken could destroy ships or snatch sailors and pull them underwater.

Similar creatures were described in ancient Greek mythology and stories from the Caribbean, Japan, and New Zealand. Why do so many cultures have tales of fearsome cephalopod-like animals? Squid and octopuses are really unusual-looking, and we don't see them very often because they are typically shy or live in deep water. If you saw one and didn't know what it was—especially a giant squid, which can grow to almost 43 feet (13 m) long—you might be a little scared of its tentacles and suction cups, too!

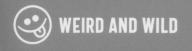
# Is AREA 51
# REAL?

Located within the Nevada Test and Training Range in Nevada, U.S.A., Area 51 is a real place. But what exactly goes on there is what has intrigued people for decades.

IN 2013, PRESIDENT OBAMA BECAME THE FIRST U.S. PRESIDENT TO USE THE WORDS "AREA 51" PUBLICLY.

## THE BACKGROUND

According to the Central Intelligence Agency (CIA), Area 51 got its name from its location in the 51st area on certain military maps that used a grid naming system. Pretty simple. In more general terms, Area 51 is located several hours outside Las Vegas in the middle of the desert. But you can't go hang out there—at least not without special clearance. Armed guards patrol the perimeter, signs remind curious visitors to keep out, and nothing can fly over it without permission from air traffic control. (However, a Russian-built satellite did take pictures of it in 2000.)

Part of the mystery of Area 51 is all the secrecy. Why can't civilians come near it? And why is it so carefully guarded? Some believe there must be something important going on there for it to be so hush-hush. Technically, it is an open training range for the U.S. Air Force. Behind its fences, there are airplane runways more than two miles (3.2 km) long. A nearby site was used to test nuclear weapons from the 1950s to the 1990s, and journalists have speculated that Area 51 was also part of that testing.

One thing we do know for sure: The space was created during the Cold War between the United States and the Soviet Union at least in part for testing and development of aircraft. This included the high-altitude U-2 reconnaissance plane (in other words, a spy plane) and other supersonic and stealth aircraft. Other stealth planes were developed at Area 51, but it's not known if there is any research currently being carried out at the facility.

THE SOVIET UNION WAS A COUNTRY IN EUROPE AND ASIA THAT WAS SPLIT UP INTO SEPARATE REPUBLICS IN 1991.

# LITTLE GREEN MEN

When people ask about Area 51, they're *probably* not really asking about planes, or even spy craft. That's because Area 51 is best known for the conspiracy theory that alien spacecraft—and the bodies of alien pilots—are stored there and used for research. The legend goes that a spacecraft crashed in Roswell, New Mexico, U.S.A., in 1947, and the alien bodies and space-craft were transported to Area 51 from more than 600 miles (965 km) away. Some people continue to claim they've seen unidentified flying objects (UFOs) near the site.

Eventually, in the 1990s, the military provided some answers. Something *did* crash in the area in 1947, but it wasn't an alien spacecraft. It was equip-ment used as part of a top-secret project to detect Soviet nuclear bomb tests. And those alien bodies? Civilians might have observed crash test dummies para-chuted from the top-secret aircraft.

And the other UFO sightings? People may be catching glimpses of human-made tech. Some of the aircraft the military tests at Area 51 look as if they came from outer space. In fact, the U-2 spy plane was flying three times higher than commercial airlines flew in the 1950s, and its look is definitely futuristic.

But even if there are answers to the mysteries surround-ing Area 51 and its UFO sightings and the crash near Roswell, New Mexico, there are still plenty of people who are skeptical. A 2019 poll found that 68 percent of U.S. adults think the government likely knows more than it's telling us about UFOs. But U.S. government officials say that's not the case. And they recently announced that what many people have reported as UFO sightings are actually surveillance operations made by foreign governments—or simply weather balloons.

THERE ARE NO GAS STATIONS ON THE ENTIRE STRETCH OF THE EXTRATERRESTRIAL HIGHWAY.

MORE UFO SIGHTINGS ARE REPORTED ALONG THE EXTRATERRESTRIAL HIGHWAY THAN AT ANY OTHER PLACE IN THE WORLD.

**ALIENS ACTIVITY AREA**

**EXTRATERRESTRIAL 375 HIGHWAY**

## ROUNDUP
## THE EXTRATERRESTRIAL HIGHWAY

Also known as Nevada State Route 375, the Extraterrestrial Highway is a 100-mile (160-km) loop from Las Vegas that runs near Area 51. It got its nick-name from all the UFO sightings reported by people traveling it. Check out some of the strange tourist sites you can see along the way.

>> First stop: The Alien Research Center is actually a gift shop where you are greeted by a two-story-tall metal alien.

>> Refreshments: You can stop at a snack shack for some "Martian poop–flavored" soda.

>> A place to stay: Little A'Le'Inn (Get it? It's pronounced "Little Alien") is a motel that "welcomes Earthlings."

# What's the DEAL with the BERMUDA TRIANGLE?

**The Bermuda Triangle is a place that doesn't officially exist.**

It refers to an area roughly within a 500,000-square-mile (1.3-million-sq-km) "triangle" in the Atlantic Ocean, marked by the southern tip of Florida, Bermuda, and San Juan, Puerto Rico. The intrigue surrounding the Bermuda Triangle stems from the more than 50 ships and 20 airplanes that are said to have mysteriously vanished in it. But the U.S. Navy and Coast Guard say there are no official maps or boundaries for the area—rather it's an area that's marked by the intersection of strange events, which may be explained by science.

## THE EVIDENCE

Reports of mysterious events occurring in the Bermuda Triangle are at least as old as the days of Christopher Columbus. In 1492, the famous explorer wrote in his logs that his compass bearings didn't work properly when sailing in the area, and he reported a glowing object coming out of the water. Since then, empty ships have been discovered in the Bermuda Triangle, abandoned for no reason. Other ships that entered the waters went missing, without a distress signal, and were never seen again.

One of the most famous Bermuda Triangle mysteries is that of five bomber planes that left from Fort Lauderdale, Florida, on a training mission in December 1945. The aviators messaged to say they were confused about their location and seemed to be off course. A Mariner seaplane was sent to look for them and it too disappeared. The U.S. Coast Guard and Navy searched the waters extensively but never found any trace of the 27 men or their aircraft.

Then, there was the U.S.S. *Cyclops*—an unsolved mystery that involves the disappearance of the ship and its 306 crew and passengers in 1918. The *Cyclops* had left Brazil headed for the U.S. but made an unscheduled stop in Barbados, an island

in the Caribbean, because the ship was overloaded. It then left Barbados and headed for Baltimore, Maryland, a U.S. port (via the Bermuda Triangle), but it was never seen again. Other ships and aircraft went missing in the Bermuda Triangle over the years, and various other reports of supernatural events have been reported.

# THE THEORIES

The unexplained events in the Bermuda Triangle have conjured up far-fetched theories of extraterrestrial involvement—such as aliens capturing humans and their planes and ships.

There are also hypotheses that are based on science: Perhaps navigators in the air and on the sea didn't account for the "agonic line"—an invisible line that connects Earth's magnetic poles. While near the agonic line, you don't need to account for magnetic compass variation—the angle between magnetic north and true north. The line moves about 12 miles (20 km) each year, and at times has run through the Bermuda Triangle. Not accounting for magnetic compass variation—or accounting for it when you don't need to—could put navigators significantly off course, which could lead to disaster.

One recent scientific theory suggests gas might be to blame for some of the mysteries of the Bermuda Triangle. Large deposits of methane gas rise up from the ocean floor, and the gas bubbles are capable of pushing water away from ships, causing them to sink. When the flammable methane rises into the air, it could even cause an airplane's engine to ignite, leading to a disastrous explosion or crash.

But that still doesn't explain why some of these shipwrecks or plane crashes have never been found. The culprit could be rogue waves, which can occur in the Bermuda Triangle. Rogue waves can reach heights of 100 feet (30 m) and are capable of destroying every last bit of ships and airplanes, leaving no evidence of them behind.

And then there's extreme weather. Atlantic tropical storms and hurricanes pass right through the Bermuda Triangle and are quite capable of destroying ships to the point that they'd never be seen again.

So, which of these explanations is the right one? Or, is it a combination of multiple different explanations? Here's what the professionals have to say.

# OFFICIAL EXPLANATION

The U.S. Navy and U.S. Coast Guard have stated that there are no supernatural explanations for disasters at sea. They attribute the disasters to a combination of forces of nature and human error, and say that there is no evidence that the events that have occurred in the Bermuda Triangle are any more mysterious or unusual than in any other parts of the ocean. After all, accidents do happen in the ocean. Every year a few dozen big ships sink or have collisions. And there's an estimated three million shipwrecks scattered across the ocean floor.

## SPEAKING OF DANGEROUS WATERS ...

Sailors might consider the Bermuda Triangle smooth sailing compared to Drake Passage. The 600-mile (1,000-km)-wide waterway between the southern tip of South America and Antarctica's Shetland Islands that connects the Atlantic and Pacific Oceans was important to early seafarers before the Panama Canal was opened in 1914. The passage—believed to contain some of the roughest waters in the world—is 11,000 feet (3,400 m) deep, icy cold, and often windy. Violent storms are common in the passage, and waves are known to reach four stories tall. On the positive side, the passage is full of plankton, so sailors are often treated to spotting whales, dolphins, and seabirds there for the feast.

# Will we ever be able to TALK TO ANIMALS?

## The answer depends on what you mean by "talk."

DOGS HAVE EVOLVED TO RECOGNIZE INDIVIDUAL HUMAN FACES AND READ A PERSON'S FACIAL EXPRESSIONS.

If you're wondering if humans will ever be able to hold a conversation out loud with an animal, the answer is probably no. This is mostly because humans have bodies built for speech and other animals don't.

When you speak, you use your vocal cords. These are folds located inside your larynx, a tube in your throat that forms an air passage to your lungs. When you speak, you emit, or send out, air. This air passes through your vocal cords, causing them to rub together and vibrate, making sound. You then use your mouth to shape the sound.

Most animals, on the other hand, don't have body parts that can form this kind of speech. Instead, they rely on cries, body language, and other forms of communication. But even if they did have the right body parts, that doesn't mean they would be fully able to use speech to communicate with us. For example, take birds—many birds can mimic human speech, thanks to a body organ known as the syrinx. Just like you control the air flowing through your vocal cords, a bird can control the air that passes over its syrinx. However, even the most "well-spoken" birds are on record as learning only about 150 human words total. This may be because what truly controls our speech isn't our vocal cords—it's our brains.

Your brain translates your thoughts into words. To do this, it forms ideas, translates them into language, then passes this information to another part of your brain that controls your mouth's movements. Other animals' brains direct them

MANY BIRDS CAN RECOGNIZE THE DISTINCT CALLS OF THEIR YOUNG.

to experience the world differently, and to communicate in different ways. For example, many animals communicate through scent rather than vocal cries. These differences in communication could make holding a conversation very difficult!

## COULD TECHNOLOGY HELP US UNDERSTAND ANIMALS?

Some scientists are working on ways to bridge the communication gap between humans and other animals. One way they hope to do this is by designing artificial intelligence (AI) programs that can decode animal cries. Some researchers have created technology that lets them analyze rodent squeals and pig grunts to determine what an animal might be feeling. They hope to expand on this to develop ways to understand more and more about animal cries, or even listen in on communication happening between animals.

Of course, not all communication is vocal. Because of this, other researchers are hoping to analyze an animal's body movements—such as the special dances many bees use to communicate with each other. Perhaps one day humans will even be able to communicate with animals using specific scents.

SOME PETS HAVE LEARNED TO USE BUTTONS TO "SPEAK" HUMAN. EACH BUTTON PLAYS A RECORDING OF A HUMAN VOICE WHEN PRESSED.

## WILL HUMANS BE ABLE TO COMMUNICATE WITH ANIMALS IN OTHER WAYS?

The answer to this question is a definite yes—in fact, we already communicate with animals. Just because they aren't able to form human speech doesn't mean they can't understand it; many animals are able to learn human words and even follow commands. Dogs are an especially great example of this. In fact, over time, dogs and humans have evolved to understand each other's body languages as well. Studies have shown that puppies are born with the ability to follow human gestures, such as pointing. And apes, such as gorillas and chimpanzees, are able to learn sign language or other symbols used for communication. In fact, many apes have been able to not only learn these forms of communication, but also pass them on to other apes as well.

# Will we ever be able to REVERSE AGING?

**Maybe! But it's not a sure thing—and it almost certainly won't be possible anytime soon.**

ARCHAEOLOGISTS DISCOVERED A POTION IN AN ANCIENT CHINESE TOMB THAT WAS INTENDED TO GIVE THE PERSON WHO DRANK IT IMMORTALITY (IT DOESN'T SEEM TO HAVE WORKED).

For thousands of years, humans have wondered if immortality could be possible. Today, we are closer than ever to understanding what causes aging. In every person's cells, there are microscopic, threadlike structures called chromosomes. The ends of these chromosomes are known as telomeres.

As you live, your cells are constantly creating new cells by copying and dividing themselves. This process, which is called replication, makes sure that your body can stay healthy and renew itself. Whenever a cell replicates, so do the chromosomes inside it. However, replicating causes the ends of the chromosomes—the telomeres—to get shorter. This shortening is what causes some of the parts of the aging process. So, if scientists could develop a way to stop telomeres from shortening, it might mean that they could stop aging ... or even reverse it. However, we don't know if this is really what would happen—or if it's even possible!

In the meantime, experts have turned to modern medicine to help people live longer. Science helps us live healthier lives and understand our bodies better. It also helps us fight off and heal things that hurt us, like illnesses or injuries. Because of this, humans are reaching longer and longer life spans. In fact, some scientists think that some humans alive today could live to be 150 years old!

## Why do we get
## WRINKLES and GRAY HAIR?

As humans age, their bodies start to change in different ways. Layers of fat under the skin start to disappear, and the skin itself creates fewer oils. The skin also starts to produce less of a substance called collagen. Collagen keeps the skin firm. Without it, and with less fat tissue and less moisture, wrinkles can appear. Wrinkles also often appear over time from repeated movements—like smiling, frowning, or squinting. In that way, they can be evidence that a person has been living life to the fullest!

Change can also happen in a person's hair. Every hair on a person's body connects to their skin, called the root. The place where this root grows from a person's skin is known as the follicle. There, there are special cells known as pigment cells, which produce melanin—the substance that gives your body color. However, over time, pigment cells die off. When this happens, hair can start to contain less color, or even become more transparent, appearing silver, gray, or white.

So, is it just humans that undergo these changes? Yes and no. While animals don't usually develop wrinkles over time (although many are born wrinkly!), some may have skin that gets a bit looser as they get older. But many animals do get gray hair—only it often appears in different places! An older dog or cat might become gray around its snout and face.

Humans tend to live longer lives than many animals. But there are some animals that seem almost ageless! Scientists even think the secrets of immortality may lie with these cool critters.

》》 Feeling jelly? One type of jellyfish, *Turritopsis dohrnii,* is also known as the "immortal jellyfish." This is because it can actually make itself age backward, going from an adult back to its immature form—a polyp.

》》 Naked forever: Scientists interested in immortality have been studying naked mole rats, as their health doesn't appear to be linked to their age. In fact, some researchers think that it might be possible for naked mole rats to live forever—although they do tend to pass away from other causes.

》》 Super sponges: Deep in the oceans, one kind of animal may have been living long before the world's first cities were even built! Scientists think that some deep-sea glass sponges may be 18,000 years old.

》》 Long-lived shark: Scientists have encountered Greenland sharks that may be around 500 years old—meaning they were born before the United States existed!

# SUPERPOWERS FOR REAL

Wouldn't it be awesome if we could borrow the superpowers we see in comic books and movies, and read about in books? Maybe there's no such thing as a special cape that makes you fly, but some people glide in special wingsuits. And even though we can't leap tall buildings in a single bound like Superman, we can put on special shoes that let us bounce like a kangaroo. Inventors are coming up with more and more gadgets that are getting us closer and closer to having superpowers—and they're super cool!

## So, without further ado, could a human ever ...

### ... JET WITH A JET PACK?

Iron Man uses jet boots and "repulsor rays" (powerful blasts of energy) to zip through the air. British inventor Richard Browning created his own real-life body-controlled, jet-engine-powered, wind-guided suit to set a world record in 2019 by flying 85 miles an hour (137 km/h)! The suit was 3D printed, and the record was set over water near England's Brighton Pier. Browning thinks that, with some modifications, a similar suit could fly twice as fast.

### ... HOP LIKE A KANGAROO?

Sure, kangaroos don't have superpowers, but their hops are pretty powerful. Red kangaroos can cover 25 feet (7.6 m) in a single leap, and they can jump six feet (1.8 m) high. What if you could wear shoes that made you extra springy? Well, you can. Kangoo Jumps are essentially ski boots attached to springy hoops that compress and expand with each step. The shoes are touted as a good workout, but they also put an extra-big spring in your step.

## ... FLY WITH A WINGSUIT?

Humans have wanted to take to the skies for centuries. And we've succeeded in propelling ourselves and floating through the air with hot-air balloons, planes, parachutes, and hang gliders. But there's an even more streamlined way to ride air currents, and that's with a wingsuit. If you've ever seen a flying squirrel or a sugar glider, you'll know these animals have folds of skin that extend along the sides of their bodies to help them glide from tree branch to tree branch. Wingsuits are made of a superlight material and work on the same principle.

Wingsuit wearers can take to the skies by skydiving from a plane or—even more extreme—jumping from a cliff, bridge, or other high point and gliding to the land below, something called BASE jumping. It's risky business. You first need to be an experienced skydiver before you even consider jumping in a wingsuit. Then, you have to complete special wingsuit training. And, of course, when you do jump, you wear a parachute, just in case.

## ... ZOOM LIKE BATMAN?

Batman has a super ride like no other, the Batmobile. In 2022, a Vietnamese architect made a replica of the Batmobile that is fully electric. It has falcon-winged doors that open up rather than out. And while parts of the car are handcrafted, some were made with a 3D printer!

## ... SHOOT SPIDERWEB FROM A WRISTBAND?

One of Spider-Man's superpowers is his ability to shoot incredibly strong spiderwebs out of his wrists to help him swing from buildings and make giant nets to catch bad guys. It would be pretty nifty to have a gadget that would do this. One company does make a wristband that shoots "web"—or strong wire—with a powerful magnet on the end so that it sticks to something several yards away. Want to point out that field trip permission slip on the fridge to your mom? Use your Spidey-Sense, and don't bother getting up from the kitchen table to draw it to her attention.

## ... SWIM LIKE AQUAMAN?

Never challenge Aquaman to see who can get to the other side of the pool the fastest. After all, according to comic book lore, he can swim 6,800 miles an hour (10,950 km/h). But there is a way to up your own speed. Grab hold of an underwater scooter and let the propellers send you cruising at speeds of 2.5 miles an hour (4 km/h). OK, so Aquaman—and even Olympic swimmers—would leave you in his wake, but you can still get the feel of zipping through the water like a superhero.

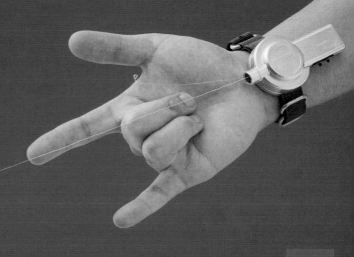

# What makes some PLACES FEEL SPOOKY?

Fear not! There could be a scientific explanation behind the spine-tingling sensation you feel in a "haunted" house.

Have you ever had the heebie–jeebies? That feeling of being nervous when you're in a room or some other space for no specific reason other than it just feels ... creepy? Or have you ever seen something unexplained or even ghostly? Don't be scared—science is here! We've learned there are some scientific explanations for some common ghost "sightings," feelings of a ghostly presence, or just general eerie vibes.

## SCARY SOUNDS

Infrasounds are sounds that fall below the audible range of humans. They can be created by earthquakes; volcanic activity; lightning; certain animals, including elephants, whales, and hippos; and human-made objects, like diesel engines, wind turbines, and loud speakers. Without us even knowing it, these infrasounds can cause us to feel anxious, sorrowful, or paranoid. An acoustic scientist in England recently produced infrasound with a pipe and tested it on an audience at a concert. Later, he asked audience members to describe their reactions to the music, and 22 percent reported feeling sorrowful and nervous. Some even got chills down their spines during the musical pieces.

## CREEPY MOLD

Toxic mold sounds like the thing of nightmares, but in addition to being bad for your respiratory system, it could also affect your thinking. Mold can cause neurological symptoms and lead to confusion and even irrational fear. A scientist in the United States is studying the link between toxic mold and people seeing ghosts. Houses thought to be haunted are often old and have mold. He theorizes that when people see ghosts, they are really experiencing the effects of inhaling mold.

## CLEAR THE AIR

Carbon monoxide can not only make you think you're seeing things, it's downright dangerous. Carbon monoxide detectors keep homes safe by alerting us when levels are dangerous—like, for instance, when you accidentally leave a gas stove on. But if you're exposed to carbon monoxide for too long, the odorless, colorless gas can cause hallucinations and an unexplained feeling of dread.

## GHOST STORIES

Perhaps one of the most common reasons why we feel a spooky presence is because we've been told that we might. The power of suggestion is quite powerful. After hearing a ghost story before bedtime, do you sometimes feel a little more jumpy? Our minds can easily imagine seeing a ghost or thinking one is nearby because we're already open to the suggestion. One study asked people to assess their feelings after touring a theater. Before their tour, one group was told the theater was haunted, while the other group was told it was being renovated. Not too surprisingly, the people who were told it was haunted reported having more intense experiences during their tour.

And on that note, when we do get jumpy, even though we might be scared, we might also feel excited. This is because of a chemical in our brain called dopamine, which is normally associated with pleasure but is also released when we're scared. It helps explain why some people love the thrill of haunted houses: Even though they're terrified, they're having fun at the same time.

## Are there GHOSTS in the White House?

President Harry S. Truman would have said yes. In 1946, the president heard a knock on his bedroom door in the middle of the night. He wrote a letter to his wife, Bess, who was not at the White House with him at the time, stating that he went to check on the noise and no one was there. After he went back to bed, he heard footsteps. He checked again, and there was still no one there. Later, the Secret Service said they were not on the floor at that hour. President Truman was convinced the White House was haunted, writing in his letter, which is archived at his presidential library, "You and Margie [his daughter] had better come back and protect me before some of these ghosts carry me off."

**MYTHS BUSTED**

# MYTHS BUSTED

# IS THE FAMOUS PHOTO OF THE LOCH NESS MONSTER A FAKE?

It's one of the most famous black-and-white photos in the world—a long-necked creature lurking in the waters of Scotland's Loch Ness. For nearly a century, it was proof for many that the monster was real. Alas, the photo was a hoax. But there's much more to this story, and the debate around the Loch Ness Monster isn't even close to over.

## LONG AGO, BEFORE THE PHOTO ...

There have been reports of a monster swimming in Loch Ness for thousands of years. Ancient people in what is now Scotland made stone carvings of an animal with flippers. And a biography from the year 565 of St. Columba, an Irish missionary who traveled in Scotland, includes a story about a monster that bit a swimmer and was ordered by Columba to go away. According to the story, it did, but there continued to be tales of monster sightings over the years.

## NESSIE CAUGHT ON CAMERA

By 1933, the legend of a monster in Loch Ness was popular again. A couple reported seeing an animal in the water, which they said looked like a dragon or prehistoric monster. A few months later, a big-game hunter tried to find the monster, and he reported discovering large animal foot-prints. It turns out the hunter had actually used a stuffed hippopotamus foot to make the tracks.

The hoax didn't stop the interest. The next year, an English physician made the infamous grainy photo of the "Loch Ness Monster." When people saw it, they thought it might be a plesiosaur, a pre-historic marine reptile that went extinct at the same time as the dinosaurs, around 65 million years ago.

The truth of the photograph wasn't finally revealed until the 1990s. The hunter had paired up with the physician to make a model, using a plastic and wooden head and attaching it to a toy submarine. Still, to this day, people are on the lookout for the Loch Ness Monster, aka Nessie. Scientists have even used sonar and underwater photography to look for it, and more than 1,000 people have claimed to have seen it.

# PREHISTORIC POSSIBILITY

A new bit of scientific evidence gives some Nessie believers hope that there could be a monster in Loch Ness. Plesiosaurs, which look a bit like the Loch Ness Monster in the photo and as described by those who claim to have seen it, were long-necked reptiles that grew to 40 feet (12 m) In length and were long believed to live in seas during the Jurassic period. But recently, scientists confirmed that the animals also lived in fresh water. So maybe Nessie is a plesiosaur that somehow managed to dodge extinction?

It's an intriguing idea, but scientists have poked a few holes in the theory. For starters, there'd need to be whole families of plesiosaurs for the species to survive, and surely, they'd be easy to spot in a lake. Also, Loch Ness was formed about 10,000 years ago—well after the extinction of the giant marine reptiles. Before that time, the area was covered in ice.

But animals long thought to be extinct have been rediscovered before. The coelacanth, a type of bony fish, was believed to have been extinct for millions of years. Then, in 1938, South African naturalist Marjorie Courtenay-Latimer discovered one among some catch by local fishermen. Loch Ness Monster enthusiasts are holding on to hope that maybe someday Nessie, too, will make an official appearance, but the facts show that Nessie is indeed just a myth.

A fossilized coelacanth. Scientists thought the bony fish had been extinct for millions of years until a fisherman caught one in 1938.

# GLOSSARY

## WHAT DOES THAT WORD MEAN?

There are a lot of words in this book. Here are some of the more complicated ones, and their meanings.

**ARTIFICIAL INTELLIGENCE (AI)** the ability of machines to mimic the ways in which humans learn and solve problems

**ASTEROID** a rocky object, smaller than a planet, that orbits the sun

**AUGMENTED REALITY (AR)** technology that combines a digital experience—like visuals or audio—with real life

**BACTERIA** a group of tiny, single-celled organisms

**BIOLOGICAL INTELLIGENCE** the ability of living things—like humans— to solve problems and learn

**BIOMIMICRY** the practice of engineering new things based on inspiration from the natural world

**BLACK HOLE** a place in the cosmos where gravity is so strong that nothing—including light—can escape its pull

**CHEMICAL** a substance that is made of atoms or molecules; it cannot be broken down without changing its properties. Water is a chemical.

**COMET** a frozen cosmic object that orbits the sun

**CONSERVATIONIST** someone who protects wildlife or the environment

**DARK MATTER** matter that can't be seen or detected by current technologies

**DNA** a molecule that contains a living thing's genetic information

**EVOLUTION** a slow change over time; the process by which living things change over many generations

**FOSSIL** the remains of an organism that have been preserved in rock

**GREENHOUSE GAS EMISSIONS** gases, like carbon dioxide, that come from human activities and warm Earth's atmosphere

**GONDWANA** a supercontinent, or giant landmass, that existed hundreds of millions of years ago

**HIEROGLYPHICS** ancient Egyptian writing that uses pictures and symbols to represent words

**LIGHT-YEAR** the distance that light can travel in a year; a unit of measurement used to describe very far distances in space

**MATTER** something that has volume (takes up space) and mass (can be weighed)

**MOLECULE** the smallest possible unit of a substance that still has all the traits of the substance; made up of two or more atoms

**NEBULA** clouds of dust and gas in space where stars are born

**NEURONS** nerve cells that relay information around your body and brain

**PANGAEA** a supercontinent, or giant landmass, that existed hundreds of millions of years ago, after Gondwana. It combined all the continents currently on Earth.

**SPAGHETTIFICATION** the stretching that occurs when something falls into a black hole

**SUPERNOVA** an exploding, dying star

**THEORY** in science, a well-founded, rigorously researched explanation of a phenomenon in the world

**VIRTUAL REALITY (VR)** an interactive world that exists in a completely digital realm

**WORMHOLE** a hypothetical tunnel through time and space

# INDEX

# INDEX

# INDEX

# PHOTO CREDITS

Photography/Stocksy/AS; 99 (UP), NASA Goddard/NASA; 99 (LO), Paul Paladin/AS; 100, rul8let/AS; 101 (UP), Lori Epstein/age fotostock; 101 (LO LE), mykolastock/AS; 101 (LO RT), Fotos593/SS; 102 (LE), Martin Capek/AS; 102 (RT), Serggod/AS; 103 (UP), NASA Goddard Space Flight Center/Chris Smith (KBRwyle)/Science Photo Library; 103 (LO LE), © & ™ Lucasfilm Ltd.; 103 (LO RT), Eric Psomoulis/SS; 104 (UP), ESA-S.Corvaja; 104 (LO), ESA/NASA-S. Cristoforetti/R. Rossi; 105 (UP), ESA/NASA; 105 (CTR), ESA/NASA/Roscosmos; 105 (LO), ESA/NASA; 106 (UP), Nature Peacefu/AS; 106 (LO), Mark Garlick/Science RF/AS; 107 (UP LE), JPL/USGS/NASA ; 107 (UP RT), Graphinate/AS; 107 (CTR), allen/AS; 107 (LO), melanie/AS; 108, Jag_cz/AS; 109 (UP), Riko Best/AS; 109 (CTR), Ondrej Prosicky/SS; 109 (center A), SuperStock/ASP; 109 (center B), U.S. Air Force; 109 (center C), GB Venture/SuperStock/ASP; 109 (LO), Sekar B/SS; 110-111, JSC/NASA

CHAPTER 5: 112-113, idal/iStockphoto/GI; 114, Olena/AS; 115 (UP LE), yurakrasil/AS; 115 (UP RT), Cemile Bingol/GI; 115 (LO), nobeastsofierce/AS; 116, costazzurra/AS; 117 (UP), Es sarawuth/AS; 117 (LO), Tricky_Shark/SS; 118 (LE), totojang1977/AS; 118 (RT), John Erhardt/iStockphoto/GI; 119 (UP), Vitaly Titov/AS; 119 (CTR LE), Dana.S/SS; 119 (CTR), Lost_in_the_Midwest/AS; 119 (CTR RT), Claudio Giovannini/EPA-EFE/SS; 119 (LO LE), cunaplus/AS; 119 (LO RT), Mandy Sim/ASP; 120, Daniel M Ernst/SS; 121 (UP), Goffkein/AS; 121 (LO), rvlsoft/AS; 122, Alexander/AS; 123 (UP LE), molenira/AS; 123 (UP RT), Thamrongpat Theerathammakorn/Moment RF/GI; 123 (LO LE), phonlamaiphoto/AS; 123 (LO RT), Nuki/AS; 124 (UP LE), audrius merfeldas/iStockphoto/GI; 124 (UP CTR), kolesnikovserg/AS; 124 (UP RT), Asaf Eliason/SS; 124 (LO), Optinik/SS; 125 (UP LE), Cosmin Manci/SS; 125 (UP RT), Kateryna Kon/Science Photo Library RF/GI; 125 (LO), Regien Paassen/SS; 126, DanieleGay/SS; 127 (CTR), JSC/NASA; 127 (LO LE), NASA; 127 (LO), DM7/AS; 127 (LO RT), Keith Homan/ASP; 128 (UP), bez_bretelky/SS; 128 (CTR), Valerija Polakovska/SS; 128 (LO), Paul Gerrard/Moment Editorial/GI; 129 (UP LE), Erickson Stock/SS; 129 (UP RT), wiangya/SS; 129 (CTR), Erickson Stock/SS; 129 (LO), Heritage Images/Hulton Archive/GI; 130, Kaspars Grinvalds/AS; 131 (UP), DDevicee/AS; 131 (CTR LE), immimagery/AS; 131 (CTR RT), inkoly/iStockphoto/GI; 131 (LO LE), charnsitr/AS; 131 (LO RT), WENN Rights Ltd/ASP; 132 (LO LE & LO RT), Cas Holman; 132 (UP), Beth Flatley; 133 (LO, UP LE & UP RT), Cas Holman; 134 (UP), nerthuz/AS; 134 (LO), unlimit3d/AS; 135 (UP), muratart/SS; 135 (CTR LE), AlxeyPnferov/iStockphoto/GI; 135 (CTR RT), Space Creator/AS; 135 (LO), MSB.Photography/AS; 136 (LE), CBS Photo Archive/GI; 136 (CTR), Alex Rublinetsky/AS; 136 (RT), Artem_Graf/AS; 137 (UP LE), Tom Durr/SS; 137 (UP RT), aperturesound/AS; 137 (CTR), RHJ/AS; 137 (LO), Everett Collection, Inc.

CHAPTER 6: 138-139, Sharon Dominick/E+/GI; 140, carballo/SS; 141 (UP), marieclaudelemay/iStockphoto/GI; 141 (LO), Pixel-Shot/AS; 142 (UP), Parvin/AS; 142 (LO), fizkes/AS; 143 (UP LE), danheighton/AS; 143 (UP RT), Tang Ming Tung/Digital Vision/GI; 143 (LO), Arazdurdyev Konstantin/SS; 144 (LE), Sergey Nivens/AS; 144 (RT), Jakub Krechowicz/SS; 145 (UP LE), Zdan Ivan/SS; 145 (UP RT), Prostockstudio/SS; 145 (LO), Africa Studio/AS; 146, sam/AS; 147 (UP LE), vladimirfloyd/AS; 147 (UP CTR & UP RT), Bocskai István/AS; 147 (music notes), Julija/AS; 147 (LO), botulinum21/SS; 148-149, Rafael/AS; 148 (LO LE), deagreez/AS; 148 (LO RT), onimate/AS; 149 (UP), Cheryl Casey/AS; 149 (CTR), galina_kovalenko/AS; 150, ewapee/AS; 151 (LE), Wayhome Studio/AS; 151 (B), breakingthewalls/AS; 151 (C), vvoe/AS; 151 (D), Sergiy Serdyuk/AS; 151 (E), sbw19/AS; 152-153, Kovalenko I/AS; 153 (UP LE), Roni/AS; 153 (UP RT), Jason/AS; 153 (LO), ExQuisine/AS; 154, Aroastock/AS; 155 (UP LE), Sashkin/AS; 155 (UP RT), zoka74/AS; 155 (CTR), Roman Samokhin/AS; 155 (center A), fantom_rd/AS; 155 (center B), crisod/AS; 155 (center C), Michelle/AS; 155 (center D), Patryk Kosmider/AS; 155 (LO), daphot75/AS; 156 (UP), Mix and Match Studio/AS; 156 (CTR), teen00000/AS; 156 (LO), Goffkein/AS; 157 (UP LE), schankz/AS; 157 (UP RT), Michae Allen/SS; 157 (CTR), Monkey Business/AS; 157 (LO), Mix and Match Studio/SS; 158, Mix and Match Studio/AS; 159 (UP), Lachina; 159 (CTR), Serggod/AS; 159 (LO), Seventyfour/SS; 160, Marco/AS; 161 (UP), Jatuporn Tansirimas/AS; 161 (LO), Hannamariah/SS; 162-163, New Africa/AS; 162 (UP), verte/AS; 162 (LO), freshidea/AS; 163, Yeti Studio/AS

CHAPTER 7: 164-165, MoMo Productions/Digital Vision/GI; 166, ink drop/AS; 167 (UP), Patrick Zweifel/AS; 167 (LO), fim design/AS; 168, bluedesign/AS; 169, gerasimov174/AS; 170 (LE), yamonstro/AS; 170 (RT), Eric Isselée/AS; 171 (UP), NASA/JSC/Bill Brassard; 171 (center A), Donald Miralle/GI for Lumix/GI; 171 (center B), Craig Beruldsen/AFP via GI; 171 (center C), Alex Mustard/Nature Picture Library; 171 (LO), Warm_Tail/SS; 172, Yulia Buchatskaya/AS; 173 (UP), Hugh O'Neill/AS; 173 (center A), daboost/AS; 173 (center B), stevanzz/AS; 173 (center C), Daniel Thornberg/AS; 173 (center D), duski93/AS; 173 (center E), Ievgen Skrypko/AS; 173 (LO), Arkadij Schell/iStockphoto/GI; 174, John Macdougall/AFP via GI/GI; 175 (UP LE), Al Bello/GI; 175 (UP RT), Lordn/SS; 175 (LO), photomelon/AS; 176 (UP), suzz/SS; 176 (LO), EQRoy/SS; 176-177, Nadzeya Pakhomava/AS; 177 (A), New Africa/AS; 177 (B), Neil Harrison/Dreamstime; 177 (C), Panagiotis Karapanagiotis/Dreamstime; 177 (D), michal812/AS; 177 (E), TMAX/AS; 177 (F), VRVIRUS/AS; 177 (G), JackF/AS; 178 (UP), oksana2010/SS; 178 (UP RT), LaptevArt/AS; 178 (LO LE), mimagephotos/AS; 178 (LO CTR), andersphoto/SS; 178 (LO RT), Ezhonok/Dreamstime; 179 (UP LE), Denis-Huot/Nature Picture Library; 179 (UP RT), kunchit1969/AS; 179 (CTR), Irina Bg/AS; 179 (LO),

New Africa/AS; 180 (UP), Julien Tromeur/AS; 180 (LO A), mtsaride/AS; 180 (LO B), Sashkin/SS; 180 (LO C), aboutsung/SS; 180 (LO D), Trong Nguyen/SS; 180 (LO E), Tatiana Popova/SS; 181 (UP LE), ohrim/AS; 181 (UP CTR), lexey Kuznetsov/AS; 181 (UP RT), Neveshkin Nikolay/SS; 181 (LO LE), New Africa/AS; 181 (LO RT), 3desc/AS; 182 (UP), Matthew Rakola; 182 (LO LE), Andy Shell/AS; 182 (LO CTR), Pakhnyushchyy/AS; 182 (LO RT), Sepia Times/Universal Images Group via GI; 183 (UP), Nastasic/Digital Vision Vectors/GI; 183 (center A), simonmayer/iStockphoto/GI; 183 (center B), warren_price/AS; 183 (center C), Padma Sanjaya/SS; 183 (LO), Feng Yu/AS; 184 (music notes), Julija/AS; 184 (LO), Africa Studio/AS; 185 (UP), Lightfield Studios/AS; 185 (LO), TCreativeMedia/AS; 186 (UP), Alexander Raths/AS; 186 (CTR), Olha/AS; 186 (LO), Anna Sedneva/AS; 187 (UP LE), Maks Narodenko/AS; 187 (UP RT), Denis Nata/SS; 187 (CTR LE), Roman Samokhin/SS; 187 (CTR RT), Abramova Elena/SS; 187 (LO), yuriygolub/AS; 188-189, Andrey Prilutskiyh/AS; 189 (UP), Blue Lemon Photo/AS; 189 (CTR), Okea/iStockphoto/GI; 189 (LO), Africa Studio/AS

CHAPTER 8: 190-191, koya979/SS; 191, Anna Lukina/AS 192, Tim Laman/NGIC; 193 (UP LE), De Rebus Naturae/AS; 193 (UP RT), Kucharski K. Kucharska/SS; 193 (center A), jps/SS; 193 (center B), GDM photo/AS; 193 (center C), axfi1/AS; 193 (LO), Naturbild AB/Johner RF/GI; 194, Jeremy Dixon; 195 (UP), Dr. Hon Weng Chong; 195 (LO), Jeremy Dixon; 196, Franco Tempesta/© National Geographic Partners, LLC; 197 (UP LE), agephotography/AS; 197 (UP RT), ©Universal/Courtesy Everett Collection; 197 (LO), Digitalstormcinema/Dreamstime; 198, Delmaine Donson/peopleimages/AS; 199 (UP LE), Wirestock/AS; 199 (UP CTR), Jeff Stamer/AS; 199 (UP RT), Images-USA/ASP; 199 (LO), Stocktrek Images, Inc./ASP; 200 (UP), Ilya Shulika/SS; 200 (LO), Roger Holden Photography/Stockbyte Unreleased/GI; 201 (UP), Fergregory/Dreamstime; 201 (center A), broukoid/SS; 201 (center B), iunewind/SS; 201 (center C), Thomas Pajot/AS; 201 (LO LE), Peter Unger/iStock Editorial/GI; 201 (LO CTR), miroslav_1/iStock Editorial/GI; 201 (LO RT), iStock Unreleased/GI; 202, Alessandro Lonati/Bridgeman Images; 203 (UP), WindVector/SS; 203 (CTR), Mike Hill/Stone RF/GI; 203 (LO), shubhamtiwari/SS; 204, Susan Schmitz/SS; 205 (UP LE), rtbilder/SS; 205 (UP RT), Mayskyphoto/SS; 205 (CTR), Samu/AS; 205 (LO), Photoboyko/AS; 206, koosen/AS; 207 (UP), perfectlab/SS; 207 (center A), underocean/AS; 207 (center B), Frans Lanting/NGIC; 207 (center C), David Shale/Nature Picture Library; 207 (center D), Saul Gonor/Blue Planet Archive; 207 (LO LE), icsnaps/SS; 207 (LO RT), Amelia/AS; 208 (UP), buy this/SS; 208 (CTR), Jeff Gilbert/SS; 208 (LO), Panther Media GmbH/ASP; 209 (UP), Talent for Adventure/AS; 209 (CTR), Van Daryl Gallery, LLC; 209 (LO LE), JonMilnes/SS; 209 (LO RT), HeroTech Pte. Ltd.; 210-211 (ghosts), Fotomay/SS; 210 (LE), Denis Belitsky/SS; 210 (LO RT), titima157/AS; 211 (UP), Arthur/AS; 211 (CTR), onebluelight/E+/GI; 211 (LO), Bill Chizek/AS; 212-213, Science History Images/ASP; 213 (UP), MichaelTaylor3d/SS; 213 (LO), bluehand/AS

Since 1888, the National Geographic Society has funded more than 14,000 research, conservation, education, and storytelling projects around the world. National Geographic Partners distributes a portion of the funds it receives from your purchase to National Geographic Society to support programs including the conservation of animals and their habitats. To learn more, visit natgeo.com/info.

For more information, visit nationalgeographic.com, call 1-877-873-6846, or write to the following address:

National Geographic Partners, LLC
1145 17th Street NW
Washington, DC 20036-4688 U.S.A.

More for kids from National Geographic: natgeokids.com

*National Geographic Kids* magazine inspires children to explore their world with fun yet educational articles on animals, science, nature, and more. Using fresh storytelling and amazing photography, *Nat Geo Kids* shows kids ages 6 to 14 the fascinating truth about the world—and why they should care. **natgeo.com/subscribe**

For rights or permissions inquiries, please contact National Geographic Books Subsidiary Rights: bookrights@natgeo.com

Designed by Kathryn Robbins

Hardcover ISBN: 978-1-4263-7573-6
Reinforced library binding ISBN: 978-1-4263-7585-9

The publisher would like to thank the book team: Kathryn Williams, project editor; Lori Epstein, photo manager; Scott Vehstedt, fact-checker; Joan Gossett, senior manager, production editorial; and Lauren Sciortino and David Marvin, associate designers.

Printed in China
24/PPS/1